# Examining Identity in
# SPORTS
# MEDIA

# Examining Identity in

# SPORTS

# MEDIA

Editors

## HEATHER L. HUNDLEY
California State University, San Bernardino

## ANDREW C. BILLINGS
Clemson University

Los Angeles | London | New Delhi
Singapore | Washington DC

*For information:*

SAGE Publications, Inc.
2455 Teller Road
Thousand Oaks,
    California 91320
E-mail: order@sagepub.com

SAGE Publications India Pvt. Ltd.
B 1/I 1 Mohan Cooperative
    Industrial Area
Mathura Road, India
New Delhi 110 044

SAGE Publications Ltd.
1 Oliver's Yard
55 City Road
London, EC1Y 1SP
United Kingdom

SAGE Publications
    Asia-Pacific Pte. Ltd.
33 Pekin Street #02-01
Far East Square
Singapore 048763

Printed in the United States of America

*Library of Congress Cataloging-in-Publication Data*

Examining identity in sports media / editors, Heather L. Hundley, Andrew C. Billings.
    p. cm.
Includes bibliographical references and index.
ISBN 978-1-4129-5459-4 (cloth)
ISBN 978-1-4129-5460-0 (pbk.)
    1. Gender identity. 2. Gender identity in mass media. 3. Communication in sports. I. Hundley, Heather L. II. Billings, Andrew C.

HQ1075.E95 2009
306.4'83—dc22                              2008046375

This book is printed on acid-free paper.

09   10   11   12   13   10   9   8   7   6   5   4   3   2   1

| | |
|---|---|
| *Acquisitions Editor:* | Todd R. Armstrong |
| *Editorial Assistant:* | Aja Baker |
| *Production Editor:* | Brittany Bauhaus |
| *Copy Editor:* | Jovey Stewart |
| *Typesetter:* | C&M Digitals (P) Ltd. |
| *Proofreader:* | Sally Jaskold |
| *Indexer:* | Michael Ferreira |
| *Cover Designer:* | Bryan Fishman |
| *Marketing Manager:* | Carmel Shrire |

# Contents

# Acknowledgments

While this project has required a great deal of work, it has been a lot of fun as well. We label this a positive experience largely because of the tremendous people we had the privilege of collaborating with on *Examining Identity in Sports Media*. Sage Publications has proven to be quite supportive of this work; we particularly thank Todd Armstrong for serving as an advocate, counselor, and expert for the book from its conception. We recognize and appreciate the book prospectus reviewers and draft reviewers as well for their insight and suggestions. This book is improved because of their work. We also wish to thank the contributors to this book who have advanced the dialogue about this area of sports communication in significant ways. These authors are prolific writers whose projects are many and skills are in high demand; we thank them for making this book a priority and for producing exceptional work. Additionally, we thank the institutional mechanisms that have allowed our dialogues about identity and sport to take place, ranging from the National Communication Association to the biennial Summit on Communication and Sport, which we used to flesh out the ideas you are now seeing in print.

On more individual notes, Heather would like to thank her mentor Dr. Leah Vande Berg (deceased) for always encouraging her and having faith and confidence in her abilities. In addition, she thanks Dr. Nick Trujillo for introducing her to Sport Communication and his support during the early stages of this work. She also gives endless credit to her partner, Alan Briggs, for his ongoing patience, endearing advocacy, and good-natured attitude.

Andy would also like to thank the Clemson University College of Architecture, Arts, and Humanities for supporting the project with additional release time and the Department of Communication Studies for providing other resources that were necessary to complete this book. He also particularly thanks his wife, Angela, and sons, Nathan and Noah, for helping him juggle the needs of this project with the time it takes to be a good husband and father.

We hope you find this book provocative, intriguing, and enjoyable. We also hope you recognize the large number of people who made this project become a reality.

The authors and SAGE gratefully acknowledge the contributions of the following reviewers:

Robert S. Brown, *Department of Sport Management; Daniel Webster College*

Pam Creedon, *School of Journalism and Mass Communication; The University of Iowa*

Linda K. Fuller, *Communications Department; Worcester State College*

Kelby K. Halone, *Department of Communication Studies; West Virginia University*

Allison Harthcock, *Department of Media Arts; Butler University*

Bob Krizek, *Department of Communication; Saint Louis University*

Anthony Moretti, *Department of Journalism and Mass Communication; Point Park University*

R. Pierre Rodgers, *School of Recreation, Health, and Tourism; George Mason University*

Raymond I. Schuck, *School of Communication Studies; Bowling Green State University*

Brad Schultz, *Department of Journalism; University of Mississippi*

Lawrence A. Wenner, *Film and Television Studies Department; Loyola Marymount University*

# 1

# Examining Identity in
# Sports Media

## Andrew C. Billings

## Heather L. Hundley

❖ ❖ ❖

In his 2006 best seller, *The Long Tail, Wired* magazine editor Chris Anderson argues that niche consumption is en vogue within virtually every form of mass media. Gone are the days of water cooler programming in which shows like *Friends* and *Seinfeld* secured substantial swaths of television viewers; in their place we have shows with "buzz" that secure less than half the viewers that the top sitcoms once did, along with hundreds of cable channels that draw viewers by the thousands rather than millions. Music enthusiasts are less likely to listen to Top 40 music radio stations than they are to take advantage of the thousands of options specifically tailored to their tastes, e.g., downloading obscure, non-commercial music a dollar at a time. The cinema still has blockbusters, but it also features independent "art house" options that grow each year. Yet, within all of the niche markets that define 21st century media, sport permeates immense segments of American and international culture. The Super Bowl continues to be the largest single television rating of a given year, and competition between satellite radio and television companies is often largely won and lost based on who can secure the most desirable sports contracts. Certainly, this century has given rise to niche programming—such as the X Games or Ultimate Fighting Championship—yet these new events only supplement the still-uber-popular cornerstone sports within the sports cultural zeitgeist. For instance, even with all of baseball's troubles, more people are attending the games than at any point in the long history of the game (Selig, 2007).

Dubbing major sports media events as "megasport" (those events that become part of a national fabric, such as the Indianapolis 500 on Memorial Day weekend or March Madness every spring), Eastman, Newton, and Pack (1996) explore the ramifications of an evermore-pervasive sporting landscape in which millions (sometimes billions) of people experience a joint "reality" through the lens of an often singular mass media outlet. Such events represent a mosaic of political, social, and cultural import, offering commentary on issues beyond the directly observable athletic performances. For decades, scholars have devoted considerable attention and scrutiny to the exploration of identity, particularly interrogating how mediasport (see Wenner, 2006) enacts and portrays social divides and underprivileged groups. Conclusions, of course, vary—ranging from arguments that sport (and the media surrounding it) contributes to and even exacerbates identity divisions to studies that argue sport can enact social changes that aid the advancement of underprivileged and underrepresented groups within society.

## ❖ NEGOTIATING IDENTITY IN SPORTS MEDIA

The examination of identity has a difficult and often convoluted history within academe at least partly because of its hybrid localization in scholarship. Scholars in disciplines from sociology to women's studies to global studies all rightly focus some of their works in this area. Disciplines such as kinesiology and sports management examine identity issues as well, partly because of the underlying belief that sport shapes society as much as society shapes sport, but also because many sporting entities routinely resist more progressive thinking about identity issues, making the organizations (and the individuals involved in them) ripe for examination (see Maguire, 1999, for an overview of identity in sport on a global scale).

However, it is hard to separate the negotiation of identity from how it is conveyed and shaped by media entities, and it is equally as difficult to separate media influence from the core communication messages employed by these same sports media. Thus, communication research can often be referred to as "Ground Zero" for understanding the complex messages that mediasport imparts. This book aims to provide some common understanding of the specific communicative messages embedded in media coverage while also serving as a bridge to the understanding of other disciplines that study identity and sport from sociological and psychological standpoints.

Stuart Hall (1996) claims that "identities are constructed within, not outside discourse" (p. 4); as such, these identities are duplicitous, ubiquitous, and continually in flux. These issues are important sources for learning and reinforcing social beliefs as they are salient contexts for investigating issues of identity, including ethnicity, gender, class, sexual orientation, ability/disability, and more. Consequently, sport and media inscribe numerous implicit and explicit ideologies that saturate our culture. Using a wide variety of theoretical and methodological constructs (e.g., surveys, content analyses, ethnographic research, field work, or other appropriate quantitative, qualitative, or rhetorical approaches), this edited collection examines various media to expose how the intersection of sport and media construct, reinforce, and/or perpetuate perceptions of human identities. Morris (2006) articulates the societal shaping of identity issues, using anecdotes to explain how people conceive their perception of identity—both in terms of self and otherness. The amount of media scholarship on identity tends to coordinate with the degree in which the identity form is directly observable. For instance, gender is relatively easy to note (and, hence, code, study, and analyze), while the sexuality of a person is obviously not as easily determined unless it is overtly articulated. Additionally, some discussions of identity are more ubiquitous than others. Jon Entine's (2000) examination of race, *Taboo: Why Black Athletes Dominate Sports and Why We're Afraid to Talk About It,* illustrates how issues of race and ethnicity permeate virtually any participant or consumer of sports media. In contrast, an identity issue such as (dis)ability only percolated in discussion after golfer Casey Martin sued the PGA Tour in his desire to use a golf cart at tournaments (Cherney, 2003). Otherwise this discussion of identity is primarily nonexistent in research making assumptions that sport and ability coalesce as a naturalized construct.

Scholars have a pragmatic tendency for isolating identity variables, particularly those that can be most readily recognized. As Kelby Halone mentions in Chapter 12, merely examining six identity variables (hardly an exhaustive list) amounts to over one thousand cells of potential examination. Thus, some scholars (e.g., Billings & Angelini, 2007; Billings & Eastman, 2002, 2003) have attempted to provide foundational analyses of gender, ethnicity, and nationality as singular variables that later can be amalgamated, while other scholars (e.g. Billings, Angelini, & Eastman, 2008; Boyd, 1997; Hauck, 2006) focus on the complex intermingled roles of identity within singular sports case studies. Both approaches are useful if not foundational to the more complex understanding of identity that must be addressed in the 21st century.

Identity politics (see Mohanty, Alcoff, Hames-Garcia, & Moya, 2005; Nicholson & Seidman, 1996), which first became part of the public consciousness in the 1970s, was largely an attempt to offer increased opportunities for inequities provided for certain underprivileged, underrepresented, or underutilized groups of people, most commonly in terms of racial and gender biases as a response to the civil rights movement and second-wave feminism. Such conceptions have expanded both in terms of scope and goal orientation over the subsequent decades, noting that hegemony entrenches notions of difference depending on cultural, social, and political contexts and understandings. Most notably, identity has been more self-denoted, suggesting a negotiation of who a group self-identifies as belonging. Recently, scholars (Hogg & Reid, 2006) have combined postulations of social identity (Tajfel, 1972; Tajfel & Turner, 1986) and self-categorization (Turner, Hogg, Oakes, Riecher, & Wetherell, 1987) to argue that group "norms" are conceived through the negotiation of these issues.

Social norming provides the impetus for examining not only media content and effects as they relate to identity but also the inherent tie to mediasport (Wenner, 2006), as sports are consumed by millions of television viewers, radio audiences, newspaper readers, magazine subscribers, and Internet users. For instance, the two largest world television spectacles (Olympics and World Cup) draw global audiences in the billions (Gordon & Sibson, 1998; IOC Marketing Fact File, 2008), numbers that dwarf the ratings of perceived American mega-programs such as *American Idol*, which attracts nearly 28 million weekly regular viewers (Robertson, 2008).

Because of the ubiquitous nature of mediasport, the opportunity also exists for billions of people to be exposed to new cultures, ideas, and social perceptions that are inherently linked with beliefs about identity including gender, sexual orientation, ethnicity, nationality, aging, religion, and many other ways in which a person self-identifies. Sometimes this exposure comes in the form of witnessing a race competition in which people rarely interact within their local communities (take, for instance, a person growing up in a small, monolithically White U.S. town who also is a fan of professional basketball); at other times exposure consists of new conceptions of identity groups in which they already interact (take for instance a Middle Eastern perspective on Olympic beach volleyball "uniforms" and their relation to women's issues). The direct effects, i.e., the hypodermic needle, approach to media is certainly not being endorsed here; however, it is also not such a logical leap to believe that people who follow national and international sports in the media also are (re)formulating their own beliefs about identity groups: the grand "negotiation" in which we refer that is perpetually in flux and constantly updated based on personal experiences.

❖  SCHOLARSHIP ON IDENTITY

This book explores issues of identity within mediasport—conceptions of gender, ethnicity, nationality, sexuality, (dis)ability, etc.—without the use of dichotomous value-laden notions of good/bad or right/wrong. The chapters within the book utilize a wide variation of theoretical constructs and methodological approaches, examining one or more issues of identity and analyzing how mediasport holds the power to shade our judgments about people. We contend that identity is an extensive negotiation that is always changing, always being interpreted and reinterpreted, and always contested by various entities. Whether the context of the mediated situation is a movie, television program, series of newspaper commentaries, or other mass media formats, the negotiation of identity can be addressed using different epistemological approaches with the underlying theme being that social identity (Tajfel & Turner, 1986) can be influenced by the way mediasport frames or sets an agenda (see Goffman, 1974; McCombs & Shaw, 1972).

Notions of identity are intermingled and interminably complex to the point that many media gatekeepers have indicated they let the visual image do the work (see Billings, 2008). As a result, gender identity is reduced to biological differences (such as breasts or an Adam's apple) and reinforced with social constructions (wearing makeup, long hair, and gender-based clothing) as evidenced in visual cues; ethnicity is typically reduced to perceived skin pigment; and sexual orientation is left to a viewer's increasingly flawed conceptions of "gaydar," based on stereotypes of effeminate men or masculine women. This book delves into many of these issues with fervor and a sense of detail that is necessary to gain even a rudimentary understanding of what constitutes self or otherness. Without question, our examination of identity variables is not exhaustive but only scratches the surface on what should be a dense dialogue about how sport, media, and identity triangulate a unique nexus of investigation that shapes everyday actions and understandings.

Many studies of identity have functioned as "scrutinizations" of social divides, essentially determining ways in which we divide ourselves biologically, culturally, socially, and politically and then uncovering inequities in media treatment by these different partitions. The most objective form of division has also been the most investigated: the gender variable. While differences between sex (largely defined biologically) and gender (largely defined within social constructions of masculine and feminine notions and expectations) have been discussed for decades, research has largely employed biological divisions because sport, in its very nature, enacts men's and women's sport as two separate entities. Even in events such as Wimbledon (tennis) championships or the Olympics in which both men and women compete, the events are divided by gender and function primarily as separate events. As such, the preponderance of mediasport studies has examined how entrenched notions of masculinity often result in less prominence and respect for women's sport. Advancements for women's sport have occurred in terms of opportunities to compete; O'Reilly and Cahn (2007) describe the post-Title IX era as a "spectacular transformation . . . in which the right to play sports and receive resources commensurate with men's sports is rarely disputed" (pp. xi–xii). Nonetheless, media coverage of women's sport has not increased in salience. For instance, people can find television channels highlighting women's sports, yet they tend to be less prominent than similar outlets for men. Where men's athletics frequently are aired on the big four broadcasting networks (ABC, CBS, NBC, and FOX) along with the cable network ESPN, women's sports often are relegated to secondary channels; for instance, men's golf is routinely offered on broadcast networks such as CBS, NBC, and ABC, while women's golf is usually located on the Golf Channel or ESPN2. Studies have also shown that the discourse used by media gatekeepers is substantially different between men and women, often serving to diminish women's athletic achievements.

Another prime area of mediasport scholarship on identity has been the examination of race or ethnicity. Again, even agreeing upon common definitions of race and ethnicity is a yeoman's task in many ways, as people who consume mediasport largely operationally define race as skin color, while other scholars argue for much more complex unpacking of this identity variable (Carrington, 2007). Despite increased comprehensive understanding of ethnicity and the problems inherent with artificial assemblage of identity groupings, sportscasters and other media gatekeepers largely continue to describe the action with stereotypical Black/White categorical distinctions, often resulting in an amalgamation of disparate ethnicities into overarching categories defined solely by one's skin color. Thus, athletes such as Fijian golfer Vijay Singh, Cablinasian golfer Tiger Woods, and French basketball player Tony Parker are frequently all subjected to biases applied to "Black" athletes even though each has a distinctively different ethnic background.

New York University sociologist Troy Duster argues that race is predominantly a cultural invention, postulating that "if you believe these differences are real, why wouldn't you slip into the thinking that performance, in the classroom or on the basketball court, is also explainable by genetic or biological differences?" (Dokoupil, 2007, p. 14). Duster is essentially arguing the cause of many ethnic findings in mediasport, which tend to show discourse differences that often can be reduced to distinctions of genetic versus learned athletic ability. Edwards (1969, 1973) claims that such discussions are not only inaccurate, they are also damaging in the inverse, seemingly arguing that Blacks lack diligence and cognitive abilities and that Whites lack the physical genetics to excel at the highest levels of modern athletics. As the argument tends to be summarized, Whites are portrayed as smart and Blacks as athletic; the problem occurs when the inverse is presumed not to be true. The damage permeates all races within modern culture because, for instance, by buying into the notion that Black athletes are genetically superior to them, "the White race thus becomes the chief victim of its own myth" (Edwards, 1973, p. 197). Indeed, it is not an insurmountable, cognitive leap to claim that portrayals of White athletes as born leaders of team sports (i.e., "natural" point guards in basketball or quarterbacks in football [Wonsek, 1992]) can impact non-White participation enacting self-fulfilling prophecies in leadership positions within organizational structures.

A third area of identity scholarship in mediasport involves the close analysis of nationalism. Bairner (2001) contends that the power of sport-induced nationalism is vast, with the capability to influence millions of people internationally, and scholars have found this to be true as well. Unlike gender and ethnicity, nationality (at least within international sports competitions such as the World Cup or the Olympics) can be overtly defined by the apparel worn by an athlete, creating an "us versus them" dichotomy with the potential to impact social and political views (O'Donnell, 1994). Indeed, nationalism can be a primary reason for consumers of mediasport to care about an event they would otherwise not know anything about, as millions of people routinely cheer on divers, snowboarders, and badminton players in the name of patriotism.

However, constructions (and related analyses) of identity in mediasport are not merely limited to gender, ethnicity, and nationality. Other forms of identity have been examined as a form of sub-niche, not because they are less important but because they are harder to uncover or much less easily decipherable via a media outlet. Issues such as economic status, religion, sexual orientation, political convictions, and social views are not identity forms that are directly observable by looking at the body or correlating uniform. As such, the issues surrounding these social divides tend to percolate within discussions of other forms of identity and many times rightly so (as, for instance, a discussion of Middle Eastern religious beliefs usually directly relates to views on gender roles).

A double-edged sword persists within mass media, as gatekeepers often feel uninformed on all forms of identity or have determined that increased awareness of these perceived social divides would only exacerbate tensions (e.g., continually pointing out the race of an athlete as a primary story could seem problematic depending on the treatment). The result is a "dropped conversation" about identity that includes both (a) the lack of any cogent dialogue about identity when it is appropriate—and sometimes primary to storytelling—within the sporting context, and (b) the surface-level dialogue that functions as discourse within other spheres of modern sport media in the United States.

The mere existence of a book such as ours underscores the degree to which discussing identity would bring added salience to the construction of identity in mediasport. The notion of power underscores all of these chapters—the power to shape public opinion, the power to reach millions of people, the power to help an individual cognitively shape a "reality," however flawed that conception may be. As Billings, Brown, Crout, McKenna, Rice, Timanus, and Zeigler (2008) write, "It appears that history is not always written by the winners; it is also written by those with the television rights" (p. 229). This book furthers this notion, arguing that any form of mediasport that has the power to reach millions also has the potential for tremendous social influence. The consumers of these messages certainly have free will to resist these overt and covert agendas, yet sport is also known as the world's most pervasive form of escapism, consequently resulting in millions of people who are more likely to consume identity-oriented messages in a peripheral rather than central processing route (see Petty & Cacioppo, 1986).

## ❖ CHAPTER OVERVIEWS

The rest of this volume contains various methodologies and epistemologies that arise from inside and outside of the communication discipline. Each chapter is structured with the same headings (such as "Methods" and "Results") to show that regardless of the approach to studying identity in sport, each has a specific theoretical frame and methodology that is employed to ultimately yield worthwhile results. This inclusiveness is a primary aim of the book, with the goal being that any person who has taken foundational courses in communication should be able to logically follow the arguments presented, whether that person is an advanced undergraduate or a seasoned academician.

The opening chapters focus on one of the largest divides in identity analysis: gender. Chapter 2 offers insights on gender through a more specialized and localized lens as Marie Hardin and Erin Whiteside examine "morality tales that naturalize a broader cultural hegemony," specifically as they relate to both gender and sexuality. Hardin and Whiteside use the case of Pennsylvania State University basketball coach Rene Portland to address how print media (both newspapers and magazines) symbolically allowed for homophobia to become entrenched within college sport, particularly in regard to the female athlete. Such analyses show how the "default" option for many journalists is to rely on "traditional" and often outdated gender roles to determine senses of sexual normality.

Kim Bissell then continues the dialogue about gender identity in mass media in Chapter 3 with an examination of sports media effects on adolescent girls. She ties issues of self-esteem and self-worth to the participation and consumption of sport, illustrating the double-edged sword within sports media, as learned media effects can result in both positive and/or negative responses about one's notion of self, ranging from perception of attractiveness to the conception of what a "healthy" body could or should be.

In Chapter 4, Lindsey Meân examines organizational gender entrenchment and the online identities these entities adopt and, in doing so, discusses the most widely played sport on the planet: soccer/fùtbal. Meân studies the Federation Internationale de Football Association (FIFA) and World Cup Web sites in terms of production and content values, finding vast differences by gender. She concludes that "the continued re/production of women's soccer as primarily about femaleness undermines women's identities as athletes." The examination also emphasizes the scope of mediasport, with billions of people across every inhabitable continent interested in events such as the men's and women's World Cups.

Then in Chapter 5, we witness an in-depth examination of how "sport has long stirred the drink of gender identity" within beer commercials, written by Lawrence Wenner. In examining the intersections of gender, sport, media, and beer, Wenner claims that "it is the sanctity of this cultural space that has allowed brewers to pander for years to men with 'beer babes' from the 'Swedish bikini team' to the Coors twins." Analyzing a "six-pack" of beer company practices, Wenner claims that media productions such as beer advertisements tend to define masculinity or femininity in terms of the negative argument—that being a man is defined as being not feminine and vice versa.

Bryan Denham and Andrea Duke's chapter on newspaper coverage of doping allegations surrounding seven-time Tour de France champion Lance Armstrong serves as a bridge from the negotiation of gender to the negotiation of nationality. Touching on both of these intertwined issues using content analytic methods, Denham and Duke contend that while the U.S. media portrayed Armstrong as a hero who symbolically defined American values, the international media judged Armstrong much more harshly, emphasizing allegations of drug use and both directly and indirectly comparing his "rogue" warrior status to current U.S. policies toward Iraq and beyond. The chapter underscores the notion that sport does not take place in a vacuum, especially when the most-watched sporting events in the world are international: the Olympics, the World Cups, and, in this case, cycling's greatest spectacle, the Tour de France.

Chapter 7 features the work of Michael Butterworth as he studies the theatrical text employed within the 2004 movie *Miracle*. Bairner (2001) argues that "sport and nationalism are arguably two of the most emotive issues in the modern world" (p. xi), and Butterworth dissects these two concepts jointly in the screen-written and directed narrative of a non-fictional event: the improbable U.S. victory over the Soviet Union in the 1980 Winter Olympics hockey semifinal. He concludes that the rhetorical analysis of *Miracle* exemplifies the "us versus them" themes that tend to gloss over the complexities of nationalistic identity.

Mary McDonald's contributions in Chapter 8 allow for the transition to the discussion of race, specifically within an examination of Whiteness. She notes "the exclusionary tactics and political workings, practices, and institutions of the dominant culture" that are endemic within sports media. Using examples that span a century, McDonald articulates sporting narratives that remain pervasive when discussing race in the modern culture.

This approach then is followed by a social scientific approach in Chapter 9, in which Benjamin Goss, Andrew Tyler, and Andrew Billings adopt a longitudinal content analysis to the examination a longitudinal content analysis to the examination of decades of *Sports Illustrated* covers depicting professional basketball players. While Black athletes have been increasingly depicted in more intellectual ways as time has progressed, some preconceived notions—such as Black hyper-aggressiveness—remain. The authors contend that major media gatekeepers (such as the sports magazine flagship that is *SI*) are often viewed as trendsetters, making their impacts potentially more directly meaningful.

Chapter 10 offers movie analysis in that James Cherney and Kurt Lindemann study the identity variable of disability within the 2005 documentary *Murderball*. Disability sport participation is often used for rehabilitation from spinal cord injury, in part because of the growing need for recreational outlets for physically disabled persons. Quadriplegic rugby plays a central role in this process. Approximately 8,000 people in the U.S. suffer spinal cord injuries every year, and currently between 250,000 and 400,000 people in the U.S. live with spinal cord injuries (National Spinal Cord Injury Association [NSCIA], 2003). Noting that most mainstream media images of disabled athletes "tend[s] to frame participation as helping those with spinal cord injuries 'overcome' their disability," Cherney and Lindemann postulate the account of the quadrapalegic rugby team's cinematic story as a counterbalance. Cherney and Lindemann even explore the notion of the camera's "gaze," explaining how the image being projected is not only more positive, but also more "real," especially in this documentary format.

The final two chapters in this volume attempt to move beyond the specific identity-oriented variables previously analyzed to focus on the characteristics of the people who consume the sports media messages and the theoretical implications of this consumption. In Chapter 11, the first of these synthesis chapters, authors Jennings Bryant and R. Glenn Cummins take a broader, conceptual approach in which they use social identity theory and disposition theory to study the fans who consume the mediated sporting event. They pinpoint how the perceived self-identity of a fan changes as each final score is calculated for their beloved team. The survey approach they adopt reinforces how "for sports fans, both being a fan and being viewed as a fan are critical components of a person's identity." Thus, this functions as a synthesis chapter, allowing the negotiation to come full circle—the team's play affects the fans, which affects the team's self-identity, which affects the media's portrayal of all forms of sport, including the identity issues that cannot be separated from the observable athletic performance. This negotiation is reinforced in Chapter 11 by Bryant and Cummins and is outlined in the final chapter from Kelby Halone, indicating how these variables jointly influence a notion of identity that is impossible to specifically pinpoint.

The final chapter is a forward-thinking piece about the intersection of media discourse within institutional and interpersonal theoretical structures. Halone advocates a strong stance in favor of the institutionalized nature of mediated sport. By incorporating the structure advanced by Kassing, Billings, Brown, Halone, Harrison, Krizek, Meân, and Turman (2004) in a seminal *Communication Yearbook* piece, Halone articulates how sport becomes a negotiation through the enactment, (re)production, consumption, and organization of modern sport. Identity is not just formed by the producers of the mediated image, but is formed by the athletes themselves, the people watching and reading about the athletic performance, and the overarching organized structures that allow sport to occur. Halone incorporates a call for the reexamination of sports processes within the media, providing a capstone argument for the implications of the cases listed in prior chapters.

## ❖ IMPACT OF EXAMINING IDENTITY IN SPORTS MEDIA

Given that Boyd (1997) argued over a decade ago that "sports and the discourses that surround them have become one of the master narratives of twentieth-century culture" (p. ix), the primary aim of this book is to decipher and interrogate the construction of master narratives that are conveyed within and among media outlets. Some of the chapters isolate identity variables, some offer forward-thinking textual analyses of the master narratives in which Boyd refers; all offer unique insight into the production and consumption of a topic that many sport fans spend little, if any, time pondering or conceptualizing in formal senses. These chapters collectively advance knowledge in a field that continues to receive more examination and yet in many ways still has lifetimes of intellectual questions in its future.

In all, this volume aims to use concrete examples from mediasport to further the contention that the portrayal of identity—whether it involves gender, sexuality, nationality, race, disability, or fan affiliation—is a part of a grand negotiation between those who enact, produce, consume, and institutionalize sport and the mechanisms that arise from it. Plato once observed that "you can discover more about a person in an hour of play than in a year of conversation" (Smith, 2008, p. 24). The same type of insights could be postulated regarding the mediated sporting experience, particularly when considering that most fans are consuming much more than one hour of play on a systematic basis.

The way in which mediasport is represented and consumed can speak volumes about whom and what a society strives to be; the negotiation of identity plays an integral role in this process as well. We hope this volume encourages engaging conversations about the manner in which these identity issues are discussed and formulated cognitively and behaviorally within all facets of mediasport.

## ❖ REFERENCES

Anderson, C. (2006). *The long tail: Why the future of business is selling less of more*. New York: Hyperion.

Bairner, A. (2001). *Sport, nationalization, and globalization: European and North American perspectives*. Albany, NY: SUNY Press.

Billings, A. C. (2008). *Olympic media: Inside the biggest show on television*. London: Routledge.

Billings, A. C., & Angelini, J. R. (2007). Packaging the games for viewer consumption: Nationality, gender, and ethnicity in NBC's coverage of the 2004 Summer Olympics. *Communication Quarterly, 55*(1), 95–111.

Billings, A. C., Angelini, J. R., & Eastman, S. T. (2008). Wie shock: Television commentary about playing on the PGA and LPGA tours. *The Howard Journal of Communications, 19*(1), 64–84.

Billings, A. C., Brown, C. L., Crout, J. H., McKenna, K. E., Rice, B. A., Timanus, M. E., et al. (2008). The Games through the NBC lens: Gender, ethnic, and national equity in the 2006 Torino Winter Olympics. *Journal of Broadcasting & Electronic Media, 52*(2), 215–230.

Billings, A. C., & Eastman, S. T. (2002). Nationality, gender, and ethnicity: Formation of identity in NBC's 2000 Olympic coverage. *International Review for the Sociology of Sport, 37*(3), 349–368.

Billings, A. C., & Eastman, S. T. (2003). Framing identities: Gender, ethnic, and national parity in network announcing of the 2002 Winter Olympics. *Journal of Communication, 53*(4), 369–386.

Boyd, T. (1997). Anatomy of a murder: O. J. Simpson and the imperative of sports in cultural studies. In A. Baker & T. Boyd (Eds.), *Out of bounds: Sports, media, and the politics of identity*. Bloomington, IN: Indiana University Press.

Carrington, B. (2007). Sport and race. In G. Ritzer (Ed.), *The Blackwell encyclopedia of sociology* (pp. 4686–4690). Oxford, UK: Blackwell.

Cherney, J. L. (2003). Sports, (dis)ability, and public controversy: Ableist rhetoric and Casey Martin vs. PGA Tour, Inc. In R. S. Brown & D. J. O'Rourke (Eds.), *Case studies in sport communication* (pp. 81–104). Westport, CT: Praeger.

Dokoupil, T. (2007, November 19). An uneasy race for profit. *Newsweek*, p. 14.

Eastman, S. T., Newton, G. D., & Pack, L. (1996). Promoting primetime programs in megasporting events. *Journal of Broadcasting & Electronic Media, 40*, 366–388.

Edwards, H. (1969). *Revolt of the black athlete*. New York: Free Press.

Edwards, H. (1973). *The sociology of sport*. Homewood, IL: Dorsey Press.

Entine, J. (2000). *Taboo: Why black athletes dominate sports and why we're afraid to talk about it*. New York: PublicAffairs.

Goffman, E. (1974). *Frame analysis: An essay on the organization of experience*. New York: Harper & Row.

Gordon, S., & Sibson, R. (1998). Global television: The Atlanta Olympics opening ceremony. In D. Rowe & G. Lawrence (Eds.), *Tourism, leisure, sport: Critical perspectives* (pp. 204–215). Melbourne, AUS: Cambridge University Press.

Hall, S. (1996). Introduction: Who needs "identity"? In S. Hall & P. du Gay (Eds.), *Questions of cultural identity* (pp. 1–17). London: Sage.

Hauck, D. (2006). Crouching tiger, hidden blackness: Tiger Woods and the disappearance of race. In A. Raney & J. Bryant (Eds.), *The handbook of sports and media* (pp. 469–484). Mahwah, NJ: Lawrence Erlbaum.

Hogg, M. A., & Reid, S. A. (2006). Social identity, self-categorization, and the communication of group norms. *Communication Theory, 16*, 7–30.

IOC Marketing Fact File. (2008). Retrieved November 5, 2008, from http://multimedia.olympic.org/pdf/en_report_344.pdf

Kassing, J. W., Billings, A. C., Brown, R. S., Halone, K. K., Harrison, K., Krizek, B., Meân, L., & Turman, P. D. (2004). Communication in the community of sport: The process of enacting, (re)producing, consuming, and organizing sport. *Communication Yearbook, 28*, 373–410.

Maguire, J. (1999). *Global sport: Identities, societies, civilizations*. Cambridge, UK: Polity Press.

McCombs, M. E., & Shaw, D. L. (1972). The agenda-setting function of mass media. *Public Opinion Quarterly, 36*, 176–187.

Mohanty, S. P., Alcoff, L. M., Hames-Garcia, M., & Moya, P. M. L. (2005). *Identity politics reconsidered*. New York: Palgrave-Macmillan.

Morris, M. (2006). *Identity anecdotes: Translation and media culture*. London: Sage.

National Spinal Cord Injury Association. (2003). *More about spinal cord injury*. Retrieved March 10, 2006, from http://www.handicapableperu.com/spinalcord_injuries.html

Nicholson, L., & Seidman, S. (1996). *Social postmodernism: Beyond identity politics*. Cambridge, UK: Cambridge University Press.

O'Donnell, H. (1994). Mapping the mythical: A geopolitics of national sporting stereotypes. *Discourse and Society, 4*(3), 345–380.

O'Reilly, J., & Cahn, S. K. (2007). *Women and sports in the United States*. Boston: Northeastern University Press.

Petty, R. E., & Cacioppo, J. T. (1986). *Communication and persuasion: Central and peripheral routes to attitude change*. New York: Springer-Verlag.

Robertson, G. (2008, August 14). TV networks ride Phelps' golden wake. *The Globe and Mail* (Canada), p. B1.

Selig, B. (2007, January 29). Presiding over record attendance and revenue. *Advertising Age*, S2.

Smith, M. (2008, April 25). Mouthing off. *The Advertiser* (Australia), p. 24.

Tajfel, H. (1972). Experiments in a vacuum. In J. Israel & H. Tajfel (Eds.), *The context of social psychology: A critical assessment* (pp. 69–119). London: Academic Press.

Tajfel, H., & Turner, J. C. (1986). The social identity theory of inter-group behavior. In S. Worchel & L. W. Austin (Eds.), *Psychology of intergroup relations* (pp. 7–24). Chicago: Nelson-Hall.

Turner, J. C., Hogg, M. A., Oakes, P. J., Riecher, S. D., & Wetherell, M. S. (1987). *Rediscovering the social group: A self-categorization theory*. Oxford, UK: Blackwell.

Wenner, L. (2006). Sports and media through the super glass mirror: Placing blame, breast-beating, and a gaze to the future. In A. Raney & J. Bryant (Eds.), *Handbook of sport and media* (pp. 45–62). Mahwah, NJ: Lawrence Erlbaum.

Wonsek, P. L. (1992). College basketball on television: A study of racism in the media. *Media, Culture and Society, 14,* 449–461.

# 2

# The Rene Portland Case

*New Homophobia and Heterosexism in Women's Sports Coverage*

Marie Hardin

Erin Whiteside

❖ ❖ ❖

Although Penn State University did not officially acknowledge it until 2006, the well-known reputation of Rene Portland as a homophobic women's basketball coach had been built on decades of discrimination. Portland had received national press attention in 1986 and then again in 1991 for her "no-alcohol, no-drugs, no-lesbians" policy. Susan Rogers' 1994 book *Sportsdykes* about the experiences of lesbians in sports discussed Portland's practices at length, describing them akin to a 17th-century witch hunt. According to the book, Portland cultivated a culture of fear among straight and gay players alike, who "femmed up" to keep from being berated and eventually dismissed (Brownworth, 1994). The book, along with Pat Griffin's *Strong Women, Deep Closets* (1998), acknowledged that other coaches had practices similar to Portland's and that homophobia was rampant in college sports.

Although Penn State adopted a comprehensive anti-discrimination policy in the 1990s, Portland continued to occupy one of the most high-profile coaching jobs in women's basketball for more than another decade while she harassed and dismissed players she thought were lesbian. She occasionally garnered coverage for discrimination in the alternative press, but it was not until 2005, when she dismissed a top-scoring player who subsequently filed a lawsuit, that Portland garnered widespread attention for something other than her team's performance (Biemesderfer, 1998). This was, simply, a story that was too big to be ignored.

With Portland's discriminatory practices so well known, why did it take a lawsuit for the story to get traction? As the gay rights movement has gained momentum over the past two decades, the amount and tone of overall coverage toward gay athletes and issues have improved, according to research (Armstrong, 1996; Gibson, 2004). Scholars and advocates for lesbians in women's sports, however, argue that a "don't ask, don't tell" approach still governs media coverage (Griffin, 1998; Kane & Lenskyj, 1998; Russell, 2007). Silence is still the most persistent media manifestation of homophobia and heterosexism in regard to women's sports (Gibson, 2004; Wright & Clarke, 1999).

This chapter explores what happens, however, when a story regarding homophobia in women's sports cannot be ignored. As critics of sports media texts have pointed out, coverage incorporates layers of social and cultural assumptions embedded in stories as "common sense," playing out in morality tales that naturalize a broader cultural hegemony (Kane & Lenskyj, 1998; Wachs & Dworkin, 1997). We seek to uncover the assumptions, the morality tale, and the ways these relate to the wider hegemony in relation to gender, sexualities, and sports.

## ❖ THEORY AND RELATED LITERATURE

Virtually every study that has examined coverage of women's sports has confirmed what is obvious from a glance through a newspaper sports section, magazine, or TV sports listings: the consistent symbolic annihilation of female athletes. The marginalization of women in sports media seems to be universal. This trend is apparent in children's magazines (Cuneen & Sidwell, 1998; Duncan & Sayaovong, 1990; Lynn, Walsdorf, Hardin, & Hardin, 2002), daily newspapers (Eastman & Billings, 2000; George, Hartley, & Paris, 2001; Pedersen, 2003), sports magazines (Bishop, 2003; Lumpkin & Williams, 1991), and programming on ESPN and CNN (Eastman & Billings, 2000). This denial of coverage is a denial of power for female athletes; they are constructed as generally insignificant by their failure to secure visibility (Wright & Clarke, 1999).

Of more interest to this study is not the lack of women's sports coverage but the ways female athletes are presented when they do receive media attention. This research looks at such media attention through the lens of cultural hegemony, a theory based in the work of Italian philosopher Antonio Gramsci. In general terms, hegemony is the reinforcement of certain norms and ideas that ultimately benefit the most powerful groups in a culture; these "common sense" assumptions thus normalize certain behavior or groups while making others seem unnatural or wrong (Altheide, 1984; Condit, 1994).

Hegemonic masculinity dictates sports as "naturally" and exclusively a masculine pursuit, making the image of a woman in sports a contradiction—rife with too much dissonance (Griffin, 1998; Lenskyj, 1994; West & Zimmerman, 2002). Hegemonic femininity positions women as opposite to everything masculine; thus, the ideal woman is, at her core, powerless and non-threatening (Kuhn, 1985). Women who participate in competitive sports, then, are ultimately perceived as deviant in terms of femininity and, by extension, sexuality (Caudwell, 1999; also see Chapter 4 in this volume).

Depictions of women in sport, then, are "softened" by de-emphasizing athleticism. Women's sports scholar and advocate Pat Griffin (1998, p. 53) generalized media-created images of female athletes to that end, including that of the "girl next door" (Mia Hamm, Michelle Kwan), "bitchy slut" (Tonya Harding), "beauty queen" (Anna Kournikova), and "wife and mom" (Chris Evert, Lisa Leslie). Women whose sports involve the most overt demonstrations of power (such as football or ice hockey and, to a lesser degree, basketball) are rendered invisible in popular culture through "erasure"—diminished coverage of these sports (Kane & Lenskyj, 1998). Women in power sports are more often labeled lesbian because of the "mannish" qualities of participation (Caudwell, 1999). After all, they play like men—might they also have the same sexual appetites as (heterosexual) men (Russell, 2007)?

❖  LESBIANS IN WOMEN'S SPORTS

Homophobia has been defined as an "irrational" fear and intolerance of gays and lesbians, but women's sports advocates have instead suggested that it is a "very logical response to the power of sport" for women (Kane & Lenskyj, 1998, p. 200; also see Griffin, 2002). Homophobia is a weapon of sexism because it preserves the gender hierarchy and defines accept-able female behavior (Griffin, 2002). The acceptance of lesbians in sports threatens masculine hegemony because it disrupts the masculine-feminine role dichotomy (Kane & Lenskyj, 1998).

Homophobia and heterosexism (the ideology that heterosexuality is the only normal, natural orientation) is reinforced most often through silence; other forms of sexuality go unacknowledged (Barber & Krane, 2007; Wright & Clarke, 1999). Even women's sports advocates often remain silent about homophobia (Schell, n.d.). The "don't ask, don't tell" climate that dominates women's sports allows prejudice and fear to rule (Griffin, n.d.-a). The fear to which Griffin (1998) refers is of what she calls the "lesbian boogeywoman"—a "media-created and promoted" unnatural, mannish predator who lurks in every female locker room. Griffin argues that the "boogeywoman" image scares female athletes and their parents, keeps women's sports advocates on the defensive, and discourages solidarity among women. It "is cast as a threat not only to 'normal' women in sport, but to the image and acceptance of women's sport altogether" (p. 54).

Thus, female athletes often go to great lengths to make sure they are not stamped with the "lesbian label" (Hicks, 1994, p. 57). This includes displaying the symbols of hegemonic femininity: long hair, painted fingernails, makeup, and dresses, for instance (Caudwell, 1999). Homophobia is so rampant at the institutional level in college sports that in the fall of 2006, the NCAA hosted a "think-tank" conference on the topic. One participant, a college player who is lesbian, told of being sub-jected to homophobic comments during a Division I summer basketball camp; she chose to play in the closet. Discussions also centered on "neg-ative recruiting," a scare tactic used by some recruiters to label rival schools and programs as accommodating to lesbians (Griffin, n.d.-b).

### Sheryl Swoopes and Coverage of Lesbians in Sports

The general silence surrounding lesbians in sports was broken in a powerful way, however, in 2005. Sheryl Swoopes, a player for the Women's National Basketball Association (WNBA) who has been one of the most famous female basketball players in the U.S. in recent decades, came out as a lesbian in that year.

Swoopes' announcement was met with a combination of silence and general ambivalence by the sports/media complex. The WNBA's (loud) silence on Swoopes was not surprising in light of its marketing, which generally uses "model-like" (i.e., hetero-sexy) players to endorse the league (Griffin, n.d.-a; Heywood & Dworkin, 2003). Many sports journalists quickly sidelined Swoopes in favor of a discussion of how "easy" it is for a lesbian athlete to come out in comparison to a gay male (Zirin, 2005).

General coverage of lesbian players has followed the familiar pattern of silence, sidelining, or stereotyping. Although the general visibility of lesbians has increased with mainstream media proclaiming the arrival of lesbians into Americans' collective consciousness, Forbes, Lathrop, and Stevens (2002) suggest that to equate that with a positive shift in attitude is premature. In fact, they and others argue that a new cultural strategy, as reflected in media accounts, presents lesbianism as an insignificant issue in women's sports, thus denying its relevance (Armstrong, 1996; Forbes, Lathrop, & Stevens, 2002).

This is not to say that news accounts of women's sports never focus on lesbianism as an issue or on lesbians as central characters; occasionally, they do. Analyses of these types of stories, however, have revealed that they frame lesbianism—not homophobia—as *the* problem in women's sports; such framing guarantees that sportswomen remain divided instead of developing a collective athletic consciousness (Burroughs, Ashburn, & Seebohm, 1995; Hargreaves, 2000; Kane & Lenskyj, 1998).

Griffin (1998) suggests that stories that reflect negatively on lesbian athletes or coaches may be motivated by homophobia and a "homosexual backlash"—a pushback against increasing visibility of lesbians (p. 61). Sports journalists may approach stories with an anti-gay bias; for example, a study by Harry (1995) found that anti-homosexual attitudes were linked with a belief in sports as socially beneficial and as defining masculinity.

Kane and Lenskyj (1998) argue that coverage of lesbian-related issues and athletes that is not overtly homophobic may still reinforce heterosexism through the use of popular liberal humanist rationales: denial of a problem, "other side of the coin" arguments, and arguments that sexual orientation is a private issue (ironic in the face of the demand on female athletes to demonstrate their femininity/heterosexuality in order to be marketable). Such coverage, while embracing the "balance" so cherished in the journalistic establishment, "continues to ignore the thorny questions of sexuality, power and privilege as they play themselves out in women's sport, and thus perpetuates the barriers to women's bonding and empowerment" (Kane & Lenskyj, 1998, p. 201).

## The Rene Portland Story: Coverage of Homophobia in College Sports

A unique feature of the Rene Portland story, in contrast to other recent events such as Swoopes' 2005 announcement and the 2007 allegations of misconduct by Louisiana State University coach Pokey Chatman, is that denying homophobia as an issue in news coverage was virtually impossible; homophobia was at the heart of the events and subsequent lawsuit in 2005 and 2006. Further, the liberal humanist rationale (Kane & Lenskyj, 1998) of *sexuality as a private issue* would also be difficult to advance in coverage of this story. The Portland case involved allegations that the *public display of heterosexuality* was demanded of players, making sexuality as an issue of power central to the story.

The unfolding of events and history behind the Portland case led us to believe this story demanded that journalists recast assumptions and prefabricated morality tales in relation to gender, sexualities, and sports. In other words, we entered this project with the hope that this story could expose cracks in the prevailing hegemony and open the way for truer depictions and empowerment of lesbians in sports.

### Background

Portland became the coach of the Penn State women's basketball team in 1981. She eventually became the sixth-winningest Division I coach of all time, a four-time Big Ten Coach of the Year, and a two-time WBCA (Women's Basketball Coaches Association) National Coach of the Year (Portland, 2005).

It was less than five years after she took the job that Portland made public comments about her "no lesbians" policy. In a 1986 interview with the *Chicago Sun Times,* Portland said she would not tolerate lesbian players (NCLR fights, 2005). A *Philadelphia Inquirer* article in 1991 that confirmed Portland's policy attracted national attention, but "none of the reports went beyond Penn State to the broader issue of homophobia in women's sports" (Brownworth, 1994, p. 79).

Stories of Portland's discrimination continued. The executive director of the WBCA and former players confirmed that Portland benched and dismissed players if she suspected they were lesbian. A 1998 article in the gay-oriented publication *The Advocate* cited a former assistant coach who said Portland promised recruits' parents the team was lesbian-free (Biemesderfer, 1998).

The story about Portland disappeared from the mainstream press until 2005 when a dismissed player, with the support of the National Center for Lesbian Rights, filed a lawsuit with the Pennsylvania Human Relations Commission against Portland and the Penn State athletic department (NCLR Fights, 2005). The player, Jennifer Harris, charged Portland—who is White[1]—with discriminating and then dismissing her because Portland believed she was a lesbian. Harris, who denied being a lesbian, also charged Portland with discriminating on race; Harris is Black. The university launched an investigation and fined Portland $10,000 in 2006, and the lawsuit was settled under confidential terms in 2007. At the end of a losing season that year, Portland promptly resigned.

❖  METHODOLOGICAL APPROACH

The purpose of this study is to describe the ways in which national sports print media challenge or reinforce hegemonic assumptions in relation to sexual identities. We used a textual analysis to accomplish this goal, using news coverage of the Rene Portland lawsuit in national publications from the day the lawsuit was filed (October 11, 2005) through March 2007, when Portland resigned. The lawsuit was chosen primarily because it generated news coverage on sexuality; the study does not focus on coverage of the lawsuit itself, but rather the issues of sexuality that could not be ignored by reporters covering this story. Understanding the journalistic process and assuming that reporters cannot achieve true objectivity, we looked to how writers presented the story as indicators of broad value systems.

**Sample**

The data gathered came from national print media covering the lawsuit, specifically *The New York Times (NYT)*, *USA Today*, and *Sports Illustrated*. Further, we included stories sent out over the wire by the Associated Press (AP), because these stories could have been run in newspapers across the United States (and around the world). We chose to focus on these publications because of prominence, both in circulation and status, and the idea that such publications often set the national news agenda for news and sports (Kiousis, 2004). The search originally included two other news publications of national stature, the *Los Angeles Times* and *The Washington Post*, but stories about the Portland case were not found in either publication.

In order to collect a comprehensive list of articles related to the lawsuit, we completed several searches. We first accessed the LexisNexis and NewsBank newspaper and magazine search engines and searched for the key term "Rene Portland" within the date range of October 11, 2005, to April 1, 2007. Stories not bylined by the AP, or by *The New York Times*, *USA Today*, or *Sports Illustrated*, were discarded. Because we could not guarantee that every story printed was also uploaded to those two databases, we conducted a similar search in the archive section of the online versions of each publication and included in the sample any additional articles that did not appear in the LexisNexis and NewsBank searches to arrive at a total sample of 54 articles. The sample included both news stories and opinion columns. Of the newspaper articles, all appeared in the sports section of their respective publications.

### Procedure

Initially, both of us independently analyzed the articles before we came together for discussion and evaluation of potential themes. We adopted a multi-step strategy of coding offered by Baptiste (2001), in which the researcher first codes in such a way that stays close to the text, applying "tags" or labels to paragraphs or ideas within the story that closely relate to the words in the text. We used NVivo software to code, categorize, and arrive at possible themes. NVivo can assist in the textual analysis process in the coding stages through its organizational functions; however, NVivo does not provide an interpretative function, thus leaving the tasks of analysis and interpreting meaning that is central to the textual analysis process in the hands of the researcher (Spencer, Ritchie, & O'Connor, 2003).

Following the initial coding process, we reviewed the codes and analyzed them for similarities, organizing them into broader categories. Finally, the categories were related to the theoretical framework guiding the study, and we arrived at the final themes, which are defined as something that "captures something important about the data in relation to the research question" (Braun & Clarke, 2006, p. 82). The process was what some qualitative researchers call iterative, meaning that the researchers returned to various steps in the process as we discussed and refined our themes (Spencer, Ritchie, & O'Connor, 2002). When we disagreed on a theme, we discussed our different readings in order to preserve, rework, or discard the theme based on our review of the texts and the theory.

### ❖ RESULTS

The analysis produced three main themes that we called (1) homophobia as unjust and outdated, (2) the privatization of sexuality, and (3) denying or discounting lesbian identity.

**Homophobia as Unjust and Outdated**

The articles we examined all accepted the premise that discrimination based on sexual orientation in sports is wrong; further, homophobia was framed as a relic of the past that U.S. society has since rejected. This manifested itself in references to "civil rights" and "gay rights," to "inclusion" and "equality," and to the Portland case as a signal that homophobia is no longer tolerated in women's sports (Lieber, 2006a; Lieber, 2006c; Longman, 2007). One column, for instance, asserted that "Harris put the entire homophobic sports culture on notice . . . university administrators have to be wary of the empowered athlete ready to fight for justice" (Roberts, 2007a). The most striking example of the argument that homophobia is not tolerated in modern sports came from *USA Today* columnist Christine Brennan, who referred to Penn State's failure to fire Portland, and then added: "shocking as that is in 2006" (Brennan, 2006). Brennan then described Portland's public statements in 1991 to the *Philadelphia Inquirer*, and suggested that homophobia in our current day and age is outdated by adding:

> When she was saying this back then, she found some takers, especially in the living rooms of Middle America. One wonders, however, what she is finding today in a world that is more open-minded and, presumably, far more surprised to hear such stark words of discrimination. (p. 2C)

Writers also suggested that Portland's reputation as a top coach had been tarnished because of her discrimination. Some articles identified Portland as someone who will be remembered as much for her legacy of discrimination as for her on-court achievements, often using language that suggested this legacy was negative. For instance, one writer described Portland's career as being "overshadowed by accusations that she discriminated against homosexual players" (For the Record, 2007). About one-fifth of the articles included information on Portland's ignominious history, recounting past interviews she gave in which she condemned homosexuality. A few also included former players who experienced abuse. One, an article in *USA Today*, provided quotes from five former Penn State players about Portland's abuse (Lieber, 2006b).

Another way these articles suggested that homophobia is wrong was through the use of contextual information about the lawsuit itself. The stories often included several pieces of information from the NCLR (National Center for Lesbian Rights) lawsuit and subsequent investigation that painted Portland in a negative light. For instance, articles consistently used the passage that Portland created a "'hostile, intimidating and offensive environment' based on Harris' perceived sexual orientation," a passage taken directly out of the University's internal investigation (e.g., Armas, 2006b, ¶ 3). Most AP stories, which were written by one reporter based in the Penn State area, used boiler-plate background paragraphs that recounted Portland's history of public "no-lesbian" comments and added that several people who had been affiliated with Portland's program "have told various news out-lets of conversations with Portland in which they alleged the coach made comments indicating bias against lesbians" (e.g., Armas, 2007a, ¶ 19). Further, most stories gave Portland's response to the allegations far less space than Harris' charges. For instance, AP stories that out-lined Penn State's investigation and subsequent findings simply stated that "Portland disagreed with the school's findings" (e.g., Armas, 2007a, ¶ 16; e.g., Armas, 2007b, ¶ 16).

## ❖ COMPARISONS TO RACIAL JUSTICE

Another way homophobia was presented as unjust was through comparisons to racism. Columnists have suggested that homophobia should be addressed in the same way they believe racism has been eradicated in sports. Sports have been framed in recent decades as exemplar (i.e., "leveling the playing field") in terms of providing equal opportunity for African Americans and Latinos; by framing homopho-bia as an injustice similar to racism that should be eradicated in sports, writers extend the mythology of sports as an ideal model for a broader American society. For instance, one *USA Today* columnist recounted the story of Jackie Robinson breaking the color barrier with some support of his White teammates, which led to the "betterment of society" (O'Connor, 2005, ¶ 27). Another columnist argued that if the Portland case had focused on race instead of sexuality, Portland would have been fired because racism is not tolerated (Brennan, 2006).

### The Privatization of Sexuality

Our analysis, however, does not suggest that these writers were ultimately framing sexual identity in similar terms to racial identity. Issues of racial identity in sports are part of public discourse; examples include focus on the social influence of athletes such as Tiger Woods and on the ways in which athletes of color have been framed by radio talk-show hosts such as Rush Limbaugh and Don Imus. In contrast, the articles we studied sought to depoliticize and privatize sexuality, ultimately making analogies between Sheryl Swoopes and Jackie Robinson irrelevant.

For instance, when talking about how a locker room should be a bias-free sanctuary, one *New York Times* columnist explained that "team boundaries should be safe havens . . . a refuge from the outside bias and ridicule that exists more than ever as sports become ethnically, religiously and racially diverse" (Roberts, 2007b). In failing to acknowledge sexuality as an identity that also diversifies sports, the writer renders sexuality invisible and unacknowledged.

Generally, what we interpreted as the privatization of sexuality manifested itself in two ways: the focus on race over sexuality and the missing parallels and labels in the identifying process.

## The Focus on Race Over Sexuality

The initial lawsuit alleged discrimination on the basis of race and sexuality, although it is an important distinction that race was *secondary* and used in support of the primary allegation. Harris charged that Portland was *more likely* to target Black players than White players for harassment based on perceptions of femininity or sexuality (NCLR fights, 2005).

Penn State's internal investigation found that Portland did create a hostile and intimidating environment for those she thought to be lesbians, but the investigation dismissed the race charge altogether. Before that report came out, however, reporters focused primarily on the race charge, despite the lawsuit's primary focus on homophobia. One indicator of this focus was the order in which the charges were presented; the allegations about racism were often presented first.

We do not mean to suggest that charges of racism should not be taken seriously by journalists, but given the lawsuit language and Portland's history of homophobia (and lack of history related to racism) the choice by journalists to prioritize the allegations of discrimination based on race over those related to sexual identity is significant. Sometimes, references to homophobia or to lesbianism were skirted entirely in favor of the race angle as in a *New York Times* brief, printed following the initial charges (Sports briefing, 2005); the article summarized the discrimination lawsuit this way: "Harris, who is black, said in the filing that Portland repeatedly asked her to change her appearance to look more 'feminine'" (p. D4).

Further, even after Penn State dismissed the charge of racism, reporters continued to emphasize Harris' race and to reference the racism charge. For instance, in a column on the university report, a

*USA Today* columnist wrote: "This week at Penn State, the university president reprimanded women's basketball coach Rene Portland for discriminating against a black player by creating a 'hostile, intimidating, and offensive environment' because of that player's perceived sexual orientation" (Brennan, 2006).

## Missing Parallels

Because race is such a highly charged and highly politicized issue, when reporters commented on Harris' race (Black), they always subsequently included Portland's race (White). Not once was Harris' race mentioned without a parallel mention of Portland's racial identity. This parallel labeling process contrasted sharply with how reporters identified Harris and Portland in terms of sexuality, an equally relevant identity given the charges of discrimination based on sexual orientation. Although Harris' denial of being a lesbian was reported in stories as soon as the homophobia allegations were outlined, reporters did not offer a subsequent identifier for Portland, leaving a hole that was especially noticeable in contrast to the race labels, which often appeared in the same stories. There was no mention of Portland's sexuality, no mention of an attempt to ascertain her sexuality, and no mention or recognition of why this was not pertinent information. Typical of the pattern we found is an Associated Press story that ran at the conclusion of the university's internal investigation (also note the primary emphasis on the allegations of racism):

> The school began its investigation in October after former player Jennifer Harris accused Portland of discrimination based on race and sexual orientation. Harris, who is black, left Penn State last spring and transferred last fall at [sic] James Madison University in Virginia. Harris also filed a federal lawsuit against Portland and the university, contending that Portland wanted Harris to look "more feminine" and that Harris was treated differently because she was perceived to be a lesbian. Harris has said she is not gay. Portland, who is white, has firmly denied allegations of discrimination and said that Harris' departure was purely related to basketball. (Armas, 2006a, ¶ 4)

Like this example, other articles did not leave us to assume that Portland was White because she was charged with discriminating against a Black player; they did, however, leave us to assume she was heterosexual because she was discriminating against someone she thought was a lesbian.

**Denying and Discounting Lesbian Identity**

Reporters' references to Harris' claims regarding her own sexuality (and not to Portland's) was one theme in the larger trend of denying and discounting lesbians in sports. About one-third of the articles in the sample included the qualifier about Harris' sexuality, often included directly after recounting the charges in the lawsuit. The following excerpt from *USA Today* illustrates the oft-repeated claim: "Harris contends in the suit that Portland discriminated against her because the longtime coach perceived her to be a lesbian. The suit alleges that Portland tried to force Harris, who says she is not gay, to leave the team" (Armas, 2006c, ¶ 5).

These references to Harris' sexuality helped legitimize coverage of this story and, in this sense, support hegemonic assumptions about compulsory heterosexuality. Articles suggested to readers that we should care because Harris was not a lesbian; in other words, if being accused of being lesbian could happen to a nice, respectable student like Harris, it could happen to anyone (Lieber, 2006c). Another *New York Times* column told readers that "Harris didn't have to be a lesbian to be outraged by Portland" (Roberts, 2007a). Further, the *USA Today* article with quotes from five former Penn State women's basketball players recounting their experiences with discrimination by Portland included only two who were identified as gay or as having lesbian relationships during their time playing for Portland (Lieber, 2006b).

In truth, whether Harris was actually gay was immaterial to the lawsuit—less relevant, in fact, than Harris' race. Only one article—an AP story that ran in *USA Today*—recognized this. The story used a quote from NCLR attorney Karen Doering about Harris to make this point clear: "It's not a matter of whether she is [lesbian] or not. Rene Portland believed that Jen is a lesbian, and Jen is not the first to be caught up in a net of discrimination based on perceived sexual orientation" (Armas, 2005 ¶ 9).

**Missing Coverage**

Another way lesbian identity in sports was denied was in the stories that were *not* written. *Sports Illustrated*, the most prominent sports-focused publication in the U.S., ran only a brief on the Portland story in its "For the Record" (2007) section (on the same page, ironically, as its famous "Sign of the Apocalypse" feature). Reporters generally kept their stories tightly contained to the Portland-Harris lawsuit which was, according to the writers who consistently mentioned Harris's sexuality,

not even about a gay woman in sports. Only four stories that mentioned the Portland case related it (albeit marginally) to the larger problem of homophobia in women's sports; this is surprising given the fact
that the Portland story provided a "news peg" for reporters to do such
stories. One of the three stories focused on negative stereotypes of lesbians in sports, recounting the 2007 case involving allegations of sexual
impropriety against LSU coach Pokey Chatman (Longman, 2007).
Another included the Portland case as part of a larger story about
young athletes standing up for their religious or moral convictions
(Roberts, 2007b). The third, which seemed to be the most sincere
attempt to address the problem of homophobia in sports, trivialized it,
however, by making fun of Portland's "gaydar" as "obviously hay-
wire" and suggested that hiring male coaches might be the safest route
(Roberts, 2007a). The fourth, a *New York Times* feature on Rutgers coach
C. Vivian Stringer, sought to cast discrimination based on sexuality as
not grounded in homophobia but in abuse of power:

> People often refer to the gay issue in women's sports as the elephant in the
> room, but let's remember that the Portland and Chatman cases can be
> seen as abuse of position and power, a far-too-common occurrence in all
> walks of sport. (For Stringer, 2007, p. D3)

## ❖ DISCUSSION

Multiple accounts in academic literature illuminate the ways in which
closeted lesbians live a fearful, scared, and lonely existence; female
athletes who are not lesbian also live in fear of the "lesbian label." The
lesbian stigma, reinforced by a "logical response to the power of sport"
for women—homophobia—is effective in dividing and discouraging
female athletes and advocates (Kane & Lenskyj, 1998, p. 200; also see
Griffin, 2002). In response, activists and scholars have called for the
public discussion of homophobia to challenge masculine hegemony;
coverage of the Portland lawsuit could have provided the catalyst for
that discussion. Instead, coverage reinforced hegemonic strategies in
relationship to homophobia, including denial of a problem and the
framing of sexuality as a private issue, justifying continued silence
about hegemonic sexual politics in sports.

### Reinforcing Heterosexism

We were encouraged to see that the articles we analyzed were
not overtly homophobic and, as we illustrated earlier, were critical of

discrimination based on sexuality. This coverage, in a departure from the findings of previous studies, does not seem to blame lesbians for Portland's discrimination. This is not surprising, however; the ideology of liberal pluralism incorporates the ideals of equality, fairness, and individual rights as essential in U.S. culture.

The problem, however, was in the presentation of homophobia as passé and gay rights in sports as taken-for-granted. Kane and Lenskyj (1998) argue that denying homophobia as a problem or asserting that sexual orientation is a private matter reinforces heterosexism; we believe that this research illuminates the ways in which those themes are embedded in coverage that can, on its surface, promote a civil rights agenda in regard to issues of sexuality.

Simultaneously assuming civil rights for gays and lesbians as a given but also positioning these athletes as deviant—or "special cases" on an otherwise level playing field—reinforces their marginalization. We argue that such coverage is the equivalent to "new racism" in sports coverage, an idea that we live in a so-called "color-blind" society that condemns overt forms of racism; the logic then follows that since race is no longer an issue, any problems in minority communities are due to individual flaws rather than systemic inequities.

The stories and columns we examined did not engage in serious discussion of the systematic and widespread problem of homophobia in sports, thus denying the problem and missing a critical window for coverage. We realize that the journalistic process is a complicated one; gatekeepers exist at many levels—from that of the reporter, to copy editors, sports editors, and publishers; given the overwhelming tradition of silence on the issue, we could argue that any coverage of this issue is progress. The lack of engagement with this story on any meaningful level, however, is discouraging. By refusing to address larger issues of homophobia, media accounts essentially reinforced lesbianism as an insignificant issue and reinforced the overall silence that shrouds homophobia in sports, cloaking issues of alternative sexualities and lesbians (and gays) where they cannot become accepted and empowered. The emphasis on the racial component to this story—which by any account did not deserve the prominent framing it received—is also evidence of the discomfort, resistance, and perhaps even fear of journalists in dealing with stories about homophobia.

The media accounts we studied also reinforced heterosexism by making Portland's racial identity visible but allowing her sexuality, assumed "normal," to remain invisible. At the same time, many media accounts also prominently "normalized" Harris, allowing her to be typecast more as the "girl next door" (i.e., harmless) than as a potential "lesbian boogeywoman," undeserving of sympathy (and perhaps rightfully run out of Portland's locker room). Thus, these media accounts reinforce the notion of compulsory heterosexuality—the idea that heterosexuality is normal and universal. The emphasis on Harris' denial of being gay leads us to wonder how much more this story may have been marginalized in the mainstream press had Harris been open to the "lesbian boogeywoman" stereotype.

### ❖ MOVING BEYOND DENIAL

It is regrettable that journalists at major media outlets, with the time and resources to go beyond the tip of the iceberg (Portland), chose not to and instead gave this story bare-bones coverage; even the storyline was obscured by a peripheral issue. Not a single stereotype was challenged in the coverage; all were left intact. The closet door for lesbians remains shut.

Even so, we remain hopeful that attention to the Portland story has and will crack the door; the NCAA think tank and other activity demonstrate that. Further, what happened to Portland may, indeed, prompt coaches and administrators to more closely examine the women's sports culture in their programs.

So, how can things change? Obviously, journalists need to cover this story differently. We do not believe they will, however, until women's sports advocates decide that they will no longer silently tolerate homophobia and heterosexism from the inside or the outside. We are not blaming women's sports advocates, however; their silence is well-grounded in the knowledge that any woman who also calls herself an athlete is threatening. Challenging prevailing ideology is never easy. We hope that critical reflection on the Portland legacy and its coverage will aid the process.

### ❖ REFERENCES

Altheide, D. L. (1984). Media hegemony: A failure of perspective. *Public Opinion Quarterly, 48,* 476–490.

Armas, G. (2005, October 12). Penn State to review anti-lesbian complaint. *USA Today.* Retrieved June 5, 2007, from http://www.usatoday.com/sports/college/womensbasketball/bigten/2005–10–12-penn-state-complaint_x.htm

Armas, G. (2006a, April 13). Penn State finishes discrimination investigation of coach Rene Portland. Retrieved June 5, 2007, from Lexis-Nexis Universe/Sports News database.

Armas, G. (2006b, April 18). Penn St. fines coach $10,000 for "hostile" treatment of player. Retrieved June 5, 2007, from Lexis-Nexis Universe/Sports News database.

Armas, G. (2006c, May 18). Penn State coach accuses group of trying to exploit bias case. *USA Today*. Retrieved June 5, 2007, from http://www.usato day.com/sportscollege/womensbasketball/bigten/2006-05-18-portland_ x.htm

Armas, G. (2007a, February 5). Ex-Penn State player, Portland settle discrimination complaint. *USA Today*. Retrieved June 5, 2007, from http:// www.usatoday.com/sports/college/womensbasketball/bigten/2007-02-05-pennstate-settlement_x.htm

Armas, G. (2007b, March 23). Rene Portland resigns as Penn State basketball coach. Retrieved June 5, 2007, from Lexis-Nexis Universe/Sports News database.

Armstrong, L. (1996). Mainstreaming Martina: Lesbian visibility in the 1990s. *Canadian Woman Studies, 16*(2), 10–20.

Baptiste, I. (2001). Qualitative data analysis: Common phases, strategic differences. *Qualitative Social Research, 2*(3). Retrieved July 4, 2007, from http://qualitative-research.net/fqs/fqs-eng.htm

Barber, H., & Krane, V. (2007). Creating inclusive and positive climates in girls' and women's sport: Position statement on homophobia, homonegativism, and heterosexism. *Women in Sport & Physical Activity Journal, 16*, 53–56.

Biemesderfer, S. C. (1998, August 18). Hoop schemes: As long as the bouncing ball is leading to the bank, many women are choosing to play from the closet. *The Advocate*, p. 20.

Bishop, R. (2003). Missing in action: Feature coverage of women's sports in *Sports Illustrated. Journal of Sport and Social Issues, 27*, 184–194.

Braun, V., & Clarke, V. (2006). Using thematic analysis in psychology. *Qualitative Research in Psychology, 3*, 77–101.

Brennan, C. (2006, April 20). Penn State didn't learn from Duke. *USA Today*, p. 2C.

Brownworth, V. A. (1994). The competitive closet. In S. F. Rogers (Ed.), *Sportsdykes: Stories from on and off the field* (pp. 75–86). New York: St. Martin's Press.

Burroughs, A., Ashburn, L., & Seebohm, L. (1995, August). Add sex and stir: Homophobic coverage of women's cricket in Australia. *Journal of Sport & Social Issues, 19*(3), 266–284.

Caudwell, J. (1999). Women's football in the United Kingdom: Theorizing gender and unpacking the butch lesbian image. *Journal of Sport & Social Issues, 23*, 390–402.

Condit, C. (1994). Hegemony in a mass-mediated society: Concordance about reproductive technologies. *Critical Studies in Media Communication, 11*(3), 205–223.

Cuneen, J., & Sidwell, M. J. (1998). Gender portrayals in *Sports Illustrated for Kids* advertisements: A content analysis of prominent and supporting models. *Journal of Sport Management, 12*, 39–50.

Duncan, M. C., & Sayaovong, A. (1990). Photographic images and gender in *Sports Illustrated for Kids. Play and Culture, 3*, 91–316.

Eastman, S. T., & Billings, A. (2000). Sportscasting and sports reporting: The power of gender bias. *Journal of Sport and Social Issues, 24*, 192–213.

Forbes, S. L., Lathrop, A. H., & Stevens, D. E. (2002). A pervasive silence: Lesbophobia and team cohesion in sport. *Canadian Woman Studies, 21*(3), 32–42.

For Stringer, only one thing left to do. (2007, April 2). *The New York Times*, p. D3.

For the record. (2007, April 2). *Sports Illustrated, 106*(14), p. 26.

George, C., Hartley, A., & Paris, J. (2001). Focus on communication in sport: The representation of female athletes in textual and visual media. *Corporate Communications, 6*, 94–102.

Gibson, R. (2004). Coverage of gay males, lesbians in newspaper lifestyle sections. *Newspaper Research Journal, 25*(3), 90–95.

Griffin, P. (1998). *Strong women, deep closets: Lesbians and homophobia in sport.* Champaign, IL: Human Kinetics Books.

Griffin, P. (2002). Changing the game: Homophobia, sexism and lesbians in sport. In S. Scraton & A. Flintoff (Eds.), *Gender and sport: A reader* (pp. 193–208). New York: Routledge.

Griffin, P. (n.d.-a). *Reflections on the significance of Sheryl Swoopes coming out as a lesbian.* Retrieved June 14, 2007, from the Women's Sports Foundation Web site: http://www.womenssportsfoundation.org

Griffin, P. (n.d.-b). *Negative recruiting and homophobia in sport.* Retrieved September 1, 2008, from the Women's Sports Foundation Web site: http://www.womenssportsfoundation.org/Content/Articles/Issues/Homophobia/N/Negative-Recruiting-and-Homophobia-in-Womens-Sport.aspx

Hargreaves, J. (2000). *Heroines of sport: The politics of difference and identity.* New York: Routledge.

Harry, J. (1995). Sports ideology, attitudes toward women, and anti-homosexual attitudes. *Sex Roles, 32*, 109–116.

Heywood, L., & Dworkin, S. (2003). *Built to win: The female athlete as cultural icon.* Minneapolis: University of Minnesota Press.

Hicks, B. (1994). Lesbian athletes. In S. F. Rogers (Ed.), *Sportsdykes: Stories from on and off the field* (pp. 57–74). New York: St. Martin's Press.

Kane, M. J., & Lenskyj, H. J. (1998). Media treatment of female athletes: Issues of gender and sexualities. In L. Wenner (Ed.), *MediaSport* (pp. 186–201). New York: Routledge.

Kiousis, S. (2004). Explicating media salience: A factor analysis of *New York Times* issue coverage during the 2000 U.S. Presidential election. *Journal of Communication, 54*(1), 71–87.

Kuhn, A. (1985). *The power of the image.* London: Routledge.

Lenskyj, H. J. (1994). Sexuality and femininity in sports contexts: Issues and alternatives. *Journal of Sport & Social Issues, 18*, 356–376.

Lieber, J. (2006a, May 11). Portland vigorously defends her integrity and Penn State program. *USA Today*, p. 3C.

Lieber, J. (2006b, May 11). Others make allegations. *USA Today*, p. 3C.

Lieber, J. (2006c, May 11). Harris stands tall in painful battle with Penn State coach. *USA Today*. Retrieved 5 June 2007, from http://www.usatoday .com/sports/college/womensbasketball/2006-05-11-jennifer-harris_x.htm

Longman, J. (2007, April 19). Chatman case raises mistrust during recruiting season. *The New York Times*, p. D1.

Lumpkin, A., & Williams, L. D. (1991). An analysis of *Sports Illustrated* feature articles, 1954–1987. *Sociology of Sport Journal, 8*, 16–32.

Lynn, S., Walsdorf, K., Hardin, M., & Hardin, B. (2002). Selling girls short: Advertising gender images in *Sports Illustrated for Kids*. *Women in Sport & Physical Activity Journal, 11*, 77–100.

NCLR fights three decades of anti-gay harassment at Penn State (2005, Winter). *National Center for Lesbian Rights Newsletter*, p. 1.

O'Conner, I. (2005, October 29). Male athlete who comes out in prime will be brave pioneer. *USA Today*. Retrieved June 5, 2007, from http://www .usatoday.com/sports/columnist/oconnor/2005-10-29-oconnor-keepingscore_x.htm

Pedersen, P. M. (2003). Examining stereotypical written and photographic reporting on the sports page: An analysis of newspaper coverage of inter-scholastic athletics. *Women in Sport & Physical Activity Journal, 12*, 67–75.

Portland, R. (2005). *Penn State 2004–05 lady lion basketball yearbook* (pp. 36–42). University Park, PA: Penn State Athletics.

Roberts, S. (2007a, February 8). A player serves notice to homophobic sports culture. *The New York Times*, p. D1.

Roberts, S. (2007b, March 28). Youngsters' defiance is a lesson in acceptance. *The New York Times*, p. D1.

Russell, K. (2007). "Queers, even in netball?" Interpretations of the lesbian label among sportswomen. In C. C. Aitchison (Ed.), *Sport and gender identities: Masculinities, femininities and sexualities* (pp. 106–121). New York: Routledge.

Schell, L. A. (n.d.). *(Dis)empowering images? Media representations of women in sport*. Retrieved June 14, 2007, from the Women's Sports Foundation Web site: http://www.womenssportsfoundation.org/Content/Articles/Issues/ Media%20and%20Publicity/D/DisEmpowering%20Images%20%20Medi a%20Representations%20of%20Women%20in%20Sport.aspx

Spencer, L., Ritchie, J., & O'Connor, W. (2003). Analysis: Practices, principles and practices. In J. Ritchie & J. Lewis (Eds.), *Qualitative research practice: A guide for social science students and researchers* (pp. 199–218). Thousand Oaks, CA: Sage.

Sports briefing. (2005, December 22). *The New York Times*, p. D4.

Wachs, F. L., & Dworkin, S. L. (1997). "There's no such thing as a gay hero": Sexual identity and media framing of HIV-positive athletes. *Journal of Sport & Social Issues, 21*, 327–347.

West, C., & Zimmerman, D. H. (2002). Doing gender. *Gender & Society, 1*(2), 125-151.

Wright, J., & Clarke, G. (1999). Sport, the media, and the construction of compulsory heterosexuality: A case study of women's rugby union. *International Review for the Sociology of Sport, 34,* 227–243.

Zirin, D. (2005, November 4). Sheryl Swoopes: Out of the closet—and ignored. *The Nation.* Retrieved June 14, 2007, from http://www.thenation.com/doc/20051121/sheryl_swoopes_out_of_the_closet

## ❖  NOTE

1. Racial, not ethnic, terms were used throughout coverage of the Portland story; thus, those are the terms we chose to use throughout this analysis.

# 3

# Exploring the Influence of Mediated Beauty

*Competitive Female Athletes' Perceptions of Ideal
Beauty in Athletes and Other Women*

## Kim L. Bissell

❖ ❖ ❖

Over the past few decades, an overwhelming amount of research has been devoted to studying adolescent girls, the nature of their development, and the factors influencing their ability to grow into well-adjusted, healthy individuals. The increase of scholarly interest in this area corresponds with alarming statistics that reveal the large number of adolescent girls suffering from anorexia, bulimia, and other forms of disordered eating and appearance anxiety. These illnesses and harmful patterns of behavior typically result from negative or low self-esteem and a desire to conform to societal and cultural pressures that dictate thinness as the ideal form of physical beauty. Researchers have observed a link between certain types of media exposure that endorse and promote this standard of attractiveness and the likelihood of young girls to become dissatisfied with their body and develop these disorders (see e.g., Harrison, Taylor, & Marske, 2006). Other work has explored the potentially positive benefits such as higher self-esteem that girls who participate in sports might experience (see e.g., Zimmerman, 1999). This project addresses and explores the relationship among female adolescent athletes, their media consumption, and their self-esteem and seeks to discover whether sports participation plays a role in these girls' perceptions of ideal beauty in others.

❖  THEORY AND RELATED LITERATURE

Physical attractiveness is celebrated in American society. General interest magazines publish special issues of the most beautiful people in the entertainment industries, and sport magazines publish entire issues devoted to swimsuits and models. Numerous researchers have analyzed the importance of physical attractiveness in personal perception (Berscheid & Walster, 1974, 1978; Cash, 1981; Riggio, Widaman, Tucker, & Salinas, 1991) and have found that attractive individuals are evaluated more favorably by others (Miller, 1970; Riggio, Widaman, Tucker, & Salinas, 1991). Furthermore, attractive people are viewed as having more desirable personalities (Dion, Bersheid, & Walster, 1972), are preferred as dating partners (Byrne, Ervin, & Lamberth, 1970), and are typically more successful in social interaction (Reis, et al., 1982). While trying to scientifically measure ideal beauty more objectively may prove to be challenging, many scholars (Sypeck, Gray, & Ahrens, 2004; Thompson, Heinberg, Altabe, & Tantleff-Dunn, 1999) suggest that the media contribute to the development and reinforcement of ideal beauty and attractiveness through the repetition of appearance-oriented norms and values. Even if individuals were to have their own ideas about what is considered beautiful and attractive, the pervasiveness of mediated messages may resonate more loudly with adolescent girls. Studying and understanding such judgments allows for insight into ideal beauty in American society and may offer some insight with regard to the way adolescent girls might perceive beauty in themselves and others. The underlying objective of this project is to assess how or if adolescent sports participation is at all influential in shaping the way girls think about beauty in others.

Young girls are said to lose confidence, self-esteem, and independence at an early point in adolescence, largely due to harmful cultural messages and societal pressures (Pipher, 1994). During this critical period, they experience a loss of self-image and develop skewed attitudes about their competence and image (Gilligan, Rogers, & Tolman,

1991). Pipher (1994) attributes this psychological tailspin to a "girl-poisoning" culture that ultimately requires them to sacrifice their true selves in order to become what society demands. It is during this time when adolescent girls are already feeling tremendous pressure and anxiety as it relates to their changing bodies that the images of adolescent beauty in the media serve to reinforce the singular ideal as it relates to body shape and size (Labre & Walsh-Childers, 2003). Currie (1999) found in her content analysis of teen magazines, published in Canada (*Teen, Seventeen, YM,* and *Sassy*), that in three of the four magazines more than half of the editorial content was dedicated to stories about fashion, beauty, celebrities, and romance. Labre and Walsh-Childers (2003) found in their qualitative analysis of online magazines targeted toward adolescent girls that three dominant themes were most evident in the content: beauty is a requirement, beauty is achieved through products, and we can help you find the right products. The resources available to adolescent girls are exploding, and the potential influence the media and other sources have on adolescent girls' self-esteem is only increasing; thus it is necessary to examine the factors influencing the phenomenon itself.

Concern about attractiveness and body image is certainly not new for college-aged and adult women as scholars have been studying the problem in a non-media context for decades (Birtchnell, Dolan, & Lacey, 1987; Cash & Green, 1986; Dolce, Thompson, Register, & Spana, 1987; Garner, Olmsted, Polivy, & Garfinkel, 1984); however, empirical studies have documented a rise in appearance anxiety and body image disturbance in increasingly younger girls. Female adolescents in particular undergo great changes biologically, cognitively, and emotionally during puberty. They become much more concerned with their body image and appearance as they experience certain hormonal disruptions (Santrock, 1998). They oftentimes use popular media to help them construct self-identities and make sense of their world (Butler & Zaslow, 2002). There is little doubt that adolescent girls are rigorous consumers of many types of media, and this consumption affects their perception of reality (Douglas, 1995; Stern, 2005). Research has shown that 83% of teenage girls report spending a mean of 4.3 hours a week reading magazines (Levine & Smolak, 1996), and 70% of girls who regularly read magazines endorse them as important sources of beauty and fitness information (Levine, Smolak, & Hayden, 1994). Younger adolescents spend approximately 25% of their time watching television (Liebert & Sprafkin, 1988) and are consequently exposed to television characters and images that reinforce notions about the importance of thinness and attractiveness. In their experiment testing the influence of exposure to ultra-thin and average-sized magazine models, Clay, Vignoles, and Dittmar (2005) found that exposure to both types of models was related to lower body satisfaction and decreased self-esteem in adolescent girls. Exposure to attractive models, regardless of their body size being ultra-thin or average, triggered more negative feelings about self.

Adolescent girls grow increasingly susceptible to the messages and cultural norms that the media perpetuate (Fouts & Burggraf, 1999), as the mass media are the most potent and pervasive communicators of social and cultural standards in America (Heinberg, 1996). Currently, these media messages depict extremely thin women and propagate an attractiveness ideal as a cultural norm that is neither healthy nor attainable for most women. The consumption of these media and the internalization of ideal beauty and thinness interact with low self-esteem to increase the likelihood of body dissatisfaction and body image disturbance among young females (Strice & Thompson, 2001). In their analysis of beauty and thinness messages in children's media, Herbozo, Tantleff-Dunn, Gokee-Larose, and Thompson (2004) found that many of the most popular children's videos contained messages emphasizing the importance of physical appearance. What is not known is the degree to which these appearance-oriented messages are found in media consumed by adolescent girls. Bissell and Birchall (2006) found in their body-shape analysis of 8-to-18-year-old girls' favorite television programs that shows viewed by older girls in the sample (i.e., 14 to 18 years of age) tended to have the greatest proportion of thin-ideal characters, primarily because much of what they reported watching was programming targeted toward older audiences. Those in the younger bracket of the sample watched more programming with "average-sized" characters such as *Full House, The Suite Life of Zack and Cody,* or shows with a larger main character such as in *That's So Raven.* Although it is clear that a number of factors—including media—influence an individual's propensity to develop a skewed perception of ideal beauty, exposure to media that emphasizes these appearance attributes has been shown to significantly predict a belief in beauty as a societal norm.

During the adolescent time of emotional and physical maturation and uncertainty, there is reason to believe that girls who actively engage in sports will have higher self-esteem than their non-athletic peers. Sports participation affords girls the opportunity to develop physical competence and de-emphasize the importance of physical attractiveness as the greatest measure of their self-esteem (Nelson, 1994). In a sport environment, girls can learn the value of teamwork, community involvement, and form meaningful friendships (Feldman & Elliott, 1990). Participation in sport may help them avoid the physical, psychological, and social pitfalls that accompany the adolescent period. For reasons not entirely clear or understood, playing sports may empower girls and help them reclaim what Gilligan has labeled their lost "voice" (Zimmerman, 1999). Sports participation may indeed act as a beneficial mediator among thinness-depicting or appearance-oriented media and low self-esteem, reducing the chances that young girls will develop eating disorders and suffer from appearance anxiety.

Given the increased prevalence of young girls in the sports arena, female athletes now have a distinctive place in the mass media. The increase of young female athletes has stimulated a growth in the mass media's production of products, services, and literature aimed at this expanding market group. A new onslaught of magazines, such as *Sports Illustrated for Kids*, has appeared on publication stands catering to the interests of these adolescent athletes. However, because athletes such as Anna Kournikova, Amanda Beard, or Jennie Finch have used the media to create or promote a more glamorized image of themselves, young girls may receive conflicting messages pertaining to the acceptance of athleticism as an attractiveness norm. One question this study seeks to answer is how or if participation in sports shapes young girls' perceptions of role models for themselves—athletes versus figures in the media—and will this subsequently affect how they view beauty and attractiveness in others? To date, no extensive research has addressed how the consumption of media interacts with the young athlete's perception of self-identity and the effect, if any, on her self-esteem and appearance anxiety.

Understanding the complex issues related to media exposure and appearance anxiety, to some extent, can be explained with cultivation theory (Gerbner, 1969; Gerbner, Gross, Morgan, & Signorielli, 2002). Overall, cultivation theory suggests that exposure and frequency of a message disseminated through a mediated form affects perception; in other words, the more media a person is exposed to, the more that person will interpret the message to be valid. Hesse-Biber, Leavy, Quinn, and Zoino (2006) examined four social psychological theories, including cultivation theory, to better understand how women are exposed to and affected by the media as they relate to body image distortion and the "cult of thinness." They argue that these theories offer a "nexus of influence and provide important clues to our understanding of the pervasive influence and impact of these industries on the development of eating disorders in women" (p. 208). While Hesse-Biber and colleagues did not study beauty and attractiveness on a more general level, they do suggest that the image-obsessed culture in which we live is partially responsible for creating culturally induced diseases that profit from women's obsession to modify their image because of their dissatisfaction with it. Lastly, they argue that it is the repeated exposure to ideal imagery in the mass media that leaves women with feelings of unhappiness and dissatisfaction.

Levine and Smolak (1996) expanded on this by stating that the "constant repetition of certain forms and themes (values) as well as the constant omission of certain types of people, actions, and stories, powerfully influences and homogenizes viewers' conceptions of social reality" (p. 250). Media frequently project images and themes of femininity, beauty, success, and body shape (Cusumano & Thompson, 1997), and it is through repeated exposure to these consistent and pervasive types of images that women become cultivated to think about beauty and attractiveness using a single framework.

A key issue with this project is the extent to which girls in this sample pay attention to the media and, more importantly, if they do not spend a great deal of time consuming media, what other activities are acting as a displacement? Certainly, in this case, involvement in a sport at a highly competitive level is going to consume great amounts of time for participants in this study, potentially taking away time the athlete might spend with the media. However, most adolescents will find some time to watch television, read magazines, listen to music, view a film, or read a book at some point throughout their day or week. Subsequently, the media may still play a role in shaping girls' sense of self and sense of appearance anxiety by presenting images representing ideal beauty and ideal thinness, even in media directed toward younger audiences. Pipher (1994) suggests that the cultural norms evident in mass media create discrepancies between an individual's true and ideal selves.

The goal of this project is to better understand the way adolescent female athletes perceive beauty in others while also examining their media use and exposure and their general self-esteem. In this case, a variety of media factors, sports participation, importance of physical beauty, and age were measured to determine which might be related to more positive appearance evaluations in others. Subsequently, the following questions were addressed:

How is media exposure related to appearance evaluations of entertainment and athletic models?

How is sports participation related to appearance evaluations of entertainment and athletic models?

How is self-esteem related to appearance evaluations of entertainment and athletic models?

How is participation in a specific sport related to self-esteem?

How does involvement in sport relate to the importance of appearance ideals?

What differences exist between participants' views of attractiveness in models and their opinions about others' views of attractiveness?


## ❖ METHODOLOGICAL APPROACH

In order to determine the relationship between sports participation, media use, self-esteem, and appearance ideals in competitive female athletes between the ages of 7 and 16, girls competing in at least one sport in three counties in the southeastern United States were recruited to participate in this study. Athletes were recruited from Division I or Division II soccer teams, optional and compulsory level gymnastics, club volleyball, club basketball, travel softball, and competitive horseback riding and spent between 8 and 16 hours a week at practice, depending on the sport and level in which each competed. A total of 66 female athletes between ages 7 and 16 participated in this study. Of the total participants in this portion of the study, 27% were African American and 73% were White. The average age of participants was 11-1/2.


### Possible Predictors of Appearance Evaluations

Exposure to television was measured by asking respondents to record the total number of days per week they spent viewing television and then report their frequency of viewing specific shows. Respondents were asked to list up to 10 television programs they viewed and then report their frequency of viewing each program listed by using the following scale (regularly, often, sometimes, rarely, or never). Television show favorites varied dramatically depending on the age of the participant, although each age group seemed to have similar viewing preferences. For example, girls between 7 and 11 years of age reported watching *That's So Raven, The Suite Life of Zack and Cody, Full House,* and *Hannah Montana,* whereas those older in the sample tended to prefer television shows on the primetime networks (*Arrested Development, Grey's Anatomy, CSI, Ugly Betty,* and *24*).

In order to get a measure of thin-ideal television exposure all of the television programs participants listed as having watched with some frequency, a thin-ideal TV viewing index was created. Approximately five minutes of each show was recorded, selecting segments in which the primary female characters were present in the scene. Using a pool of 16 undergraduate college students, each person was asked to identify the primary female characters in each clip of the television show and also assign each primary female character a body shape code ranging from conspicuously thin to conspicuously fat (1 to 5 respectively). The mean score for each show was calculated, resulting in a thinness score for each television show. Then each show's thin-ideal index was multiplied by the participants' reported frequency of viewing each show, thus creating a variable representing a thin-ideal television viewing index.

### Sports Participation

Respondents were asked several questions related to their participation in sports. This included having them report the sports they were currently competing in and listing sports they participated in or competed in during the off-season. At the time data was collected, 82% were in season with their respective sports. Of the sample, 20% reported participating or practicing their primary sport for several hours every day. Another 27% reported practicing or competing in their primary sport for several hours almost every day, and another 34% reported practicing between 1 and 2 hours almost every day. For example, members of one soccer team trained three days a week for two hours on each of those days and then often played between 1 and 3 games over the weekend. Athletes participating in fast-pitch softball played in several games each week and then reported having practice on the days they were not competing.

### Self-Esteem

Using a modified version of Coopersmith's (1967) self-esteem inventory, participants were asked to respond to 29 items related to their own feelings of self. Examples of statements included items such as "I often get discouraged in school" or "There are a lot of things I would change about myself if I could." Responses were on a 5-point scale, ranging from strongly agree to strongly disagree. The mean score on the 29-item self-esteem measure was 99.64 with a low of 83 and a high of 124. In this case, a higher number represented higher general self-esteem.

### Sociocultural Attitudes Toward Appearance

Participants were asked to answer two series of questions related to the importance of appearance attributes to themselves and the projected importance of those same appearance attributes to people they knew (Cusumano & Thompson, 1997). Participants were asked about the importance of being thin, being tall, being muscular, being athletic, being attractive, being smart, and being popular, and then were asked to indicate how important each attribute was to them using the following responses: extremely important, important, somewhat important, or not at all important. When all of the items were combined, they were not statistically reliable, so individual items were used in some of the statistical tests. The mean response for the importance of thinness for one's self was 2.05 (on a 1-to-4 scale with 1 representing extremely important), and the mean response for the importance of attractiveness was 2.18 (on the same 1-to-4 scale, with 1 representing extremely important). Of all of the traits listed (thin, tall, muscular, athletic, attractive, smart, popular), participants indicated thinness as being the most important trait for themselves, followed by being attractive and being popular.

### Attractiveness Evaluations

Since perceptions of attractiveness are a fairly subjective measure, the objective for this project was to provide adolescent girls a range of images to respond to with varying degrees of glamorization, attractiveness, and athleticism. No literature exists that documents the way adolescent athletes might respond to images of glamorized celebrities versus non-glamorized athletes; thus, another objective of this study was to address that issue—i.e., how would a specific sample respond to images like the ones used in this study? In order to measure participants' assessment of attractiveness and beauty in others, participants were shown images of 13 women and girls from a variety of venues. In some cases, the models were recognizable celebrities from popular movies or television series (e.g., Miley Cyrus, Raven-Symoné, etc.). In other cases, the models were potentially recognizable athletes (e.g., Michelle Wie, Jennie Finch). In the remaining cases, the models were probably not at all recognizable by participants but were clearly images of athletes. In order to select the 13 images used in the current study, an earlier pilot study used 30 images to test the recognizability of the models and to assess overall attractiveness. In the pilot study, 15 athletes—some known and some unknown—were selected and 15 television, movie, or music stars were selected. After viewing the attractiveness means for all 30 models, three were eliminated because there was little variability on the responses (two athletes received 10s [extremely ugly] and one television star received all 1s [extremely attractive]). From there, seven athletes and six celebrities were randomly selected from the remaining pool. For examples see representative photos on Web sites such as:

Maria Sharapova: http://www.sharapova.org.uk/maria_sharapova_photo_gallery_2.html#

Ashley Tisdale: http://ashley-pictures.com/displayimage.php?album=4&pos=17

Cheyenne Kimball: http://www.mymostwanted.com/gallery/showphoto.php/photo/312203

Participants in this study viewed a wide range of photographs of celebrities, celebrity/athletes, athletes, and non-recognizable models. The photos viewed showed some celebrities looking more glamorous and other celebrities looking more natural. Photographs of the athletes were similar: some looked more glamorous, whereas others were in action in their respective sports or were not wearing makeup or fancy clothing. The objective was to give participants an opportunity to respond to a wide range of images to assess how or if glamour and makeup might influence their perceptions of attractiveness. Participants were asked four questions about each image: Write the name of the person, if you know it; indicate how pretty YOU think she is (1=extremely pretty, 10=extremely unattractive); indicate how pretty OTHERS would think she is (same responses); and indicate how much you would like to look like this person (see Table 3.1 for means). Participants were shown one image and the series of questions on separate pages so that responses would not be confusing.

## ❖  RESULTS

### Descriptive Results

Participants were asked to list three people they thought were pretty and then describe why they thought each person was attractive. In 32% of the cases, participants listed a media personality as one person they thought was attractive. Reasons for these evaluations included responses such as: "She has such a pretty face"; "I cannot help but think she is pretty"; "She is a great singer and looks pretty too"; or "Her hair always looks perfect, and she always dressed very pretty." Participants who listed a friend or relative as one person they thought was pretty listed responses such as "(name) is just pretty; she's nice

**Table 3.1**   Means and Standard Deviations for Perceived Attractiveness, Projected Attractiveness and Desire to Look Like the Model Shown for 13 Entertainment and Athletic Models (N = 66)

| | | Attractiveness* | Projected Attractiveness** | Would Like to Look Like Model*** |
|---|---|---|---|---|
| Model#1 Maria Sharapova Pro athlete | Mean STD | 3.77 (1.44) | 4.36 (1.46) | 5.59 (1.76) |
| Model#2 Ashley Tisdale TV and movie star (Disney Channel) | Mean STD | 3.00 (1.82) | 3.22 (1.90) | 5.31 (2.64) |
| Model#3 Unknown athlete White model | Mean STD | 5.41 (1.71) | 5.54 (1.68) | 5.09 (2.54) |
| Model#4 Cheyenne Kimball Pop singer | Mean STD | 3.45 (1.50) | 3.72 (1.51) | 6.00 (2.45) |
| Model#5 Unknown athlete White model | Mean STD | 5.10 (1.41) | 5.50 (1.50) | 5.54 (2.24) |
| Model#6 Brenda Song TV and movie star | Mean STD | 3.32 (1.49) | 3.72 (1.54) | 5.68 (2.49) |
| Model#7 Unknown athlete Non-White model | Mean STD | 5.86 (2.10) | 6.04 (1.76) | 4.77 (2.61) |

**Table 3.1** (Continued)    Means and Standard Deviations for Perceived
Attractiveness, Projected Attractiveness and Desire to
Look Like the Model Shown for 13 Entertainment
and Athletic Models

| | | Attractiveness* | Projected Attractiveness** | Would Like to Look Like Model*** |
|---|---|---|---|---|
| Model#8 Miley Cyrus TV star | Mean STD | 3.41 (1.86) | 3.45 (2.01) | 4.86 (2.31) |
| Model#9 Jennie Finch Olympic athlete | Mean STD | 4.45 (1.44) | 4.04 (1.39) | 5.27 (2.39) |
| Model#10 Michelle Wie Pro athlete | Mean STD | 5.04 (1.81) | 5.04 (1.29) | 5.90 (2.20) |
| Model#11 Raven-Symoné TV and movie star | Mean STD | 4.00 (1.60) | 4.04 (1.43) | 5.05 (2.08) |
| Model#12 Terin Humphrey Olympic & collegiate athlete | Mean STD | 5.68 (1.78) | 5.36 (1.59) | 4.36 (2.61) |
| Model#13 Vanessa Ann Hudgens TV and movie star | Mean STD | 2.50 (1.10) | 2.86 (1.42) | 6.32 (2.45) |

*attractiveness evaluations were on a scale of 1-10 with 1 representing the most attractive

**projected attractiveness evaluations were on a scale of 1-10 with 1 representing the most attractive

***would like to look like the model shown was a scale of 1-10 with 10 representing the greatest desire to look like the model shown.

and funny and that makes her more pretty"; "(name) is very funny and can be annoying, but I love her because she is the best"; or "I think they have good virtues and that makes her really cool."

Participants were asked to list one attribute they liked most about themselves and list one attribute they would like to change about themselves. Responses varied on both of these items with participants indicating their athleticism, their face, their personality, their creativity, their talents, their figure, and the way they looked as being one thing they liked most about themselves. Participants listed similar attributes as something they would like to change about themselves but often described these attributes with greater specificity, such as: "My confidence around teens my own age"; "I get mad easily"; "My body"; "My legs"; "My knees are always kind of dusty"; "My popularity"; "My temper"; "My appearance"; and "Sometimes being rude, unkind or untruthful." Again, responses to these two items were open-ended so participants could list anything they wanted to in the blank space. All responses were recoded into one of several general attribute categories—personality, appearance, athleticism, academics, or other.

The adolescent athletes also were asked to list a person whom they thought would be a good role model for themselves. Responses to this question also were open-ended so that respondents could list anyone they liked. Almost half of the sample listed Miley Cyrus (*Hannah Montana* star) as a good role model for them, while the remaining half of the sample listed other music or television stars, athletic stars (soccer player Mia Hamm or gymnast Morgan Dennis), relatives, teachers, or characters in history ("Amelia Earhart because she was just one of the great feminists of the 1900s," from one participant). Respondents were asked later in the survey to list one female athlete they really admired. Responses to this question also varied but seemed to fall in line with participants' primary competitive sport. For example, some respondents listed one of their own teammates; others listed sports stars such as Mia Hamm, tennis player Venus Williams, gymnast Alexis Brion, university softball pitcher Stephanie VanBrankle, and a few others wrote comments such as: "I just think anyone who tries their best and is dedicated is a good role model for me."

### How Are Media Exposure and Appearance Evaluations Related?

Participants first viewed a photograph of tennis player Maria Sharapova in action. Of the sample, 18% were able to identify her by name. On the attractiveness scale ranging from 1 to 10, with 1 representing extremely pretty, the mean attractiveness evaluation for Sharapova was 3.77 (see Table 3.1). Participants also were asked to indicate how pretty others would think she was, and in this case the perceived attractiveness score of others was not as high, 4.36. Participants also were asked to indicate how much they would like to look like this model. On a scale of 1 to 10 with 1 representing not wanting to look like the person at all, the mean score for this variable was 5.59. Overall, attractiveness evaluations were higher for the television, movie, and music stars, and were the lowest for the non-recognizable athletes.

Using participants' reported number of days per week spent viewing entertainment television, statistical tests were conducted to determine how frequency of viewing was related to attractiveness evaluations. In 9 of the 13 cases, increased viewing predicted higher attractiveness scores for the models. For example, for model #11 (Raven-Symoné, see Table 3.1), participants who reported watching television 7 days a week gave Symoné an attractiveness score of 2.20 (with 1 representing extremely attractive); participants who viewed television 5 days a week gave her an attractiveness score of 4.67, and participants who viewed television 3 days a week gave her a score of 4.90. Similar patterns were followed for eight of the other models. However, while statistically significant differences were found in the attractiveness scores for model #9 (softball player Jennie Finch, looking more like a celebrity than she did an athlete), no consistent pattern was identified based on number of days spent viewing.

In a second test of this relationship, thin-ideal television viewing served as a predictor of attractiveness evaluations of the 13 models. Participants who spent more time watching thin-ideal programming were most likely to give the models lower attractiveness scores. For example, with model #1 (tennis player Maria Sharapova in action), those watching the most thin-ideal programming gave her an attractiveness score of 5.50, whereas those watching programming with fewer numbers of conspicuously thin characters gave her an attractiveness evaluation of 3.51. Similar patterns were repeated for four other models (Cheyenne Kimball, Jennie Finch, Raven-Symoné, and Terin Humphrey). Statistical tests indicated significant differences in the evaluations of the above five models based on their reported viewing of television shows, ranging from having very conspicuously thin characters (*Grey's Anatomy*, 1.34 on a 1-to- 5 scale of conspicuously thin to conspicuously fat) to television shows with a main character coded as larger than average (*That's So Raven*, 3.78 on a 1-to-5 scale of conspicuously thin to conspicuously fat) or shows with a main character receiving a mean code of thin but not conspicuously thin (*Hannah*

*Montana,* 2.53 on a 1-to-5 scale of conspicuously thin to conspicuously fat). These preliminary findings suggest thin-ideal viewing can be related to more general perceptions of beauty and attractiveness as those who spent more time watching thin-ideal programming were more critical in their overall assessments of the models' attractiveness.

### How Are Sports Participation and Appearance Evaluations Related?

To address this research question statistically,  type of sport was used as a grouping variable to see if athletes in specific sports had higher or lower appearance evaluations of the models. The statistics run to test this relationship revealed some interesting patterns. For example, in evaluations of an unidentifiable athlete, athletes competing in horseback riding reported the highest attractiveness score (1.50), followed by significantly lower evaluations coming from volleyball players, softball players, and soccer players, all reporting mean attractiveness scores at slightly higher than a 5. The basketball players gave this model the lowest attractive scores (7.12). However, attractiveness scores for a television celebrity (Brenda Song) had significantly less variance, meaning attractiveness scores across the sample were more similar, with the highest attractiveness evaluations coming from the gymnasts (2.33), and the lowest coming from the volleyball players (4.75). In sum, the type of sport played did not seem to be related to attractiveness scores for the entertainment models but proved to be a better predictor of appearance evaluations of the athletes.

### How Does Self-Esteem Relate to Appearance Evaluations of Models?

Self-esteem may be one of several factors that interact  with an individual's assessment of beauty and attractiveness in others. Quite possibly, an individual with higher self-esteem may be more generous in her evaluations of others because she is fairly confident in herself; however, if an individual is engaging in social comparison with a media model who is perceived to be extremely attractive, that individual's own self-esteem may decline on a short-term basis. For this study, self-esteem was measured prior to the attractiveness evaluation assessment items. With that in mind, self-esteem was used as a predictor of the attractiveness evaluations of the 13 models and used with the projected attractiveness evaluations of the 13 models. In a few tests of how self-esteem might interact with one's own desire to look like someone else, the self-esteem scale was used as a predictor of participants' desire to look like the person shown. No statistically significant patterns emerged from these tests, suggesting that for this sample, self-esteem was not related to higher or lower attractiveness evaluations of the 13 models.

### How Does Participation in a Specific Sport Relate to Self-Esteem?

For this study, the general self-esteem scale was used rather than using a body self-esteem scale. Certainly, an individual's self-esteem is something that could fluctuate from day-to-day, but as Clay, Vignoles, and Dittmar (2005) report, general self-esteem is more likely to remain relatively stable and constant within an individual, whereas body self-esteem may be more susceptible to fluctuations based on situations or the environment. Thus, this question addressed the relationship between participation in a specific sport and general self-esteem. Results indicate that the basketball players had the lowest self-esteem (83.01 on a scale of 29 to 145, with 145 representing the highest self-esteem), followed by the tennis players (89.12) and the volleyball players (92.50), and the soccer players and horseback riders had the highest self-esteem (104.63, 109.12, respectively). Earlier studies suggest that athletes in aesthetic sports such as gymnastics might have the lowest body self-esteem, whereas athletes in power or contact sports tend to have higher self-esteem (Bachner-Melman, Zohar, Ebstein, Elizur, & Constantini, 2006; DiBartolo & Shaffer, 2002; Fulkerson & Keel, 1999). However, this study measured only general self-esteem, and as stated earlier, several factors contribute to the development of higher or lower self-esteem in an individual, and involvement in a sport may only be one of those factors. Thus, these preliminary results are used only as a baseline measure to help better understand adolescent female athletes.

### How Does Involvement in Sports Relate to Appearance Ideals?

Participants were shown a list of appearance attributes (being thin, being tall, being muscular, being attractive, etc.) and were asked to indicate how important each appearance attribute was to them. Participants were then shown the same list of attributes and were asked to predict how important each was to people they knew. For this statistical test, the perceived importance that others placed on the appearance attributes was subtracted from their own rating of importance for themselves. That number, which could have been a positive or negative number, was then used in a statistical test to better understand the relationship between involvement in sports and appearance ideals. In this case, if a negative number was present, it would suggest the individual indicated a particular appearance attribute was more important to others and less important for oneself. If a positive number was present, the results indicated the attribute was more important to the individual and perceived to be less important to others; a number of 0 indicated that the perceived importance for self and others was the same (see Table 3.2 for mean differences for thinness, muscularity, and attractiveness).

For this test, participants in gymnastics, soccer, volleyball, and basketball had the greatest difference scores between the importance of thinness to themselves and to others. For example, the mean difference score for gymnasts on the importance of thinness was –2.21; the mean difference score for soccer players was also –2.17, whereas the mean difference score for softball players was .50. It is not too surprising to find athletes in this sample projecting thinness as being an important attribute to people they know. The primary objective of this question was to determine if an adolescent girl's participation in a specific sport might decrease the value or importance of appearance attributes.

In evaluating participants' perceived importance of muscularity, findings among type of sport played varied a little more than they did for the thinness attribute. The gymnasts largely felt muscularity was much more important to others (–2.02), but soccer players considered muscularity to be more important to themselves (1.12). The softball and basketball players similarly thought muscularity was a more important attribute to themselves than it was to others (1.78, 1.17, respectively). In examining the importance of attractiveness, the horseback riders and the softball players placed significantly less importance on being attractive (.14, –.17, respectively) when compared to the basketball players (.67) and the volleyball players (–1.11). The gymnasts, the only ones classified as participating in an aesthetic sport, reported attractiveness as being moderately important to them (2.67). Given these findings, no real identifiable pattern can be reported between athletes' participation in a specific sport and the importance of appearance attributes to themselves.

### What Differences Exist Between Attractiveness Evaluations by Participants and Perceived Attractiveness Evaluations by Others?

One item of interest was participants' attractiveness evaluations of the 13 models and the perceived attractiveness evaluations of others. Of interest was whether the participants might view the models more favorably in attractiveness, especially when viewing the athletic models. Similar procedures were used to calculate a difference score, representing participants' attractiveness score minus the attractiveness score for others. The attractiveness scale ranged from 1 to 10, with a 1 representing the most attractive. In this case, a negative score represented the participant giving the model a higher attractiveness score than others, and a positive score represented the participant giving the model a

**Table 3.2**   One-Way Analysis of Variance between Type of Sport and Attribute Importance

|  | Mean Difference Between Attribute Importance To Self & Others | | | |
|---|---|---|---|---|
| *Sport* | *SD* | *F* | *DF* | *Sig* |
|  | THINNESS | | | |
| gymnastics | −2.21 (.42) | | | |
| soccer | −2.17 (.39) | | | |
| volleyball | −2.03 (.21) | | | |
| basketball | −1.50 (1.87) | | | |
| softball | .50 (.79) | | | |
| horseback | −.71 (1.43) | 3.85 | 58 | *p* < .01 |
|  | MUSCULARITY | | | |
| gymnastics | −2.02 (.42) | | | |
| soccer | 1.12 (.29) | | | |
| volleyball | 1.11 (.43) | | | |
| basketball | 1.17 (1.11) | | | |
| softball | 1.78 (.57) | | | |
| horseback | .57 (.76) | 4.89 | 58 | *p* < .01 |
|  | ATTRACTIVENESS | | | |
| gymnastics | 1.05 (1.16) | | | |
| soccer | −2.00 (.37) | | | |
| volleyball | −1.11 (.27) | | | |
| basketball | −.67 (1.15) | | | |
| softball | −.17 (1.26) | | | |
| horseback | .14 (1.16) | 2.41 | 58 | *p* < .05 |

lower attractiveness score. In 10 of the 13 cases, the mean difference score was a negative number with the greatest difference being found for model #1, Maria Sharapova. Participants in this study gave model #1 a substantially higher attractiveness score than they predicted others would give her. Three of the 13 models had positive difference scores, model #9 (Jennie Finch), model #10 (Michelle Wie), and #12 (Terin Humphrey), indicating participants gave the three models a lower attractiveness rating than they projected others would give her. All three were athletes, although the photo of Jennie Finch was not of her in action. So, the results suggest participants in athletics would not lean to a more favorable attractiveness score when evaluating other athletes.

## ❖ DISCUSSION

While there is a great deal of literature available documenting the behavioral effects of the mass media on patterns of appearance anxiety, a smaller band of literature examines the role of sports participation, media exposure, self-esteem, and appearance evaluations. Further-more, scholars do know a good bit about adolescent girls' general self-esteem and body self-esteem, but very little is known about the role participation in sports might play in this relationship. This study ana-lyzed competitive adolescent female athletes' use of media and their beliefs about the importance of appearance attributes and self-esteem, and it examined how or if these factors shaped the way they viewed attractiveness in others. This survey of 66 female athletes, ages 7 to 16 years, yielded interesting but conflicting results with regard to poten-tial factors possibly related to higher or lower appearance evaluations. However, because of the uniqueness of this sample and the selectivity of their media use, the hope is that the results may prove helpful in understanding the complicated factors related to young girls' desire to adopt or emulate societal beliefs that uphold attractiveness as a very important attribute. It is further hoped that the results can guide parents, health educators, and media literacy advocates in a direction that might also prevent girls from engaging in dangerous comparisons with the media models that might result in general dissatisfaction with themselves or increased levels of body dissatisfaction.

One of the most important contributions of this project to mass communication scholars is what was learned about adolescent girls' use of the media and the relationship this media use had with their own sense of self-esteem. Because participants in our sample had such limited time with the media, especially television, their consumption of television programming was quite specific. For example, in conversa-tions with some of the athletes after their completion of the survey, sev-eral indicated knowing they would only have time to watch one television program previously recorded on a DVR (e.g., TiVo) and were able to state what their viewing pattern for that day would be. Many others also indicated great recall with regard to their viewing habits because, as they reported, they "have such little time to watch TV, when [they] do watch, [they] want to watch their favorite show". Statistical tests examining television exposure and self-esteem indicated a very clear pattern: greater exposure to television in days per week and minutes per day was related to lower self-esteem. While the survey results offer no evidence that greater TV viewing causes lower self-esteem, the statistical relationship suggests media exposure may be one of several factors related to adolescent girls' decreased levels of self-esteem. Nevertheless, those with lower self-esteem may be seeking out television as a source of comfort, so this relationship is merely suggested.

Obviously, several factors are going to be related to an individual's self-esteem, and age may be one of the key factors in adolescent girls. In this sample, it was found that the older athletes, between 14 to 16 years old, were more likely to have lower self-esteem compared to their younger counterparts. While scholars in several disciplines suggest general self-esteem is a product of multiple factors, many (Kostanski & Gullone, 2007; Serpell, Neiderman, Roberts, & Lask, 2007) suggest that weight and body shape drive adolescent girls' general sense of self. Those older in the sample are undergoing fairly dramatic changes with their bodies, and this fact coupled with their reliance on friends, older siblings, and the media as a social guide may result in lower self-esteem.

It is not surprising that younger girls perceived their interaction with the media differently than older females did. Pre-teen females, those between 7 to 12 years old, were more likely to view their media consumption as pure entertainment and may have remained oblivious to any effects the media had on their self-esteem and body image. Whereas a 9-year-old might watch *Full House* or *Raven* for simple entertainment value, a 15-year-old might view *The O.C.* or *Grey's Anatomy* and unconsciously internalize the images portrayed by those characters and then evaluate herself in terms of those character images. Consequently, older females may perceive the media to play a greater role in shaping who they have become today compared to younger females. In this sample, the younger girls were more likely to cite female athletes, rather than female television characters or media personalities, as their role models. Of the entire sample, 14% of the survey respondents listed an athlete as a great role model compared to 41% who listed a media personality. When examining these percentages by age, 67% of the sample younger than age 12 listed an athlete as a great role model while the remaining 33% (younger than 12) listed a media personality, friend, or relative as a great role model. Self-esteem, when examined by age, also was found to be quite linear, with the younger participants having more positive self-esteem and the older participants having lower self-esteem. With that said, it has not been determined how the influence of these role models interacts with the younger girls' self-esteem when they reach the critical beginning stages of adolescence. Do the relationships they have established with athletic role models lose influence as they become more aware of societal expectations associated with being female? As young girls age, do the media override and dictate their character formation, regardless of the positive influence their previous athletic role models might have had? This study surveyed many girls at various stages of their development, and it is crucial to note that their perceptions of self, media, and role models fluctuate with maturity.

While age and degree of emotional maturity are important factors as they relate to an adolescent girl's self-esteem, participation in a sport also seems to be important. Even though this sample's body self-esteem was not measured at all and their self-esteem in general was not compared with girls of similar ages who do not compete in sports, it is contended that involvement in a competitive sport serves as a displacement to outside influences, which may function as negative influences in the development of more positive self-esteem and body awareness. If participants in this study had not spent as much time practicing or competing in their respective sports, they might have filled that time watching more television and reading more magazines with potentially harmful messages about appearance ideals. Researchers in sports psychology concur with this conclusion: Boone and Leadbeater (2006) examined sports participation as a potential protective factor in the development of elevated levels of body dissatisfaction in girls. They found that involvement in a team sport served as a partial mediation of the risk of depressive symptoms, which often led to higher body dissatisfaction in Canadian girls in grades 8 through 10. While the results here do not suggest that involvement in a specific type of sport—team, individual, power, or aesthetic—led to higher or lower levels of self-esteem, observational results do support this relationship.

For several participants in this sample—across various sports—their involvement in sports represented a great deal of dedication and commitment on their parts. These athletes were not only very successful on the court, field, or mat, they also managed to maintain high grades in school and be active in their churches. For these athletes, very little else exists in their worlds: they go to school, they leave school and go to practice, then go home, do homework, and go to bed. On weekends, practice becomes competition and when the competition schedule allows it, they attend church. In speaking with several of the participants, many indicated their goal was to earn a scholarship to compete in their sport at the college level. To a large degree, these athletes were very happy with their activity level and did not seem to mind the other activities that were being displaced because of their level of involvement in sport. It is argued that because many of the participants in this sample do not represent "average" adolescents in terms of media use, social activities, etc., their involvement in sport has allowed them to develop and maintain higher general self-esteem. This seemed to be especially true of the younger athletes who had not had as much exposure or experience with societal pressures to be attractive or thin.

Clearly, more work needs to be done in this area to confirm these notions, but these findings at least provide a hint of information regarding an activity that can be used to help prevent girls from succumbing to outside negative influences that push them to think they are not attractive or beautiful to others. Furthermore, involvement in sport may help girls learn to be more accepting of others in terms of their outward appearance. However, the results here do not support such broad-sweeping claims. The athletic models received the lowest attractiveness scores of all models, but that is not to say the athletic models were perceived as unattractive. When asked to make assessments about outward appearance based on looking at a color photograph, it is quite possible the athletes would be perceived as less attractive by anyone viewing the group of photos. When compared to celebrities or television personalities, the athletic attire, lack of makeup, and a ponytail might certainly influence the way an individual is perceived in terms of her beauty. The key is in better understanding the way beauty is defined. Scholars have attempted to identify the way ideal beauty is defined, and while scholars agree that appearance norms exist in the media and are related to appearance and image issues in girls and women, researchers have not been able to fully articulate how ideal beauty is defined. We can only learn that from making assertions and assumptions based on studies such as this one. Given the way some participants responded when asked about what made an individual pretty—"They are pretty inside and out," or "They care about their body and treat it with respect," it seems at least a few of them were looking beyond outward appearance in their assessment of beauty in others. The positive outcome for media scholars and parents is knowing that the media could play either a positive or negative role in the development of an image of ideal beauty. More specifically, the media could help young girls understand the very old adage about beauty coming in all shapes, sizes, and colors.

While it is erroneous to conclude that the media are solely responsible for a negative outcome with respect to ideal beauty, the media in combination with other outside influences help shape the world in which these girls feel they have to be attractive in order to be popular or successful. Cultivation theory (Gerbner et al., 2002) offers one approach for better understanding how notions of ideal beauty have become adopted and accepted by women across ethnic and socioeconomic groups, across women from different countries, and across age groups. If the television world presents its viewers images of only attractive characters, and women and girls are exposed to these images with some frequency over a long period of time, those same viewers' worldview may be similar to the mediated view as presented to them. Harrison (2003) writes, "Media exposure will be positively correlated with perceptions of the world and its components, such that these perceptions match the way the world is portrayed in the media" (p. 257). Since examinations of entertainment media content have established that the primary female characters in many prime-time television shows are portrayed as very attractive and extremely thin, the suggestion is that frequent and long-term exposure to media containing these messages will only serve to reinforce the notion of beauty and thinness as an ideal.

While one objective of this study was to recruit a very specific sample to assess the potential factors related to self-esteem and appearance evaluations, this objective resulted in a fairly low sample size. This limits the ability to generalize the findings to a larger population or even a population similar to what was sampled here. Despite the limitations with regard to generalizability, future studies should include a comparative component so that greater generalizations can be drawn between an athletic sample and a nonathletic sample. A second limitation to this study was the measure of self-esteem. While it was geared toward adolescents, statements were made in a positive and negative way, and given the nature of the way each statement was written, it could have proven confusing to participants.

Despite the limitations, the results here shed light on a small portion of this line of research that has not received a great deal of attention in the past. Most important, the contribution here is a better understanding of the attitudes and beliefs of adolescent, athletic girls about the importance of beauty and attractiveness. Sports participation may be one very important variable that helps women and adolescents develop a sense of what is right and acceptable for them as it relates to their own appearance. Most important, if girls can be taught—via parents, media literacy campaigns, and school—that mediated constructions of beauty are not the ultimate ideal but rather that ideal beauty can be derived from internal and external character-istics, these girls may be able to be protected from years of lower self-esteem and lower feelings of self-worth. Future projects should continue examining sports media exposure, sports and exercise fre-quency, and interpersonal relationships as possible mediating variables in the development of self-esteem in women and girls.

> Participating in sport is one way that girls can develop physical competence. Girls learn to appreciate their bodies for what they can do, instead of the perceived appearance by oneself or by others. In a sport environment, girls learn to control their bodies and to rely on acquired physical skills. Partaking in sport also helps girls trust and rely on themselves and teammates while working toward common goals. (Schultz, 1999, p. 3)

## ❖ REFERENCES

Bachner-Melman, R., Zohar, A. H., Ebstein, R. P., Elizur, Y., & Constantini, N. (2006). How anorexic-like are the symptom and the personality profiles of aesthetic athletes? *Medicine & Science in Sports & Exercise, 38*(4), 628–636.

Berscheid, E., & Walster, E. (1974). Physical attractiveness. In L. Berkowitz (Ed.), *Advances in experimental social psychology* (Vol. 7, pp. 158–216). New York: Academic Press.

Berscheid, E., & Walster, E. (1978). *Interpersonal attraction.* Reading, MA: Addison-Wesley.

Birtchnell, S. A., Dolan, B. M., & Lacey, J. H. (1987). Body image distortion in non-eating disordered women. *International Journal of Eating Disorders, 6*(3), 385–391.

Bissell, K., & Birchall, K. (2006). *Playing like a girl: The perceived influence of media and parents on body self-esteem in adolescent female athletes.* Paper presented to the Instructional & Developmental Communication Division at the annual meeting of the International Communication Association, San Francisco, CA.

Boone, E. M., & Leadbeater, B. J. (2006). Game on: Diminishing risks for depres-sive symptoms in early adolescence through positive involvement in team sports. *Journal of Research on Adolescence, 16*(1), 79–90.

Butler, A., & Zaslow, E. (2002). "That it was made by people our age is better": Exploring the role of media literacy in transcultural communication. *Journal of Popular Film and Television, 30,* 31–41.

Byrne, D., Ervin, C., & Lamberth, J. (1970). Continuity between the experimen-tal study of attraction and the real-like computer dating. *Journal of Personality and Social Psychology, 16,* 157–165.

Cash, T. (1981). Physical attractiveness: The effects of physical attractive-ness, sex, and attitude similarity on interpersonal attraction. *Journal of Personality, 36,* 259–271.

Cash, T. F., & Green, G. K. (1986). Body weight and body image among college women: Perception, cognition, and affect. *Journal of Personality Assessment, 50*(2), 290–301.

Clay, D., Vignoles, V. L., & Dittmar, H. (2005). Body image and self-esteem among adolescent girls: Testing the influence of sociocultural factors. *Journal of Research on Adolescence, 15,* 451–477.

Coopersmith, S. (1967). *The antecedents to self-esteem.* San Francisco: W. H. Freeman.

Currie, D. H. (1999). *Girl talk: Adolescent magazines and their readers.* Toronto: University of Toronto Press.

Cusumano, D. L., & Thompson, J. K. (1997). Body image and body shape ideals in magazines: Exposure, awareness and internalization. *Sex Roles, 37,* 701–721.

DiBartolo, P. M., & Shaffer, C. (2002). A comparison of female college athletes and nonathletes: Eating disorder symptomatology and psychological well-being. *Journal of Sport & Exercise Psychology, 24*(1) 33–41.

Dion, K., Bersheid, E., & Walster, E. (1972). What is beautiful is good. *Journal of Personality and Social Psychology, 24,* 285–290.

Dolce, J. J., Thompson, J. K., Register, A., & Spana, R. E. (1987). Generalization of body size distortion. *International Journal of Eating Disorders, 6,* 401–408.

Douglas, S. (1995). *Where the girls are.* New York: Times Books.

Feldman, S., & Elliott, G. (Eds.). (1990). *At the threshold: The developing adolescent.* Cambridge, MA: Harvard University Press.

Fouts, G., & Burggraf, K. (1999). Television situation comedies: Female weight, male negative comments, and audience reactions. *Sex Roles, 46*(1/2), 439–442.

Fulkerson, J. A., & Keel, P. K. (1999). Eating disorder behaviors and personality characteristics of high school athletes and non-athletes. *International Journal of Eating Disorders, 26,* 73–79.

Garner D. M., Olmsted, M. P., Polivy, J., & Garfinkel, P. E. (1984). Comparison between weight-preoccupied women and anorexia nervosa. *Psychosometric Medicine, 46,* 255–266.

Gerbner, G. (1969). Toward "cultural indicators": The analysis of mass mediated message systems. *AV Communication Review, 17,* 137–148.

Gerbner, G., Gross, L., Morgan, M., & Signorelli, N. (2002). Growing up with television: Cultivation processes. In J. Bryant & D. Zillman (Eds.), *Media effects: Advances in theory and research* (pp. 43–68). Mahwah, NJ: Lawrence Erlbaum.

Gilligan, C., Rogers, A. C., & Tolman, D. L. (Eds.). (1991). *Women, girls and psychotherapy: Reframing resistance.* New York: Harrington-Haworth.

Harrison, K. (2003). Television viewers' ideal body proportions: The case of the curvaceously thin female. *Sex Roles, 48,* 255–264.

Harrison, K., Taylor, L. D., & Marske, A. L. (2006). Women's and men's eating behavior following exposure to ideal body images and text. *Communication Research, 33*(6), 507–529.

Heinberg, L. J. (1996). Theories of body image: Perceptual, developmental, and sociocultural factors. In J. K. Thompson (Ed.), *Body image, eating disorders, and obesity: An integrative guide for assessment and treatment* (pp. 27–48). Washington DC: American Psychological Association.

Herbozo, S., Tantleff-Dunn, S., Gokee-Larose, J., & Thompson, K. J. (2004). Beauty and thinness messages in children's media: A content analysis. *Eating Disorders, 12*(1), 21–34.

Hesse-Biber, S., Leavy, P., Quinn, C. E., & Zoino, J. (2006). The mass marketing of disordered eating and eating disorders: The social psychology of women, thinness and culture. *Women's Studies International Forum, 29,* 208–224.

Konstanski, M., & Gullone, E. (2007). The impact of teasing on children's body image. *Journal of Child and Family Studies, 16*(3), 307–319.

Labre, M. P., & Walsh-Childers, K. (2003). Friendly advice? Beauty messages in web sites of teen magazines. *Mass Communication & Society, 6,* 379–396.

Levine, M. P., & Smolak, L. (1996). Media as a context for the development of disordered eating. In L. Smolak & M. P. Levin (Eds.), *The developmental psychopathology of eating disorders: Implications for research, prevention, and treatment* (pp. 235–257). Mahwah, NJ: Lawrence Erlbaum.

Levine, M. P., Smolak, L., & Hayden, H. (1994). The relation of sociocultural factors to eating attitudes and behaviors among middle school girls. *Journal of Early Adolescence, 14,* 471–490.

Liebert, R. M., & Sprafkin J. (1988). *The early window: Effects of television on children and youth* (3rd ed.). New York: Pergamon Press.

Miller, A. G. (1970). Role of physical attractiveness in impression formation. *Psychonomic Science, 19,* 241-243.

Nelson, M. B. (1994). *The stronger women get, the more men love football.* New York: Harcourt.

Pipher, M. (1994). *Reviving Ophelia: Saving the selves of adolescent girls.* New York: Putnam.

Reis, H., Wheeler, L., Spiegel, M., Kernis, N., Nazlek, J., & Perri, M. (1982). Physical attractiveness in social interaction II: Why does appearance affect social experience? *Journal of Personality and Social Psychology, 43,* 979–996.

Riggio, R., Widaman, K., Tucker, J., & Salinas, C. (1991). Beauty is more than skin deep: Components of attractiveness. *Basic and Applied Social Psychology, 12*(4), 423–439.

Santrock, J. W. (1998). *Adolescence* (7th ed.). New York: McGraw-Hill.

Schultz, A. M. (1999). You go girl! The link between girls' positive self-esteem and sports. *The Sport Journal, 2*(2). Retrieved January 3, 2009, http://www .thesportjournal.org/article/you-go-girl-link-between-girls-positive-self-esteem-and-sports

Serpell, L., Neiderman, M., Roberts, V., & Lask, B. (2007). The shape and weight-based self-esteem inventory in adolescent girls with eating disorders and adolescent controls. *Psychotherapy Research, 7*(3), 315–319.

Stern, D. M. (2005). MTV, reality television and the commodification of female sexuality in *The Real World. Media Report to Women, 33*(2), 13–21.

Strice, E., & Thompson, K. (2001). Thin-ideal internalization: Mounting evidence for a new risk factor for body-image disturbance and eating pathology. *Communication Directions in Psychological Science, 10*(5), 181–183.

Sypeck, M. F., Gray, J. J., & Ahrens, A. H. (2004). No longer just a pretty face: Fashion magazines' depictions of ideal female beauty from 1959 to 1999. *International Journal of Eating Disorders, 36*, 342–347.

Thompson, J. K., Heinberg, L. J., Altabe, M., & Tantleff-Dunn, S. (1999). *Exacting beauty: Theory, assessment, and treatment of body image disturbance.* Washington, DC: American Psychological Association.

Zimmerman, J. (1999). *Raising our athletic daughters: How sports can build self-esteem and save girls' lives.* New York: Random House.

# 4

# Making Masculinity and Framing Femininity

## FIFA, Soccer, and World Cup Web Sites

### Lindsey J. Meân

S occer, or football as it is known outside the United States, is the most popular sport in the world. Often referred to as "the beautiful game," soccer comprises many countries' national sport and thus provides a key site for the re/production of traditional forms of aggressive and competitive national and masculine identities (Sudgen & Tomlinson, 1994). Therefore, soccer has actively excluded and resisted the entry of women, especially in countries with a long history of the game (e.g., England). A major news and television event, soccer attracts huge audiences, receives high production values,[1] and provides significant marketing and merchandising opportunities. Equally, soccer's world regulating organization, the Fédération Internationale de Football Association (FIFA), has been acknowledged to be a transglobal socioeconomic force that shapes cultures (Sklair, 1991). Yet, FIFA remains deeply masculine, heterosexual, and predominantly White.

    Reflecting soccer's position as the world's dominant sport, the FIFA World Cup (known as The World Cup) is the biggest international (single) sport competition. Held every four years, a record 204 national teams from six world regions have registered for the preliminary competition, seeking a place in the 32-team "finals" of the 2010 World Cup (see http://www.fifa.com). The World Cup is widely considered to attract the largest audiences of any sporting event, including the Olympic Games. However, exact viewing figures for global markets are hard to verify and estimations are fraught with commercial imperatives, making comparisons problematic.[2] The cumulative television audience for the 2006 World Cup has been estimated at over 26 billion (Infront Sports & Media, 2007), while the 2004 Athens Olympics reported an unprecedented cumulative figure of 34.4 billion (International Olympic Committee [IOC], 2008) including Internet viewings that are expected to boost 2008 viewing even higher. However, the significance of cumulative versus actual audience numbers remains debatable, and specific World Cup matches have generally exceeded global audiences for individual Olympic events.

As an organization, FIFA has the international prominence of the IOC, but it also has the power to regulate soccer throughout the world as the organization that sits at the top of the hierarchy that comprises soccer: six world regional confederations (such as the Union of European Football Associations [UEFA] for Europe and the Confederation of African Football [CAF] for Africa, 208 affiliated national associations, and within-nation local associations). One might get close to understanding the power and influence of FIFA by thinking of it as the National Football League (NFL) on a global scale in a world where football was the number one sport (for all nations, on television, in schools, and on the streets). Consequently, the global sociocultural and economic influence of FIFA is not surprising. Yet the nature and extent of the impact of soccer on wider sociocultural discourses and identities remain underestimated.

The influence of FIFA is exerted through multiple levels of symbolic re/presentation and action, with an increasingly significant mediated site of global[3] influence being FIFA's Web site (http://www.fifa.com). Available in four languages (English, French, German, Spanish), FIFA.com offers up-to-date and immediate global, national, and local (club) news and information in ways that transcend geographic and time barriers. Web sites are considered unique, mediated sites that provide an illusion of democratization and active participation while being packaged and constructed to guide consumption (Graham & Hearn, 2001; Jansson, 2002). As such, Web sites are increasingly acknowledged as powerful sources for the construction of meaning that appear to be especially influential with sporting audiences

(Scherer, 2007), given their strong identification with sport categories and definitions (Meân, 2001; Walsh & Giulianotti, 2001; Wenner, 1991). Thus, one set of powerful cultural discourses about gender, race, and sexuality (that is, one ideological position) becomes available to members of all cultures in the guise of one language or discourse they can understand: soccer.

## ❖ THEORY AND RELATED LITERATURE: DISCOURSES, IDENTITIES, AND THE CONSTRUCTION OF GENDER

Sport is a powerful, familiar, and highly naturalized discourse that has become more prominent with the extensive rise in media coverage over the last 15 to 20 years. The same time period has seen a large increase in the participation of women as both athletes and sports fans, yet there has been little substantive change in the re/presentational practices deployed in sports media with respect to gender, race, ethnicity, and sexuality. (The notion of re/presentation is used to concisely but actively invoke the cyclical and constructive nature of the practices through which objects, events, and people are presented, represented, and re-presented.)[4] Instead, re/presentational practices have increased the spectacularization and hyper-masculization of male sport and male bodies (e.g., enhancing speed and aggressiveness) and continued to undermine female athleticism (e.g., sexualization and feminization). Culture, categories, and shared understandings are constructed through re/presentational practices, thus language and media practices are crucial re/producers of ideology, discourses, and identities (Hall, 1997; Potter, 1996). Sport is a key site for masculine identities (Messner, 1988), it's ideological and re/presentational significance further apparent in its common cultural deployment as a metaphorical and intertextual referent (Shapiro, 1989). As such, the media now comprise a predominant site for the construction and maintenance of the central social discourse that is sport, and sport remains a powerful site in the re/production of the traditional, hegemonic gender order, particular highly masculinized sex-typed sports like soccer.

As a primary site for the re/production of gendered identities, sport remains a disputed ideological terrain. The cultural prominence of sport, especially soccer, accounts for its significance as a globalized discourse that implicitly and explicitly constructs wider social practices, such as gender. Discourses are part of the process through which power and prevailing hegemonies are re/produced, serving to maintain and resist dominant definitions and identities (Foucault, 1970, 1972).

Identities are embedded in discourses, hence ideologies. As a consequence, an emotional link exists between identities and the discourses in which they are embedded; that is, we have an emotional commitment to the discourses from which our identities arise. However, given its cultural and ideological prominence, I argue that sport is a particularly powerful form of discourse (Meân, 2001), termed *foundational* or *"self-constituting"* (Maingueneau, 1999, p.183). The emotional link between foundational discourses and identities runs extremely deep and beyond the habitual patterns of emotional commitment typical of less powerful discourses (Maingueneau, 1999), accounting for the strong resistance to women's entry into sport, particularly male sex-typed sport. Indeed, foundational discourses are extremely hard to resist and question as they provide fundamental and naturalized explanatory frameworks for wider social and cultural practices.

Foundational discourses are so highly naturalized that their rudimentary assumptions and practices are rarely systematically scrutinized or questioned. As such, sport is often framed as *mere* leisure and entertainment, and as a site that reflects rather than constructs culture. This position has inevitably led to the acceptance or disregard of the gendered (and racialized) nature of sporting discourses as natural and normative, even by those typically strongly opposed to discriminatory ideologies and practices. This is not surprising since we are subject to re/producing the hegemonies that oppress us (van Dijk, 1993). Thus, while we may resist the prominent versions of masculinity and femininity, we also are likely to re/produce them (Foucault, 1972; van Dijk, 1993), especially given that discourses provide limited ways to describe and discursively re/produce people, objects, events, etc.

Of course, while we may scrutinize the media or organizations, it is people who are *doing* the action; that is, it is people who write, speak, and perform organizations, the media, etc. (Cameron, 1998). The highly masculine nature of sporting organizations (Shaw, 2006) makes this pertinent given that talk and text are social practices that construct and re/produce identities, categories, and discourses in ways that are strategic, motivated, and have social and political consequences (Potter, 1996). The construction of identities, category boundaries, and discourses are therefore part of the everyday, routine action (re/production) of all social texts, including language, discursive practices, and interactions. In turn, the routine management of membership and its entitlements are part of the action of defining, gatekeeping, and constructing category boundaries (Gumperz, 1982); acts of power (Foucault, 1970) are achieved at the "invisible" levels of ritual, language, and other symbolic and discursive practices. As such, identities, category membership, and entitlements are not natural, but achieved and constructed. Therefore, soccer as a category has to be constructed and maintained as hegemonically male, especially given its powerful, ideological position as the epitome of national and male identities and, thus, heterosexuality (Caudwell, 1999).

Thus, as the Web site of the organization that is synonymous with and central to the practice of soccer, FIFA.com provides a powerful site for the re/production of the discourses and meanings that define soccer, its identity categories, and discursive practices. The deployment of familiar narratives, practices, and intertextual relations are a significant part of establishing meanings and guiding interpretations within shared categories or communities (Jansson, 2002). However, due to their strong identification with the category, sporting audiences or communities are highly familiar with key sporting narratives and practices while simultaneously being especially susceptible to the meanings re/presented in sporting texts (Scherer, 2007; Wenner, 1991). Equally, Web sites have a number of characteristics that make them particularly powerful re/producers of meanings, as they provide a (false) sense of active participation (Graham & Hearn, 2001; Jansson, 2002). As part of this, the users are self-selected and therefore likely to strongly identify as *proper* members of the soccer community. Thus, while FIFA.com is a significant site for the re/production of soccer through shared identities, meanings, narratives, and, hence, category definitions, it could provide a powerful site for the disruption of traditional meanings and the establishment of alternative definitions.

### Making Masculinity Through Femininity

Constructing soccer as *the* standard male category requires that femininity is "othered" (framed, resisted, and constructed outside category norms) because categories do not exist in isolation but in oppositional, dichotomous relations (Lakoff, 1987). The nature of categories, their meaning, and their status are not natural, but constructed. Thus, even the predominant discourses and category definitions require continued re/production to maintain the status quo. As such, the othering of female athletes protects category boundaries, ensuring that sporting masculinity and heterosexuality remain untouched by the increasing proximity of femininity. A major strategy of category construction, therefore, has been the exclusion or symbolic erasure of women within mediated re/productions of sport (Kane & Lenskyj, 1998), cognitively rendering women invisible within the category of soccer. Nonetheless, the presence of women in sport makes the issue of sexuality highly significant, given that the body provides a powerful site for the performance of gender and sexuality as well as sport. Resultantly, the increasing participation of female athletes has rendered problematic the traditional link between the body, masculinity, and heterosexuality in sport (Caudwell, 1999; Vertinsky, 2006).

Protecting hegemonic masculinity and heterosexuality has led to othering strategies that automatically or implicitly question the heterosexuality of female athletes or feminizes and eroticizes them. Consequently, the female athletic body becomes highly significant as the site at which heterosexuality is achieved through the performance of hegemonic femininity (Hall, 1988). This simultaneously protects and distinguishes the performance of hegemonic masculinity by diminishing the threat of alternative forms of athletic femininities—either heterosexual or lesbian. As a consequence, there has been comparatively little media coverage of female athletes who do not fit the hegemonic versions of femininity and/or heterosexuality, while the actual media coverage of women athletes remains mitigated by hetero/sexualization and the paradoxical re/presentation of power and traditional femininity (see e.g., Christopherson, Janning, & McConnell, 2002). Similarly, there is little coverage of women athletes performing male sex-typed sport (such as soccer outside the United States) and/or performing sport in what are deemed masculine ways (Dworkin & Messner, 1999). Accordingly, women soccer players are rarely shown performing the aggressive, competitive action that typifies the male game of soccer.

## FIFA and the Category of Soccer

Accepting sport, hence soccer, as a foundational discourse acknowledges its significance within the symbolic systems that comprise culture. Considering the significance of language and discursive practices in constructing culture and knowledge (Hall, 1997; Potter, 1996), the relationship between language, cognitive categories, and thought (Lakoff, 1987), and the sociopsychological significance of identity categories (Turner, Hogg, Oakes, Reicher, & Wetherell, 1987), it is not surprising that language deployment and discursive action enact (mobilize or work up) the underlying nature of categories and their membership. Even the basic naming or *lack* of linguistic marking of men's soccer and tournaments reveals how the men's game is re/produced as the standard, as the key or prototypical member of the cognitive category of soccer. In contrast, the linguistic marking of *women's* soccer and the *Women's* World Cup indicates deviation from the category standard, meaning most people "think male" in relation to soccer. Such symbolic practices may be seen as reasonable and merely reflecting the "reality" of audience preferences and the status of men's, women's, and youth soccer. However, categories are not natural but constructed; audiences for sporting events are built and interest is constructed, and language and discursive practices are strategic and motivated. Even the biggest events—like The World Cup or the Super Bowl—are marketed and audience interest is created through news, advertising, narrative building, and production techniques that frame the event for consumption (Wenner, 1998). Indeed the lack of interest and poor production values of U.S.A. televised soccer coverage demonstrate that there is nothing *natural* or *given* about sport audiences or spectacular action.

❖ METHODOLOGICAL APPROACH

A key site for the everyday, routine construction of masculinity, soccer serves to mobilize action and ideas that are intertextually linked to wider discourses about gender (Meân, 2001; Meân Patterson, 2003). However, to do this requires that soccer itself be re/produced as a hegemonically masculine category. As noted earlier, the global significance of FIFA as a key re/producer of the category of soccer, the characteristics of digital media, and the strong identification of the fans, supporters, and spectators combine to suggest that FIFA.com comprises a powerful site for the re/production of the shared meanings, definitions, understandings, and practices that are soccer. Critical discourse analysis (CDA) therefore provides a useful approach for an analysis of the gendered category construction and practices re/produced at FIFA.com. Given that Web sites are large, the analysis focused on the Web site's key elements. A priori selections included: FIFA.com's home page (as the entry point that guides readers; http://www.fifa.com); the World Cup home page (given the significance of the tournament; http://www.fifa.com/worldcup/index.html); and the Women's World Cup home page (for comparative purposes; http://www.fifa.com/womenworldcup/index.html). Other elements were emergent, guided by the content of the new Web site in part reflecting the experience of the users (implied readers), comprising: the News Centre (Latest News and Features; http://www.fifa.com/newscentre); world soccer (http://www.fifa.com/worldfootball/index.html); the men's and women's World Cup tournament logos (throughout FIFA.com); and the Latest Photos (http://www.fifa.com/newscentre/photo/photolist.html). An e-mail newsletter from FIFA.com announcing FIFA's new Web site also was included.

## Results: FIFA on the World Wide Web

On June 1, 2007, "FIFA.com and FIFAworldcup.com merged to create a super site—FIFA.com" (FIFA.com newsletter, personal communication, June 6, 2007). The FIFA e-mail newsletter announcing this "significant development in online football" only included the men's game. Promoting the 2010 World Cup™ qualifications, the message urged fans to use the Web site and not "miss a kick of the action." In contrast, women's and youth soccer were missing from the action. Failure to promote or encourage fans to engage with women's soccer or the imminent Women's World Cup tournament renders them invisible and outside of the main action, effectively re/producing the category of soccer, fan identities, and interests as exclusively male. Similarly, failure to promote the imminent male youth tournaments (U-17 and U-20 World Cups) exclude youth soccer from the main category, re/producing a particular version of masculinity. Excluding the imminent women's (September 2007) and male youth (June/July 2007) tournaments as objects of interest alongside The World Cup strategically separates the men's tournament. The absence discursively communicates to the user that—as a fan—they should have no interest in the women's or youth tournaments and that identities are embedded in the men's game. This is a powerful re/producer of the category given the strong identification of soccer fans (Walsh & Giulianotti, 2001).

Masculine identity re/produced in soccer is a hegemonic form of aggressive and competitive masculinity that is strongly tied to national identities. Therefore even male youth soccer has a complex relationship with the men's game and also is often excluded from central category membership to protect the powerful, aggressive form of masculinity of the *real* game (i.e., the men's game). Indeed, at 17 to 18 years of age, the best male players are already participating in the adult game at club and even international levels. As such, the structure of soccer (and most sport) outside the United States ensures an almost universal lack of interest in youth soccer. Consequently, it is essential that the entry of women, girls, and boys into the main category is resisted as, in essence, their ability to perform the category (i.e., the aggressive masculinity of soccer) would effectively undermine masculinity.

## Inclusions: More Presence, Same Practices

Compared to the previous FIFA.com Web site, women's soccer had a much stronger presence in the basic informational content of the new FIFA.com. The previous Web site provided little if any substantive information on women's leagues and fixtures and "World Football" contained no detail about the women's game, effectively excluding it from the category. However, despite the increase in basic information incorporated into the new FIFA.com, women remained excluded from the routine discursive action and re/presentational practices that re/produced the category of soccer.

The new FIFA.com home page format comprised seven "Latest News" items plus one large image rotating through a photograph for each news item. This production technique stood out as the most sophisticated across the Web site and was used only on the main home page and the World Cup main page, denoting the value placed upon the men's tournament and re/producing it as the standard. During the six days sampled (in June 2007), 1 of 37 news items (2.7%) was about women's soccer. The full women's item, "Bundesliga stars up for the cup" (FIFA.com, posted June 12, 2007), was actually posted within the Women's World Cup pages, positioning it outside the supposedly generic main news pages of the "News Centre" and thus effectively framing it outside the main category. Equally, while the item did include positive linguistic power markers, it referred to the players as "the girls from Frankfurt," simultaneously highlighting the saliency of their femaleness and framing it as non-threatening by diminutive language selection (given gender-neutral and/or non-diminishing alternatives such as team, players, women, etc). Diminutives symbolically infantilize the women players (Duncan & Messner, 1998), mobilizing gendered discourses that frame them as less powerful and outside the category in spite of the presence of power markers. Indeed, the combining of power and feminizing markers promotes a sense of increasing gender equality while concurrently diminishing the threat of women's sport (Christopherson, Janning, & McConnell, 2002).

The male predominance as "News" (97.3%) clearly constructed the category as male, making the women's game effectively invisible and excluding it from routine membership in the category. The male game as the everyday, normative subject of the "News" discursively constructs it as the object of action, happenings, and interest (i.e., newsworthiness). In contrast, the news items about the women's game were linked to the Women's World Cup, even if the main topic of the article was not directly about the tournament. Linking the news to the Women's World Cup can be viewed as promoting the tournament, but it also frames the action as special, or nonroutine, rather than about everyday category membership. The routine nature of male soccer as "news" (and the women's as not) achieves a normative framing of the women's game and players in opposition to the action of the men's game. Such oppositional framing re/produces the standard as male and women as outside the category; this maintains the status quo of masculinity and femininity as dichotomous while undermining the threat of the alternative versions re/presented by the participation of women in soccer.

Covering a range of broad and specific topics across international (FIFA), world regional (e.g., UEFA), club teams, and individual players, the news framed soccer, its fans, and their interests as global in nature. Nonetheless, the range of interest was not constructed as including women's soccer (2.7%). The news is not a natural category, rather it also is constructed according to interrelated notions about what is deemed newsworthy (by reporters, producers, etc.), what has come to be considered news (by producers, consumers, etc.), and how these events are constructed as news products (Christopherson, Janning, & McConnell, 2002). Thus the "News" is subject to the discourses, identities, and ideologies of the individuals who "do" the news, re/producing newsworthy soccer action (97.3%) as being about men, masculinity, and FIFA.

In contrast, the "Features" section contained more items about women: two of six main items (33%) and 8 of 53 additional items (15%). A low turnover section of the Web site, only four items (all male) were posted during June 2007 (replacing the two women's items as main news) while 24 were from December 2006. The lack of up-to-date items combined with the anecdotal, biographical, and personal nature of many items suggests that "Features" provided the lighter side of the game and was not part of the main action of the "News Centre," concurrently framing women's soccer as less substantial, outside the main news category, and therefore outside the soccer category.

While the coverage of women's sport in the press, broadcast news, and highlight shows varies, figures from Duncan, Messner, Willms, and Wilson (2005) have shown a reduction in U.S. broadcast media coverage of women athletes as news in 2004 (6.3%) compared to 1999 (8.7%), which was an increase from 1989 (5%) and 1993 (5.1%). Additionally, these low figures are likely to include the spikes in female athletic coverage that occur around broadcasts of the Olympics, women's tennis, and the widely watched 1999 Women's World Cup. Print and press coverage typically report similar or lower figures (e.g., Bishop, 2003). However, at FIFA.com, the 2.7% coverage of women's soccer in the news and the substantive inclusion of women within the "Features" section (33% and 15%) suggest that the re/presentation of women remains especially problematic, arguably reflecting the strong resistance of soccer as a male sex-typed category. Further, while researchers have noted a reduction in the trivializing and humorous nature of women's sport coverage, there is evidence that powerful differences remain in the portrayal of men's and women's sport (Billings, Halone, & Denham, 2002; Duncan, Messner, Willms, & Wilson, 2005).

## FIFA World Cup

As noted earlier, the 2010 FIFA World Cup South Africa main page shared the most sophisticated production format with the FIFA.com home page (seven news items plus one large "rotating" image). The World Cup news items effectively comprised audience building and tournament promotion alongside items involving key FIFA organizational members and South African political figures. Audience building and excitement were evident in the construction of the countdown ("1096 days and counting," June 11, 2007, Web site item), a "clock" that counts down the days until the final phase of the 2010 World Cup tournament. This item also was posted on the FIFA.com home page, framing the newsworthiness of this event and, hence, the tournament. Of course, as the flagship tournament, one can argue that the World Cup is naturally the focus of such media attention. However, since audiences and events are built, these practices continue to construct the men's game as more exciting, valuable, and newsworthy.

The "significant figurability" of sport (Shapiro, 1989, p. 72) has made it a powerful political tool and, given its global prominence, soccer in particular has become a significant site for the intertextual re/production of ideology, politics, and national identities. In direct contrast to the women's game, the commodification of the men's game for political and organizational purposes was evident. News items and content directly linked the FIFA president and FIFA as an organization to the World Cup tournament, achieving a powerful intertextual relationship between the organization, key organizational members, and the tournament. Indeed, on June 26, 2007, two of seven news items explicitly linked FIFA President Joseph Blatter and the World Cup. Both items enacted Blatter as the embodiment of FIFA and soccer through the intertextual association of FIFA and the World Cup. The rhetorical persuasiveness of the discursive action linking Blatter, FIFA, and the World Cup was powerfully illustrated by using a form of active voicing in the item title "Blatter: Nothing Can Stop South Africa 2010!" Equally, the second item, "Blatter: Optimistic and Excited," enacts the action and excitement of the game of soccer and the World Cup tournament, while simultaneously embodying Blatter as the voice of FIFA and soccer.

Re/presenting news about Blatter and FIFA Vice President Issa Hayatou's trip to South Africa serves to simultaneously promote the World Cup and its centrality to FIFA, FIFA's identity as the embodiment of the World Cup, and South Africa as the host nation. Similarly, the items intertextually and symbiotically promote the political identities and status of FIFA (hence soccer) and the South African politicians named in the main and related items on the Web page. Links to "Media Releases" included items about the size of the tournament ("Record number of 204 teams enter preliminary competition"—posted on FIFA.com, March 30, 2007); FIFA's president ("FIFA President deems . . ."—posted January 29, 2007); and South African President Mbeki" (President Mbeki: In 2010, we will win in Africa with Africa" —posted October 24, 2006). The items mobilize discourses that simultaneously re/produce national and political identities and promote the tournament's significance and excitement. The promotion of South Africa as the host of the World Cup also was apparent in the World Cup home page feature "South Africa A-Z," which featured key cultural symbols and referents, concurrently emphasizing the national identity of South Africa and audience building through the promotion of South Africa and the World Cup as a travel and cultural destination.

## FIFA Women's World Cup

In contrast to the men's World Cup pages, the women's pages provided little sense of immediacy, excitement, or explicit links to FIFA or politics. The *lack* of political or organizational commodification of the Women's World Cup suggests that the intertextual references provided by the women's game were neither desirable nor equivalent to the intertextual power of men's soccer. FIFA as an organization was absent from the main page and there were no key FIFA members to embody or personify the organization, effectively ensuring that FIFA was not constructed as the embodiment of women's soccer (nor was women's soccer constructed as an embodiment of FIFA). Indeed, in contrast to the (men's) World Cup, President Blatter was noticeably absent from all items concerning the Women's World Cup, meaning that the powerful intertextual links between FIFA and men's soccer were not enacted with women's soccer. The lack of political and organizational commodification of the women's game suggests that it is not a member of the main category of soccer. Clearly, the intertextual relationship remains absent because the commodification of the women's game by FIFA and key FIFA members would itself enact a powerful link with women's soccer, working in turn to re/produce it as part of the main category.

A map of the 2007 Women's World Cup host nation, China, marking five cities (match sites) was provided with no caption on the FIFA.com Web site in June 2007. There were no items promoting China as a nation or host of the 2007 Women's World Cup; no photographs of key soccer or Chinese cultural symbols such as buildings, wildlife, or soccer stadia. Similarly, the lack of Chinese political presence in the news items reflected the lack of political and national intertextual value provided by the Women's World Cup. The failure to commodify the tournament to promote either soccer or national identities reflected the lack of intertextual power of women's soccer. However, as before, this failure to build intertextual links re/produces the women's tournament as lacking status, interest, and significance for soccer audiences.

One of the lowest value production formats found on FIFA.com was used on the Women's World Cup page, comprising two news stories each with a small photograph followed by a list of five news items. Posting dates indicated a low turnover, with most items older than the men's World Cup news items despite the imminence (at the time of this analysis) of the Women's World Cup (in September 2007). A lack of audience building and excitement was apparent in the comparative failure to promote or frame the Women's World Cup either on this page or the wider Web site. Like most sports fans, soccer fans are used to good production values and the framing of the game as exciting, newsworthy, and politically valuable due to its strong links to national identities. Failure to frame and enact these elements suggests that FIFA does not construct the same implied users, or narratees, for the women's and men's tournaments. As such, it fails to collaborate with or enact soccer fans' identities as including an interest in the women's game, and it does not construct fans of the women's game as members of the (main) soccer category. Given the strong identification of fans, the exclusion of women's soccer from the enactment of fan's interests and understandings is a powerful act that defines the category as male and re/produces the distinction between men's and women's soccer.

The lack of production values and promotion of the women's tournament was echoed throughout the wider Web site. Of the 49 interviews available through the "News Centre," only one was about the impending Women's World Cup, comprising the sole interview with a woman (the same item was featured on the Women's World Cup page). Concerning the former Sweden coach's move to coach China, the accompanying image did not portray her in the act of coaching (in contrast to most other images of male coaches at FIFA.com). Images and language choices frame and mobilize discourses, thus nonaction portrayals of women athletes position them as outside the category of sport. Similarly, power markers can be undermined by proximal deployment of an alternative marker, because one word or symbol can intertextually mobilize discourses (O'Donnell, 1994). This was apparent in the FIFA.com "News" item, "All in a good cause," which stated: "The 6–2 final scoreline also meant that the U.S. girls extended their unbeaten run to a stagger- ing 41 games" (posted May 15, 2007). The impressive scoreline and "unbeaten run" provide positive power markers, but the deployment of the term "girls" works to diminish the players as both athletes and women, hence the quality of the game. The item further stated that the match "transpired to be an entertaining contest." Deployment of the term "transpired" discursively framed the match as entertaining against expectations, mobilizing the predominant discourse re/ produced by media production practices that frame women's sport as less spectacular and less entertaining. This contrasts with the spec- tacular action that is re/produced as part of the male category, further constructing the gender distinction in soccer.

In contrast, a newer FIFA.com item titled "Swenson embodying Swedish spirit" (posted June 22, 2007) did re/produce a version of women's soccer that worked to construct the game and the upcoming women's tournament as exciting, both audience-building and re/ producing women's soccer as part of the main category. The item stated:

> With just over two months to go before the FIFA Women's World Cup China 2007, all eyes are turning to a Sweden team currently enjoying a red-hot run of form. Back-to-back 7–0 wins over Romania and Hungary during the qualifiers for the UEFA European Women's Championship 2009 have sent morale soaring ahead of September's showpiece event.

Imminence (i.e., "just over two months"; "September's") is used to build audiences and excitement for both the upcoming tournament and the more distant UEFA tournament. Discourses of action, excite- ment, and skill are mobilized to promote the tournament using lan- guage and narratives discursively familiar to soccer fans and typical of men's soccer reporting. Phrases such as "red-hot run of form" and "September's showpiece event" frame the women's tournament as significant and newsworthy and the game as skilled, exciting, and of interest to soccer fans. However, the language choice of "feisty" does undermine the athleticism of one player, making gender her salient categorization given that "feisty" is typically deployed in relation to women and young animals.

### World Cup Logos and Photos

Both Web pages displayed the tournament logos, the main symbols of the tournament. Similar in format across all FIFA tournaments, the logos for the men's 2010 and women's 2007 tournaments differ on significant features that discursively mobilize gendered discourses. The main image of the (men's) World Cup logo comprises a figurative male in the action of performing the highly skilled scissor kick. The ball is in the air and lines of color signify the action and movement of the ball and the male body performing the kick. Mobilizing discourses of action, this achieves a categorization of the men's game and its version of masculinity as highly skilled, exciting, and action-oriented, as this is one of the more exhilarating, accomplished, daring, and spectacular moves in soccer. In contrast, the Women's World Cup logo is more static and statuesque comprising three curved shapes balancing on top of each other, with the top curve holding a ball which, given the orange and yellow coloring, could also symbolize the sun. The women's logo lacks action, and there is no symbolism of skill or competition. Instead, the image is more aesthetic, curvaceous, and organic in form, intertextually mobilizing familiar discourses about women and women athletes (Christopherson, Janning, & McConnell, 2002). Symbolism re/presenting Chinese iconography is also intertextually referenced in the logo, further enacted by the prominent positioning of "CHINA" across the visual symbol. While the prominence of national symbolism within the logo is interesting, its dominance frames the action of the tournament as secondary to its location.

Both the men's and women's World Cup main pages included an advertisement for *FIFA* magazine. At the start of the analysis, the advertisement comprised the front cover of three magazines, all of which portrayed action images of male players. The subsequent version comprised multiple copies of one *FIFA* magazine that portrayed an action image of a male player. The predominance of male images on the magazines used in the advertisement re/produces the category and the organization as male, the action nature of the shot constructing the form of masculinity and the sport as skilled, aggressive, and competitive action. This reflects typical re/presentational practices of sport magazines (Bishop, 2003; Duncan, 1990) and wider mediated sport sites.

The likelihood of soccer fans' familiarity with mediated texts suggests that the provision of photographic imagery contributes to a shared understanding about the importance of events and action, and in turn re/produces the newsworthiness of the events and action re/presented. The men's tournament Web page provided a series of photographs for perusal and a link to more "Photos." In contrast, the women's tournament page provided neither additional photographs nor a link to more photographs. As such, the (comparative) absence of photographs of action, events, and news re/produces the women's game as lacking in action and newsworthiness. Indeed, the Web site as a whole had very few photographs related to the women's game and even fewer of on-the-field action, symbolically erasing or annihilating their presence as part of the category. This exclusion is particularly significant because digital media have the ability to provide dynamic images that promote shared understanding through familiarity to sporting audiences alongside the illusion of active participation. Equally, while this can be seen as a reflection of the lower production values used for low-status sports, low production values in themselves re/produce the low status of the sports.

### FIFA.com Photographs

Photographs and links to more photographs were available on many pages on the Web site, a notable exception being the Women's World Cup page, with a link on the "News Centre" main page to most of the photographs offered on FIFA.com. Of the 497 photographs viewed, 15 (3%) were of women players or coaches and 11 (2.2%) were general images related to the 2007 Women's World Cup (e.g., the final draw; performance of the first official song; official shop opening). The photographs relating to the men's 2010 World Cup—excluding images of key FIFA representatives—totaled 29 (5.8%; e.g., stadia construction). This may not seem like a large difference, but considering the need to build audiences and promote tournaments the comparative lack of photographs of the impending women's tournament was problematic. Of the 12 photographs of women playing soccer, seven showed women in emotional celebration. Of the five action shots available, two were considered undermining action in contrast to the successful, power tackles typically used to re/present male players. The first image, "Kerstin Stegmann (Germany) controls the ball," is problematic because it claims to be an image of skilled action but shows none as there is no ball in the image and her legs are excluded from the photo. The second undermining shot (of Atiba of Nigeria challenging Meflah of Algeria) was an action shot, but the action was of a poor, arguably illegal and unusual tackle rather than a skilled performance. Atiba is shown trying to win a ball, which is behind her, with a high, backwards, "studs up" tackle, while Meflah appears to be responding to the dangerous move by moving back off the ball (which is closer to her hands than her feet) with a grimace (of fear) on her face. While these images mobilize a number of familiar discourses about women's soccer, at the most basic level they re/produce the women's game as unskilled.

The 12 photos of women playing contrasts with 288 images of men playing soccer, of which 61 (21.2%) comprise celebration and 227 (78.8%) male action (tackles, etc.). The far greater proportion of celebratory images of women compared to action shots re/produces predominant discourses about the emotionality of women athletes, while the failure to include discursively familiar forms of action excludes women players from the category of soccer. Effectively the images framed the women's game as lacking in action and skill, re/producing discourses about women's soccer as lacking competitiveness, aggressiveness, and talent (Meân, 2001). In comparison, the multiple photographs of men in action typically portrayed the spectacular action of tackles and challenges that epitomize the aggression, competitiveness, and skill of soccer in ways that are discursively familiar and normative to soccer audiences. As a form of extrematization (Potter, 1996), such re/presentational practices re/produce the traditional hegemonic masculinity of soccer, constructing it as spectacular and "action-packed." Similarly, images of male players celebrating are discursively familiar to soccer fans, enacting the acceptable face of male emotion in soccer by framing it as part of the action.

Serving to construct the category as male and the female as other, the re/presentational practices enact women's gender (i.e., femininity) as the primary and salient identity category of female players. The substantive difference in photographs on FIFA.com suggests that selection was rhetorically and discursively motivated, since making female and male action comparable would entail crossing the gendered boundary that demarcates male and female as so distinct in soccer. The overall lack of images of women and the failure to include women performing the familiar skilled tackles excludes them from the category of soccer, reflecting similar discursive actions observed within organizations that regulate soccer in response to the presence of women (Fielding & Meân, 2008). Thus, beyond protecting masculinity through the symbolic exclusion of women, the routine mobilization of traditional gendered discourses about female players as more emotional, less aggressive, and less skilled also positions male soccer as action-packed, spectacular, skilled, and aggressive.

❖ DISCUSSION: CONCLUDING COMMENTS

Overall, it was apparent that the creators of FIFA.com had strategically worked to include women within the basic informational elements of the new Web site (compared to the old Web site). However, women were routinely excluded from the everyday making of soccer through action, news, and images, effectively enacting the main category of soccer as male. Similarly, the re/presentational practices deployed in the inclusion of women's play were undermining, trivializing the action of the women's game. Since it is within the ordinary and everyday act of "doing" categories that meanings are constructed, these actions re/produce the women's game as lacking the characteristics that define the category of soccer and serve to exclude and "other" women (Hall, 1997; Potter, 1996). The sociocognitive significance of identity categories suggests that these practices are strategic in nature (Potter, 1996; Turner, Hogg, Oakes, Reicher, & Wetherell, 1987). Thus, the practices enacted at FIFA.com serve to undermine the threat of women's participation in soccer, maintaining the status quo of a "natural" gendered demarcation in re/producing the category as hegemonic masculinity. The continued positioning of women outside the category of soccer resists the participation of women, a powerful act given FIFA's position as the dominant re/producer of the category of soccer (Foucault, 1970, 1972).

The mobilization of highly gendered discourses and the routine construction of players' identities as hegemonic versions of masculinity and femininity at FIFA.com reveal an underlying organizational framing of women's soccer as lacking in skill, action, and interest. The continued dominance and value of traditional masculinity combined with the inclusion of women at basic levels arguably serves to promote a sense of equality and inclusion yet ensures that women players remain "othered" (Christopherson, Janning, & McConnell, 2002), powerfully rendering continued discriminatory practices invisible (Foucault, 1970). Indeed, FIFA.com's failure to discursively construct shared category membership and identification with the women's game reflects the everyday, routine failure to enact the women's game as part of the category of soccer. This failure to build intertextual links re/produces the women's tournament as lacking status, interest, and significance for soccer audiences, particularly given sporting audiences' familiarity with the narratives, discursive practices, and promotional culture of soccer and the primacy of soccer for identity (Walsh & Guilianotti, 2001). Similarly, the predominant practices at FIFA.com promote the primary categorization of women players as female rather than as athletes, a gatekeeping practice that strategically mobilizes traditional gendered discourses (Gumperz, 1982). This is evident in the first official song for a Women's World Cup, "You Are the Most Beautiful in the World" (FIFA.com, 2007). Instead of focusing on competitive athleticism and the world's "beautiful game," the title deploys the intertextual reference to beauty to mobilize discourses of hegemonic femininity.

FIFA's mission states: "FIFA has a huge responsibility to reach out and touch the world, using football as a symbol of hope and integration" (posted FIFA.com). This mission statement recognizes the significance and influence of FIFA and soccer on culture and therefore its ability to promote change. However, change is not achieved through policy and statement but in the everyday action and practices that construct and define categories and identities (Hall, 1997; Potter, 1996). It is at this invisible level of power—within the symbolic and discursive processes that construct meaning—that soccer remains inherently male at FIFA.com, resisting, excluding, and framing women's soccer as outside the category. Indeed, the fundamental significance of the category as embedded within a highly naturalized, foundational discourse suggests that re/producing alternative gendered or gender-neutral meanings in soccer are likely to be especially strongly resisted. Consequently, the re/production of women's soccer as primarily about femaleness will continue to undermine women's identities as athletes, serving to protect masculinity. As such, FIFA.com's failure to routinely and systemically integrate women into the action of soccer means it has failed to fulfill FIFA's mission of being a symbol of integration, although some may perceive hope in the recent changes that (merely) increase the inclusion of women's soccer.

## ❖ REFERENCES

Billings, A. C., Halone, K. K., & Denham, B. E. (2002). "Man, that was a pretty shot": An analysis of gendered broadcast commentary surrounding the 2000 men's and women's NCAA final four basketball championships. *Mass Communication and Society, 5,* 295–315.

Bishop, R. (2003). Missing in action: Feature coverage of women's sports in *Sports Illustrated. Journal of Sport and Social Issues, 27,* 184–194.

Cameron, D. (1998). "Is there any ketchup, Vera?": Gender, power and pragmatics. *Discourse and Society, 9,* 437–455.

Caudwell, J. (1999). Women's football in the United Kingdom. *Journal of Sport and Social Issues, 23,* 390–402.

Christopherson, N., Janning, M., & McConnell, E. D. (2002). Two kicks forward, one kick back: A content analysis of media discourses on the 1999 Women's World Cup soccer championship. *Sociology of Sport Journal, 19,* 170–188.

Duncan, M. C. (1990). Sports photographs and sexual difference: Images of women and men in the 1984 and 1988 Olympic Games. *Sociology of Sport Journal, 7,* 22–43.

Duncan, M. C., & Messner, M. A. (1998). The media image of sport and gender. In L. A. Wenner (Ed.), *MediaSport* (pp. 170–185). London/New York: Routledge.

Duncan, M. C., Messner, M. A., Willms, N., & Wilson, W. (2005). *Gender in televised sport: News and highlight shows, 1989–2004.* Report to Amateur Athletic Association of Los Angeles (AAFLA). Retrieved September 10, 2007, from http://aafla.com/9arr/ResearchReports/tv2004.pdf

Dworkin, S. L., & Messner, M. A. (1999). Just do . . . what? Sport, bodies, gender. In M. M. Ferree, J. Lorber, & B. Hess (Eds.), *Revisioning gender* (pp. 341–364). Thousand Oaks, CA: Sage.

Fielding-Lloyd, B., & Meân, L. J. (2008). Standards and separatism: The discursive construction of gender in English soccer coach education. *Sex Roles, 58,* 24–39.

Foucault, M. (1970). *The order of things: An archeology of the human sciences.* New York: Vintage/Random House.

Foucault, M. (1972). *The archaeology of knowledge.* London: Tavistock.

Graham, P., & Hearn, G. (2001). The coming of post-reflexive society: Commodification and language in digital capitalism. *Media International Australia Incorporating Culture and Policy, 98,* 79–90.

Gumperz, J. (1982). *Discourse strategies.* Cambridge, UK: Cambridge University Press.

Hall, M. A. (1988). The discourse of gender and sport: From femininity to feminism. *Sociology of Sport Journal, 5,* 330–340.

Hall, S. (1997). The work of representation. In S. Hall (Ed.), *Representation: Cultural representations and signifying practices* (pp. 13–74). London: Sage/Open University Press.

Infront Sports & Media. (2007, February 6). *2006 FIFA World Cup broadcast wider, longer and farther than ever before.* Retrieved September 9, 2007, from http://www.infrontsports.com/presscenter/newsdetail/article/116/2006-fifa-wo-8.html

International Olympic Committee (2008). *Olympic marketing fact file, 2008 edition.* Retrieved September 14, 2008, from http://multimedia.olympic.org/pdf/en_report_344.pdf

Jansson, A. (2002). The mediatization of consumption: Towards an analytical framework of image culture. *Journal of Consumer Culture, 2,* 5–31.

Kane, M. J., & Lenskyj, H. J. (1998). Media treatment of female athletes: Issues of gender and sexualities. In L. A. Wenner (Ed.), *MediaSport* (pp. 186–201). London/New York: Routledge.

Lakoff, G. (1987). *Women, fire and dangerous things: What categories reveal about the mind.* Chicago: Chicago University Press.

Maingueneau, D. (1999). Analysing self-constituting discourses. *Discourse Studies, 1,* 175–199.

Meân, L. J. (2001). Identity and discursive practice: Doing gender on the football pitch. *Discourse & Society, 12,* 789–815.

Meân Patterson, L. J. (2003). Everyday discursive practices and the construction of gender: A study at the "grass roots." In A. Schoor, W. Campbell,

& M. Schenk (Eds.), *Communication research and media science in Europe* (pp. 497–515). Berlin: Mouton de Gruyter.

Messner, M. A. (1988). Sports and male domination: The female athletes as contested ideological terrain. *Sociology of Sport Journal, 5,* 197–211.

O'Donnell, H. (1994). Mapping the mythical: A geopolitics of national sporting stereotypes. *Discourse and Society, 5,* 345–380.

Potter, J. (1996). *Representing reality: Discourse, rhetoric and social construction.* London: Sage.

Scherer, J. (2007). Globalization, promotional culture and the production/ consumption of online games: Emerging Adidas's "Beat Rugby" campaign. *New Media & Society, 9,* 475–496.

Shapiro, M. J. (1989). Representing world politics: The sport/war intertext. In J. Der Derian & M. J. Shapiro (Eds.), *International/intertextual relations* (pp. 69–96). Lexington, MA: Lexington Books.

Shaw, S. (2006). Scratching the back of "Mr. X": Analyzing gendered social processes in sport organizations. *Journal of Sport Management, 20,* 510–534.

Sklair, L. (1991). *Sociology of the global system.* London: Harvester Wheatsheaf.

Sugden, J., & Tomlinson, A. (1994). Soccer culture, national identity and the World Cup. In J. Sugden & A. Tomlinson (Eds.), *Hosts and champions: Soccer culture, national identity and the World Cup* (pp. 3–12). Aldershot, UK: Arena.

Turner, J. C., Hogg, M., Oakes, P. J., Reicher, S. D., & Wetherell, M. (1987). *Rediscovering the social group.* Oxford, UK: Blackwell.

Van Dijk, T. A. (1993). Principles of critical discourse analysis. *Discourse and Society, 4,* 249–283.

Vertinsky, P. (2006). Time gentlemen please: The space and place of gender in sport history. In M. G. Phillips (Ed.), *Deconstructing sport history: A postmodern analysis* (pp. 227–243). New York: SUNY Press.

Walsh, A. J., & Giulianotti, R. (2001). This sporting mammon: A normative critique of the commodification of sport. *Journal of the Philosophy of Sport, 29,* 53–77.

Wenner, L. A. (1991). One part alcohol, one part sport, one part dirt, stir gently: Beer commercial and television sports. In L. R. Vande Berg & L. A. Wenner (Eds.), *Television criticism: Approaches and applications* (pp. 388–407). New York: Longman.

Wenner, L. A. (1998). Playing the mediasport game. In L. A. Wenner (Ed.), *MediaSport* (pp. 3–13). London/New York: Routledge.

## ❖ NOTES

1. Many people in the United States consider soccer to be untelevisual (i.e., not a good sport for the medium of television) and that this is a natural aspect of the sport. However, the televisual excitement or spectacle of any sport or sporting event is really a reflection of the production values, techniques, and strategies put into producing the program content. Thus, in most of the world,

soccer makes exciting television, reflecting its status and mediated re/production as the most exciting sport.

2. Estimated figures are often used given the difficulty in establishing actual viewing figures in many countries throughout the world. Infront Sports & Media is responsible for compiling the World Cup figures and also handle's the global sales of the TV rights; its chief executive (Sepp Blatter) is the nephew of FIFA's president (*The Independent on Sunday*, 2007). Thus, while FIFA estimates the audience for the final game at 715.1 million, verifiable figures (using 54 key surveyed markets) suggest a live audience of 260 million, with 600 million watching part of the match (Initiative Sports Futures, 2007). However, verifiable figures do exclude major audiences, such as most African countries.

3. Given soccer's international appeal, globalization is a key element of the sport. Major clubs (i.e., domestic teams) often have a stronger fan base outside their home nation. The Internet has increased this trend by enhancing access to club sites, as well as fan clubs and fanzines (fan magazines). Indeed FIFA.com reports domestic club news, reflecting the global appeal of club soccer. Equally, many soccer players play for clubs outside their home nation.

4. Re/presentation is a way of explicitly drawing attention to the mediated nature of the world, as it is presented, represented, and re-presented to us through talk and other communicative contexts. Linked to ideas concerning the production and reproduction (re/production) of knowledge, culture, and therefore, power, while the media can easily be seen as part of this process, it is also a part of *everyday* talk and practices within which we all participate (Potter, 1996), resisting or collaborating as members of shared interpretative communities or social categories.

# 5

# Gendered Sports Dirt

*Interrogating Sex and the Single Beer Commercial*

## Lawrence A. Wenner

Gender has long raised issues in and around sport. On the field, sport is largely a sexually segregated space. At elite levels, this is almost always the case. In the marketplace, male sport dominates. As fans, men are more avid and plentiful. There is much to be concerned about in this state of affairs (Crawford, 2004; Messner & Sabo, 1990). Yet, while things may be changing, we know marketers remain pragmatic. They rely on old saws about sport and gender to target an elusive and desirable male demographic. In adding beer to that mix, this study explores the familiar trinity of sport, beer, and gender and its implications for identity.

### Gender, Sport, and Commodity Culture

Sport plays in the drawing of gender identity through its narrative telling, and this is ported to narratives that culturally frame sport. In studying "mediasport," these necessarily commodified "frames" can be more important than "the game" (Wenner, 2006). Here the lens on sport and gender often focuses on gender as a "myth of difference" where "women are not seen as the fellows of men" (Pronger, 1990, p. 178). Commercialized mediasport representations are often reliant on complementary processes of "symbolic annihilation" of women and "symbolic glorification" of men (Sabo & Jansen, 1992).

We know much is problematic about the use of sex in advertising (Reichert & Lambiase, 2003). The ills range from reliance on wanton gender stereotype to gratuitous choreographies of "sexiness" to sell just about anything no matter how far-fetched the connection. In televised sports, commercials often rely on broad, brush-stroke drawings of "what men want" and "how women are" (Sabo & Jansen, 1992). Still drawings of gender and sexuality in commodity aesthetics are not fixed. In *Sportsex*, Miller (2001) points to openings for alternative readings of gender identity in sport. His analysis raises questions about new drawings of gender and sport in the commercial sphere.

While Miller's work explores the homoerotic pushing against unfettered heterosexuality, much evidence suggests that dominant heterosexual masculinity is undergoing changes in the marketplace. Recent pronouncements by brewers recognize that their stereotyped drawings of hyper-masculinity and "sexed up" women may be losing functionality (Ives, 2003; Poulton, 2004), but this has been heard before (Teinowitz, 1993). A prominent example of recent changes has been the rise of the male as a loser countertype (Farhi, 2005; Messner & Montez de Oca, 2005). Such changes in gender portrayal in the sport marketing environment portend concomitant changes in portrayals of male-female interactions with sexual relation implications.

## Beer, Sport, and Commodity Culture

Beer is a special product in the context of sport. At once, its consumption is oxymoronic with athleticism and synonymous with sport spectating (Wenner, 1991). Beer is very much a male product with men consuming more than 80% of beer (Goldammer, 2000). Its reputation as a tool of male bonding has been ported to modern sports spectatorship (Collins & Vamplew, 2002). Consequently, breweries routinely spend more than 60% of their advertising dollars in sports programming to reach men ("Alcohol advertising," 2004). The beer–sport relationship is glued, perhaps not at the hips, but at the beer belly of male sports fans.

Many concerns have been raised about beer marketing in sport. Foremost is concern over sport's role in helping to fuel earlier and more positive associations with drinking, underage and earlier drinking, and alcohol abuse (Ellickson, Collins, Hambarsoomians, & McCaffrey, 2005; Grube & Wallack, 1994; Slater, Rouner, Domenech-Rodriguez, Beauvais, Murphy, & Van Leuven, 1997; Zwarun & Farrar, 2005). Because of this, there have been calls for the NCAA (National Collegiate Athletic Association) and FIFA (Fédération Internationale de Football Association) to "just say no," or at least "not so much," when it comes to alcohol marketing and advertising dollars (Campaign for Alcohol-Free Sports TV, 2005, 2006).

Yet, the framing of moral panic over beer and alcohol can hide the obvious. In framing beer relative to sport as a social problem, there is danger in masking the caveat that both beer and sport are largely male problems. This mirrors Katz's (1999) critique that violence has been treated as a social rather than male problem. Like violence, men's tendencies towards beer and sport impact women. Herein lays the importance of taking a closer look at the beer, sport, and sex cocktail.

### The Beer, Sport, and Sex Cocktail

That beer and sport have so long gone together has created a psychic "third place" for men (Oldenburg, 1989). It is the sanctity of this cultural space that has allowed brewers to pander for years to men with "beer babes" from the "Swedish bikini team" to the Coors twins. In recent times, both beer and sport have struggled with their marketplaces. Sport has realized that in order to grow its fan base, it will need women. With its diminishing sales, beer too has needed to rethink its image and reach out to, or at least not alienate, women. As a result, many brewers have rejiggered their strategies to appeal to the more "sophisticated" consumer (Ives, 2003; Poulton, 2004).

Still, the world of beer commercials seen in sports programming remains a male "dreamworld" (Jhally, 2007). In the shadow of sport, it is the place where things play out well for men as long as there is beer. This includes sex. In familiar archetypes in this dreamworld, beer both fuels sex and serves as consolation for it. Here it is common for beer to be shown driving parties with much dancing and glancing that portends hookups. Beer is also often shown fueling men's communal gazing at women beyond their reach and softening the blow of that realization. Other familiar themes show "boys being boys" consuming beer and sport free of the shackles of women and implicitly their "civilizing" demands that must be accommodated for sex.

Beer commercials have a tough time with women. If Sabo and Jansen (1992) are right, they disrupt the glorification of men and are often symbolically annihilated. As a consequence, in this world women are often absent or seen at a distance. But this is not always the case.

What happens when beer, sport, and gender get together in a commercial? What is the nature of the male-female interaction and what does it tell us about gender identities relative to beer, sport, and sex?

## ❖ METHODOLOGICAL APPROACH: ON INTERROGATING GENDER, SPORT, AND THE BEER COMMERCIAL

Approaches to analyzing the commercial have been ported from virtually every quarter of critical inquiry. Each approach has its merits. Still, there remains an underlying "unease" about our encounters with commercial bombardment often not addressed in critical stocktaking. This hinges on feelings that we are being worked over in devious ways by fallacious connections made to enlist our sympathies. This is all not so simple as we are active readers capable of pushing back. Yet, in recognizing the necessity to push back, we also acknowledge that much is ethically problematic in our transaction with the commercial message. In recognizing these tensions, the approach here relies on a dirt theory of narrative ethics fashioned to deconstruct the commercial narrative and its reading and ethically interrogate the transaction (Wenner, 2007). The next sections consider three elements in the approach and questions raised for beer commercials in which sport and gender interact.

### Approaching Dirt, Readers, and Ethics in Commercial Narratives

#### Dirt Theory

Traceable to the work of Douglas (1966) and Leach (1976), mediated *dirt theory* advanced with the work of Hartley (1984) and Enzenberger (1972), and has been applied to mediated sport (Hilliard & Hendley, 2004; Wenner, 1994, 2004, 2007). Throughout, dirt is seen as "matter out of place." Dirt transfers power and logic from one setting to another. When we say "sex sells" or "sport is a good place in which to sell your product," we recognize the power of dirt. Dirt helps sell products through manufactured connections. While dirt may be benign, contagion from its employment can be ethically problematic. Consequently, dirt theory begins by identifying dirt, evaluating its build-up and characterization, and assessing its role in reading.

#### Reader-Oriented Criticism

There has long been a de facto concern with dirt in reader-oriented criticism as the approach hinges on what readers bring to the text.

Familiar dirt helps us make sense of new things. There are many variants of reader-oriented criticism and reception theory along the critical landscape (Machor & Goldstein, 2001; Tompkins, 1980). Most appropriate to interrogating dirt are Iser's (1974, 1978, 2006) concerns with the (1) contextualization of implied readers, (2) drawing of readers in and by the text, and (3) nature of the reading act. In beer commercials, we need to understand how marketers as authors reach out to readers through contextual understandings of sporting "interpretive communities" (Fish, 1980). As well, we need to look at the characterization of readers through on-screen textual surrogates and off-screen clues, such as direct address or camera position, that help to state preferred reading positions. Finally, reading processes need to be explored by considering the reader's vantage point and the negotiation of both gaps and redundancies in texts.

### Ethical Criticism

The third layer in analysis concerns ethics. Ethical assessments have often been resisted in literary, aesthetic, and cultural criticism as presumptuous (Carroll, 2000). More recently, ethical interrogation has come to be seen as both inescapable in narrative analysis (Booth, 1998; Eco, 1979; Gregory, 1998) and a necessary remedy to detached relativism in cultural critique (Eaglestone, 2004; Eagleton, 2003; Kellner, 2000; Zylinska, 2005). The key in this ethical turn has been the realization that ethical interrogation is not synonymous with moral prescription. Rather, the approach allows for a complementary stocktaking of ethical tensions in the text and its reading in companion with other critical concerns (Carroll, 2000). In raising questions about greater good, duties such as truthfulness or not doing harm, balance or fairness, other respecting care, justice, or other issues, ethical criticism illuminates moral flaws that also can be aesthetically defective or culturally problematic. In assessing commercial narratives, the approach is particularly well-suited to interrogating the propriety of dirt imported to the sell and the dirtiness encouraged through reading and characterizations of the reader (Wenner, 2007).

## Gendered Sports Dirt and the Beer Commercial

It should be no surprise that something called dirt theory is an inherently messy enterprise. The process depends on overlapping considerations including the nature of dirt and its functioning; dirt's relation to reading; the nature of the reading act; the characterization of the reader; and ethical problems in dirt, reading, and how they interact. Yet, the approach's components help structure the messiness of "thick

readings" (Geertz, 1973), which are more free-form and often characterize critical inquiry. Each layer of analysis drives questions about
understanding beer commercials that mix sports dirt with gender dirt.

### Finding Dirt

Mirroring the axiom "follow the money," a dirt theory look at
beer commercials that mix sport and gender must "follow the dirt."
What dirt comes from sport, and what dirt comes from gender?
Where does dirt come from, and where does it go? How is it
imported, and what is its character? How is dirt used in the construction of the narrative? How are logics of dirt from one place
appended to the logic of the sell? What fallacies or distortions come
about as a result of importing the dirt to the new setting? These and
other questions begin the hunt.

### Constructing Readers

In starting with dirt, it becomes a key overlay in approaching the
reader and in reading. Thus, one begins by examining the roles that
sport and gender dirt play in contextualizing the interpretive community for beer commercials. To this are added questions about dirt in
characterizing the reader in and by the beer commercial text. What
roles does dirt play in coaxing a preferred reading position? Finally,
dirt's role in shaping the reading act needs consideration. How do gender and sport dirt and their interaction influence the reader's vantage
point? What roles does dirt play in filling gaps and influencing how
redundancies in the text are likely to be received? These kinds of questions drive the pathway to ethical interrogation.

### Deconstructing Ethics

In interrogating ethical dynamics in beer commercials, it is worth
recognizing that a little dirt may be dust, doing little harm. A lot of dirt
covers and clogs things, doing harm. Yet a little dirt, like water in a gas
tank, can cause considerable harm. Thus, in dirt theory, ethical interrogation mostly focuses on what dirt does. Still, we need to take stock of
what the "matter out of place" really is. Is it ethically flawed prior to
importation? What issues are raised by dirt's movement, its landing, its
buildup, its workings, and its interaction with other matter?

In more specific terms, does dirt improprietously push the reader to
control reading? Has dirt influenced the liberties taken in characterizing
interpretive communities? What roles does dirt play in obfuscating

truth? How does dirt work to devalue the greater good? Has dirt worked to disrupt balance or cover up inequities? Has dirt worked against other respecting care? Are there inherent injustices that dirt works to mask? What ethical dilemmas are raised when recombinant sport and gender dirt interact? With questions like these, ethical inquiry can be expansive.

**Sampling a Six-Pack**

Many beer commercials are produced each year. Virtually all are broadcast in sports programming. Studies analyzing the beer marketing in sport have relied on content analysis (Grube & Wallack, 1994; Madden & Grube, 1994; Zwarun & Farrar, 2005). While such studies provide important surface understandings, they cannot fully interrogate the marketing message and its reading.

The approach here errs in another direction. An a priori target universe of beer commercials featuring both sports and gender was specified. Here all beer commercials in advertising industry video collections at http://www.adcritic.com and http://www.adforum.com were examined to identify a subset of spots that featured sport or athletic activity in addition to some male-female interaction with sexual relation implications.[1] This criteria was also used in searching the more public video sites of http://www.youtube.com and http:// www.ifilm .com for additional spots.[2]

Most surprising was that few beer commercials explicitly featured both sport and cross-gender interaction. Even for spots clearly aimed at the sports audience, commercials that featured sex without sport or sport without sex were far more common. The sex-without-sport spots centered on men ogling women often with trepidation or disdain but without interaction or party scenes that often featured dancing with either limited or innuendo-dependent interaction. The sport-without-sex ads centered on parodies of athletes interacting with media or groups of male sports fans enacting tales that celebrate and naturalize beer consumption, while spectating.

A six-pack convenience sample was chosen for analysis from approximately 20 spots featuring sport or athletic activity in addition to some male-female interaction with sexual relation implications. The winnowed sample chosen considers distinct, non-redundant strategies from a range of brewers. This six-pack strategy magnifies a range of strategies while putting forth a manageable number for interrogation and comparison.

❖  RESULTS: INTERROGATING SPORT,
    GENDER, AND THE BEER COMMERCIAL

The analyses that follow examine commercials aimed at the domestic American market and at foreign audiences in Europe and Australia. In the sections below, variant strategies showcasing the Heineken, Michelob Ultra, Bud Light, Coors Light, Miller Light, and Tooheys brands are considered.

### Heineken: Sex Versus Sport

Heineken's "Down Hill" ad (n.d.) bridges overlapping pairings of beer and sex with those of beer and sport. Featuring no dialogue for flexibility in the European market the short spot opens on a young man sitting on a wall in front of a residence. He waits with flowers and a six-pack of Heineken. As a soundtrack emblematic of foot-stomping by enthused fans in a stadium comes up, he eyes and moves to his "true love"—a smiling pretty woman—for a passionate sidewalk embrace marked by an unseen crowd's "ah-oh" cheer mirroring a reaction to a goal. As the embrace is consummated, the young man sees a soccer ball bounding down the street and tears away in pursuit with six-pack in hand. As the scene closes, we see the disappointed young woman left holding flowers and a throng of young men rushing after the Heineken-toting man and ball. The spot closes with the title graphic "Welcome to Champions Planet" over a soccer ball and noting Heineken as "Proud Sponsor of UEFA (Union of European Football Associations) League."

This spot is a duel in the powers of sport versus sexual dirt, and here sport wins. Significant is the importation of normative dirt into the heterosexual romance. Here flowers bring romance, while beer brings sex. Romance is left behind, and the beer is transferred to the more important pursuit of sport in the company of men. Thus the "natural" place of women is also imported into the logic of this sell. As a dirty object, the moving ball serves as an equally naturalized Pavlovian bell.

With such naturalized logics, the ad's interpretive community becomes young men drawn to packs and hedging on prioritizing relational life. The ad's young man serves as a textual surrogate. Complimenting readers, he is an action figure on a "Champions Planet," with the young woman acted upon and passive. The standpoint in reading does not allow looking back with regret in leaving love for sport. In fact, the reading position is one that demands an understanding that when duty calls, the young man must chase the ball. It analogizes to military obligation as man's duty, with women left behind.

Seen as such, a key issue in ethical interrogation hinges on notions of duty and other respecting care. Here duty to persons has lost out to duty to an object (a ball) connected to a social construction (sport). Thus, preferred reading demands the demotion of personal duty and the relegation of other respecting care to pleasure. Further, such reading necessitates revaluation that the pleasures of sport are greater (and implicitly of broader good) than those of heterosexual romance. Helping to justify this counter-ethic is the power that is assigned to sports dirt and the affinities in the interpretive community of sports fans that must be brought to bear in reading. Thusly constructed, the moral stands resolute, sport wins and beer goes with the winning team. Of course women are not on that team.

### Michelob Ultra: On Women Playing a Man's Game

Women's role relative to sport is also explored in Michelob Ultra's "Light Beer Just Got a Little Darker" ad (n.d.). This spot opens with a mix of young men and women playing touch football. There is playful "trash talk" as they line up at the scrimmage line. A pretty blonde woman ups the ante by taunting a handsome young man opposite on defense; to his displeasure, she tousles his hair and boasts, "Throw it to me. I'm going to be wide open." Next, we see the quarterback throw the enthused blonde woman a successful pass. As she revels in the catch, we hear an announcer begin reinforcing superimposed titling "The world of light beer. . . ." Before that sentence can be finished, we see the thrilled then panicked blonde woman running full steam into a flying tackle by the "dissed" young man and landing limp on the ground with a hard thump. As she lies knocked out, the redeemed man stands over her taunting, with aggressive pointing in a familiar recombinant NFL and MTV hip-hop style, "You were open, but now you are closed." Then we see other players shocked by this inappropriateness with another superimposition reinforcing the announcer finishing the sentence ". . . just got a little darker." After a short product plug break to introduce "new Michelob Ultra Amber," the narrative closes in a bar for a post-game brew. In reviewing the big play, the aggressive male tackler reminds a male teammate "no free passes" as we see the victimized blonde woman, still in her football jersey, launching an aggressive tackle to floor her nemesis. As she bounces up, the watchful, male teammate winces, "Ooh, late hit!"

Football as a man's game serves as core dirt for meaning. With this comes an animus towards women on such sacred and implicitly broader playing fields. Gendered dirt ports both male backlash towards women in traditional provinces of men and male resentment over women continuing to be able to play by different rules courtesy of sexual leverage. This influences the reading position to see this narrative as a moral of what happens when women venture into the natural place of men. This standpoint is reinforced by the ad's likely placement in football broadcasts and beer as both a male product and tool of male bonding. The reading position taps what might be thought of as a "dominant but oppositional reading" of an interpretive community, one "socially policed" into accepting women on equal footing but resenting it. In this light, the reading position demands thinking about men's resentment over complexities arising from women's sexual freedom. This is raised in capital letters with the woman announcing she will be "wide open" and the man finishing with "now you are closed." The vantage point yearns for simpler times of male monogamous conquest.

The ethical equation here is a problematic two wrongs make a right. While it is playfully employed, this eye-for-an-eye logic is often a core problem in male-female relationships. Not only is prioritizing "getting even" at odds with other respecting care, in practice it escalates rather than resolves conflict in male-female (and other) relationships. Beyond this, there is unevenness in getting even. While the man uses inappropriate force and weight advantage to land a jarring tackle in a social touch football setting, it is the woman who is called for the late hit at the close of the ad.

## Bud Light: Letting Your "Inner Carlos" Out

In many ways, Bud Light's "What Would Carlos Do?" (n.d.) spot for 2007's Super Bowl broadcast speaks to the same "dominant but oppositional" logic seen in the male backlash featured in Michelob's retaliatory tackle. Opening on a boisterous group of male pals entering an urban apartment with six-pack in hand, we see the group's leader react in surprise to a group of women laughing and chatting in the living room. The leader's wife greets him with a cheery "Hey babe, I told you I was having the girls over, remember?" We focus on the husband's disbelief as he asks: "What would Carlos do?" The answer comes through a dreamy dissolve to the comedian Carlos Mencia who acts out the scene in place of the husband. The nervier Carlos channels the husband's inner hostilities by gesticulating while telling the wife: "Hmm no, I remember you telling me that Linda needs to lose some weight and that Beth needs to send her hair back to 1982 and that Claire should stop messin' with Beth's boyfriend." Carlos' delivery is intercut with reactions of horror from the wife and girlfriends. Here, the narrative pauses for a product plug with a close-up of a pour from a chilled bottle to glass with the announced reminder: "Refreshingly smooth Bud Light—always worth it." The narrative closes with the husband's alter ego Carlos and friend cheering wildly, with beer bottle in hand and six-pack in foreground while viewing cranked-up game action on screen. In the background, we see upset girlfriends stomp out with the wife, casting a disparaging glance at the oblivious men.

As in the Heineken ad, when sport dirt enters the scene, the rules of heterosexual gender relations vaporize. Fueled by the potent combination of male camaraderie and beer, sport dirt parts these seas. A key part of the gender dirt that is imported relies on the potency of the stereotyped ongoing war between the sexes over sport and with it, archetypal guy behavior and beer consumption. With this dirt comes animus towards women for the inconveniences they cause in that natural order. As in the Michelob Ultra spot, there is realization that actual acting on this animus is taboo in present social relations. Carlos' entrance and substitution for the husband as a textual surrogate enable readers in the interpretive community to safely act out a taboo fantasy.

Thus in reading, Carlos' appearance allows aggression towards women with a smile. Reading is enhanced from the dirt of knowing the "schtick" of Carlos Mencia and appreciating strategies that have made his brand of hostile, racist, and sexist humor successful in stand-up, comedy albums, and his *Mind of Mencia* show on Comedy Central, popular with young men. The appearance of Carlos empowers "real men" in recapturing their resolve. Necessarily appended to this is not only the symbolic obliteration of other respecting care—recognizing that women's socializing is of equal value to men's—but the celebration of the hostility that enables it. Even in humor, it is hard to fathom a greater good or justice that comes from heightening the value of what is, after all, sociopathic behavior. Yet this ad has fashioned such an everyman's dream, naturalizing it as socially permissible and desirable.

### Coors Light: Ejaculating Beer Over Your Dream Girl

While there is less meanness in Coors' "Beer Babe" (n.d.) spot, it too recognizes the wilting social power that men have in heterosexual romantic relationships. Set in the sport-dirtied male shrine of the baseball stadium, our everyman textual surrogate is a nebbish of a beer-drinking sports fan. We open on our hero turning from the concession stand with beer and snacks to almost bump into an attractive, smiling young woman. She flirtingly pushes her hair from her face and comments, "Frost brewed Coors Light, nice choice . . . to whet your whistle," as she moves to the concession stand. The enamored young man spins to follow her and queries, "Yeah, (you) sure know a lot about beer, come here often?" to which she replies, "I haven't missed a game yet." We see the now totally awestruck young man react with a woozy, "Really?" followed by an anticipatory "music up" shot from his point of view where we see the young woman "strip" her sweater over her head as the camera lingers on her breasts behind a tight T-shirt. As the sweater rises, we hear our hero's internal commentary: "Whoa! Could this get any better?" As he and the audience gain their bearings, it becomes clear as the young woman slips a beer server's case over her neck that her job is hawking beers in the stadium. He continues to stare in awe as she adjusts her Coors Light cap and notes that "you're spilling your beer," which the audience sees. We see him glassy-eyed and hear his dazed internal assessment—"the beer babe"—as his gaze continues. As she heads away providing a reminder mentioning "the beer" (he is spilling), his eyes follow glued to her swaying hips and buttocks. Over this last shot is the titling "Coors Light" with "Tap the Rockies," shown in titles lower in the frame.

From "tapping the Rockies" to "whet whistles" to the prematurely ejaculated "spilled beer," this spot is more driven by sexual than sport dirt. Still, it is in this pairing that the spot garners its power. Here Coors works to incarnate Ninkasi, the ancient Sumerian goddess, and port her to the modern-day shrine for beer, the sports stadium. Thusly drawn, the beer and sport goddess strikes awe in our everyman. We see his disbelief as this non-modern creation seems too good to be true. Still, while such goddesses are not seen every day, the standpoint brought to bear is. The reading position encourages the interpretive community's participation as voyeur. We look but cannot act effectively either on our desires or on engaging with a whole human being. The picture that is drawn works to remind us of the impossibility of a functional encounter, let alone the beginnings of a male-female romantic relationship for this poor sap. Ethically, the saga that is drawn here is a flawed exercise in stereotype. Our prince is an intimidated frog that cannot get beyond the aura of his goddess. From this vantage point, there cannot be true other respecting care as the surface cannot be penetrated. To this point, the tendency of this male loser to prematurely ejaculate only exacerbates the polarities reinforced by this narrative. While he may "tap the Rockies," he is hopeless in crossing the crevasse between men and women to get the girl.

## Miller Lite: Blowing Whistles on Sexual Infractions

Similarly hopeless is the man romantic lead in Miller Lite's "Ineligible Beer in the Cooler" (n.d.) spot. Here, we open on a long shot of a young couple in bathing suits lounging on deserted sands at an idyllic tropical beach. In a closer two-shot, the shapely bikini-clad woman thanks her companion for "bringing me here" to which the man as the romantic instigator replies, "You deserve this beach" as he advances his move with a kiss and by pulling a couple of beers out of a cooler. As the beers come out, they are revealed as Bud Light and then are hit with a football referee's penalty flag. A whistle is blown followed by a shot of a stripe-shirted referee rushing in, turning to the camera gesticulating thumbs-down and saying, "I've got an ineligible beer in the cooler on Hector, less taste, very un-macho." In a two-shot, we see the young woman panicking and angry at her lover ask, "Do you know who he is?" We quickly return to the referee whipping out and handing over two Miller Lite beers while saying, "Replacing with great tasting, less filling Miller Lite, half the carbs of Bud Light." Making a further call on the infraction, the referee announces, "Wow, we also have a disproportionately hot girlfriend." He signals this offense with gestures recognizing the woman's ample breasts and drawing her hourglass figure. To this we see her feign upset and then smile. Winking at the audience, the referee notes, "I will need further review." Sitting down, he and the young woman begin flirting. She eyes his whistle asking, "Can I try that?" and grabs it for a blow, much to the amusement of all except our now humiliated hero.

Here sport-infused beer dirt saves the day, preventing our hero from making a romantic faux pas. Very "official" sports dirt in the form of the football referee intervenes. Here we learn how the game should be played. In the course of this, dirt also implies that women don't care or know much about sports. Yet, clearly in the dark about the icon of the football referee and the place of the whistle, she is more than willing to blow it. Of course, in the blowing comes much sexual dirt.

The reading position embraces an interpretive community of young, unattached male football fans aware of their social clumsiness with women. The ad reminds us that romance is not played by the clear rules of sport. Overpowering early identification with Hector the romantic as textual surrogate, the standpoint clearly shifts to that of the referee. Here, the referee plays a role similar to Carlos in the Bud Light spot. He acts out the social taboo of the lecherous voyeur, taking it a step further to hit on "another man's" woman. In reliance on this, a number of ethical problematics are raised. Foremost is the subjugation of other respecting care necessary to objectifying women. Ancillary to this is the reinforcement of one of the big lies of sexual relations, that for women no means yes. This problematic ethic is legitimized with the feigning of no turning quickly to the smiles of yes.

## Tooheys: Real Men's Bravado Meets Its Match

A more forceful woman takes over in the Tooheys "Man vs. Woman vs. Beer" (n.d.) spot for the Australian market. Posted many times over and commented upon on YouTube.com, the dialogue-free spot shows the meeting of two teams at a bowling alley bar as an occasion for archetypal male one-upmanship. Here we see a "face-off" between a group of black-leathered and tattooed toughs and more well-scrubbed ruggers in matching uniforms. There is ambiguity as to whether they have been bowling, whether a rugby match has been played, and whether the "all-black" toughs are part of a rugby squad. Music emphasizing bravado marks the start of their competition as we see one of the toughs threateningly open a beer top in the crook of his elbow and slam the opened bottle on the bar. In response, a scowling rugby player turns mean in twisting the bottle open on his forehead, leaving the cap stuck above his eyes until his teammate forcefully strikes his back to spit the cap to the bar. Escalating the matter further, one of the toughs twists a bottle open on his chest. Mean-eyed glances are exchanged and an angered rugby player starts to open a bottle with his teeth. Before tooth meets bottle, a pretty young blonde woman companion to the ruggers, who has been lurking in the background, grabs the bottle away to a bemused reaction from the leader of the toughs. She takes a deep breath and pulls the bottle well beneath the bar. As she does so, we see a close-up of the lead tough eye the action in discomfort. She faces him eye-to-eye and raises an eyebrow and offers a sexy smile for emphasis as we hear the cap pop off the bottle. As she slaps the opened bottle to the bar, one of the toughs is taken aback, seemingly by the thought that she has opened the bottle with her vagina. She punctuates the act by spitting the bottle cap from her belly button to the bar, tempering this thought, as all are impressed and laugh.

What has just happened is a complex equation. There is dirt of course from the sports setting of the bowling alley bar, rugby culture, and outlaw leather manhood. However, it is clear that the woman, as outsider, has emerged as the toughest of the tough amongst these two warring groups of men. What is perhaps most threatening is the implication that the aggression has been fueled by her vagina as a phallic counterpart. While the belly button spit attempts to mask this reading position, it is unavoidable. Indeed, many YouTube.com commentaries echoed the response, "She opened it with her cunt." The ethics of this situation too are complex. On the one hand, the outsider woman, just like many a woman competing in a man's world, has learned to play by men's rules to succeed. This fact of life is often bemoaned by women in their quest for rising rank in the professional world. Such pragmatics mark a turn away from care-based core values or duties in how one lives. More troubling perhaps is the flawed ethic of participating in a needless escalating of aggression. This naturalization of this tendency, without questioning its logic, helps to celebrate moral flaws in both men and women.

❖ DISCUSSION

In its largely segregated spaces and where the male standard has been the benchmark of excellence, sport has long stirred the drink of gender identity. This remains true when sports dirt mixes with gender dirt in commercial settings. The findings here pertain to a limited set of commercials. Indeed, the subgenre of beer commercials that explicitly contain both sports and cross-gender dirt is a small one. Still, this meeting place for gender and gender identity is important. It provides a glimmer into today's marketable man's world and how interactions with women are best characterized to effectively market the quintessentially male product of beer.

These commercials bring a number of dirty connections to the fore. There are consistent reminders that men's products are often marketed through juxtapositions with what they are not as much as for what they are. Thus, much of the dirt that is brought forward about the sport and beer mix is that this combination is quintessentially male by virtue of it not being women's place. In variant ways, this is signified in all the ads. In the Heineken spot, man leaves woman to mesh men, sport, and beer. In Michelob Ultra's touch football scenario, women, as players, are interlopers. In the Bud Light "Carlos" spot, the men, sport, and beer mixture seek sanctuary. The Coors Light goddess is so unbelievable because she is not possible on this earth. That the young woman on the beach in the Miller Lite spot does not get it is seen in her cluelessness over the football referee and his whistle. The Tooheys spot shows a bold woman as an outsider trespassing and changing the rules of a man's game of one-upmanship. Throughout, women remain the other. Women reside on Venus while men remain on Mars. And cast as Martians, the new real man seems to be losing the battle of the sexes.

This is magnified, as much in these commercials relies on the core dirt of sports, in the naturalized primacy of winning. In the Heineken spot, sport wins out over love. The Michelob Ultra spot is about winning the battle of the sexes; threatened in that war, males threatened by women respond inappropriately. In the Bud Light spot, Carlos enables voicing truth to power to win a domestic battle that is cast as a losing proposition. With the gorgeous but unintimidated women beating tough guys at their own game, the Tooheys ad provides further recognition of who is winning the battle. To this we add the picture of males hopeless in their romantic overtures and yearnings. In the Miller Lite spot, an inept man cannot get it right and is called for an "illegal beer in the cooler." In the Coors Light spot, our loser is so enamored of his dream girl that he prematurely ejaculates his beer. Each instance relies on a drawing of the male as either flawed or failed. While this does not always fit into the loser countertype as drawn by Messner and Montez de Oca (2005), it does speak to the discomfiting use of self-reflexiveness in the sale of beer to its core market of men.

The merits of this strategy are intriguing. Rather than flattering men by putting an attractive reflection of the real man of dominant hyper-masculinity forward in their commercial mirrors, or readjust to a positive take on the "new lad," advertisers in this niche seem determined to work with the notion that the gender wars have been lost by men and that women have ultimate power. Consequently, they have come to rely on the strategy that it is more effective to sell to men through the creation of an alternate space where commiseration and escape can take place. And that place is away from women where men can successfully bond with other men, sport, and beer.

There are a variety of ethical questions raised here by the use of dirt and its reading. Foremost are those about the characterization of the heterosexual relationship, a partnering that on-odds demands transparency and cooperation to be successful. Here what is featured is the norm of deception and conflict. While it is undoubtedly true that many relationships and key parts of others are reliant on deception and conflict, it is in the exclusion of transparency and cooperation that the moral compass of these spots is revealed. This has a number of troubling artifacts. Foremost, such a drawing of heterosexual relationships is reliant on well-worn stereotype and thus is deceptive. This helps legitimize men's self-preserving right to establish compensatory refuge from women, a place where male camaraderie meshed with sport and beer provide superior sanctuary. From this worldview, a dream girl such as the one seen in the Coors spot, who is on the same page as men, is not just bewilderingly unattainable but is seen as unlikely to exist.

In the end, the dirty workings of these spots do not so much contribute to Sabo and Jansen's (1992) concerns over the symbolic annihilation of women as they point to the escape route from them. Their concerns over the symbolic glorification of men do not hold up either as the men here are drawn as losers or otherwise flawed. The reliance on these archetypes both confirms and redraws Pronger's (1990) myth of difference as the guiding force in these commercials. This myth, however refashioned, continues to drive dirt and drive reading. A main ethical consequence remains, as Pronger (1990) has put it, that "women are not seen as the fellows of men" (p. 178). In a time of more clear dominant masculinity, this could be seen as an inequitable problematic. In today's world, such assessment waivers. If the world of these ads has it right, boys will be boys, not men. Women are not the fellows of boys; rather they hold power over them. And that perhaps is the moral of the story in these beer commercials. When sport and beer are involved, men gladly take the opiate, becoming boys and losing.

In moving beyond beer to other products merchandized in companion with sports, there is a further need to interrogate the sport–sex equation. One of the things left unsaid by this analysis is that gender and sexual identities are defined not only by male-female heterosexual interactions but also by same-sex friendships (men as "buddies" and women as "girlfriends") that often work to normalize heterosexual roles. Thus, there is a need to explore gender identities, with regards to beer and other products, in same-sex narratives. In what may be less polarized settings, we may find key differences in the kinds of dirt seen and their workings. Readings may be less locked-in than was the case in painting norms about male-female interactions with sexual relation dimensions. We have much to learn about the workings of dirt on gender identity. In particular, in the commercial setting, we need to know more about our abilities to recognize dirt and to resist its contagion when placement may be ethically problematic. Both ethnographic and experimental studies can help round out this picture.

Studies such as this one have inherent limitations. Certainly there is much more to be learned about how sport and gender are used in the selling of beer and other alcoholic beverages. Sport and gender are of course only one mixed drink. Other dirty mixtures used in the selling of alcohol and other sinful and not-so-sinful products deserve our attention. Sex, perhaps more than sport, is culture's penultimate dirt machine in making the sell. Our gender identities are both formed and constrained by the dirty logic that works to tint conceptions we have of ourselves through the marketing of commodities that consumers purchase and consider purchasing. That critics should give a bit more attention to how this dirt interacts with our capacities to read and interpret is self-evident as we ponder what the last gasps of late capitalism might look like. In answering part of the question of what comes after postmodernism, dirt theory encourages critical scholars to venture across the ethical bridge and leave the ambiguities of relativism to those less willing to call it as they see it.

## ❖ REFERENCES

Alcohol advertising on sports television: 2001–2003. (2004). Retrieved June 29, 2007, from Center on Alcohol Marketing and Youth Web site: http://camy.org/factsheets/index.php?FactsheetID=20

Beer babe [Television commercial]. (n.d.). New York: Mother Agency [for client Coors Light]. Retrieved June 29, 2007, from Ad Critic [now Creativity Online] Web site: http://www.adcritic.com

Booth, W. C. (1998). Why ethical criticism can never be simple. *Style, 32,* 351–364.

Campaign for Alcohol-Free Sports TV. (2005, April 1). *Coaches, CSPI urge NCAA to end beer ads on college sports.* Retrieved June 27, 2007, from the Center for Science in the Public Interest Web site: http://www.cspinet.org/new/200504011.html

Campaign for Alcohol-Free Sports TV. (2006, June 22). *Give Bud the boot from World Cup.* Retrieved June 27, 2007, from the Center for Science in the Public Interest Web site: http://www.cspinet.org/new/200606221.html

Carroll, N. (2000). Art and ethical criticism: An overview of recent directions of research. *Ethics, 110,* 350–387.

Collins, T., & Vamplew, W. (2002). *Mud, sweat, and beers: A cultural history of sport and alcohol.* New York: Berg Publishers.

Crawford, G. (2004). *Consuming sport: Fans, sport, and culture.* London: Routledge.

Douglas, M. (1966). *Purity and danger: An analysis of the concepts of pollution and taboo.* London: Routledge & Kegan Paul.

Down hill [Television commercial]. (n.d.). New York: Strawberry Frog [for client Heineken]. Retrieved June 29, 2007, from Ad Forum Web site: http://www.adforum.com

Eaglestone, R. (2004). Postmodernism and ethics against the metaphysics of comprehension. In S. Connor (Ed.), *The Cambridge companion to postmodernism* (pp. 182–195). Cambridge, UK: Cambridge University Press.

Eagleton, T. (2003). *After theory.* New York: Basic Books.

Eco, U. (1979). *The role of the reader: Explorations in the semiotics of texts.* Bloomington, IN: Indiana University Press.

Ellickson, P. L., Collins, R. L., Hambarsoomians, K., & McCaffrey, D. F. (2005). Does alcohol advertising promote adolescent drinking? Results from a longitudinal assessment. *Addiction, 100*(2), 235–246.

Enzenberger, H. M. (1972). Constituents of a theory of the media. In D. McQuail (Ed.), *Sociology of mass communication* (pp. 99–112). Harmondsworth, UK: Penguin.

Farhi, P. (2005, December 31). The frat house is now closed; TV commercials clean up and dumb down. *The Washington Post,* p. C1.

Fish, S. (1980). *Is there a text in this class? The authority of interpretive communities.* Cambridge, MA: Harvard University Press.

Geertz, C. (1973). Thick description: Toward an interpretive theory of culture. In C. Geertz (Ed.), *The interpretation of cultures* (pp. 3–30). New York: Basic Books.

Goldammer, T. (2000). *The brewer's handbook*. Clifton, VA: Apex Publishers.

Gregory, M. (1998). Ethical criticism: What it is and why it matters. *Style, 32,* 194–220.

Grube, J. W., & Wallack., L. (1994). Television beer advertising and drinking knowledge, beliefs, and intentions among school children. *American Journal of Public Health, 94,* 254–259.

Hartley, J. (1984). Encouraging signs: TV and the power of dirt, speech, and scandalous categories. In W. Rowland & B. Watkins (Eds.), *Interpreting television: Current research perspectives* (pp. 119–141). Thousand Oaks, CA: Sage.

Hilliard, D. C., & Hendley, A. O. (2004, November). *Celebrity athletes and sports imagery in advertising during the NFL telecasts.* Paper presented at the annual meeting of the North American Society for the Sociology of Sport, Tucson, AZ.

Ineligible beer in the cooler [Television commercial]. (n.d.). New York: Ogilvy & Mather Agency [for client Miller Lite]. Retrieved June 29, 2007, from Ad Critic [now Creativity Online] Web site: http://www.adcritic.com

Iser, W. (1974). *The implied reader: Patterns of reading in prose fiction from Bunyan to Beckett.* Baltimore: Johns Hopkins University Press.

Iser, W. (1978). *The act of reading: A theory of aesthetic response.* Baltimore: Johns Hopkins University Press.

Iser, W. (2006). Reception theory: Iser. In W. Iser (Ed.), *How to do theory* (pp. 57–69). Oxford: Blackwell.

Ives, N. (2003, July 31). After a wild period, beer ads sober up and put some clothes on. *The New York Times,* p. C2.

Jhally, S. (Writer, Editor, Narrator). (2007). *Dreamworlds 3: Desire, sex and power in music video* [Video]. Northampton, MA: Media Education Foundation.

Katz, J. (Writer). (1999). *Tough guise: Violence, media, and the crisis in masculinity* [Video]. Northampton: MA: Media Education Foundation.

Kellner, D. (2000). Cultural studies and philosophy: An intervention. In T. Miller (Ed.), *A companion to cultural studies* (pp. 139–153). Oxford, UK: Blackwell.

Leach, E. (1976). *Culture and communication.* Cambridge, UK: Cambridge University Press.

Light beer just got a little darker [Television commercial]. (n.d.). St. Louis: Cannonball Agency [for client Michelob Ultra]. Retrieved June 29, 2007, from Ad Forum Web site: http://adforum.com

Machor, J. L., & Goldstein, P. (Eds.). (2001). *Reception study: From literary theory to cultural studies.* London: Routledge.

Madden, P. A., & Grube, J. W. (1994). The frequency and nature of alcohol and tobacco advertising in televised sports, 1990 through 1992. *American Journal of Public Health, 84,* 297–299.

Man vs. woman vs. beer [Television commercial]. (n.d.). Sydney: Saatchi & Saatchi Agency [for client Tooheys]. Retrieved June 29, 2007, from YouTube Web site: http://www.youtube.com/watch?v=c_ZghpAP1CE

Messner, M. A., & Montez de Oca, J. (2005). The male consumer as loser: Beer and liquor ads in mega sports media events. *Signs, 30,* 1879–1909.

Messner, M. A., & Sabo, D. F. (Eds.). (1990). *Sport, men, and the gender order: Critical feminist perspectives.* Champaign, IL: Human Kinetics.

Miller, T. (2001). *Sportsex.* Philadelphia: Temple University Press.

Oldenburg, R. (1989). *The great good place.* New York: Paragon.

Poulton, T. (2004, May 17). The issue in question: Are the days of T&A over for beer? *Strategy,* p. 2.

Pronger, B. (1990). *The arena of masculinity: Sports, homosexuality, and the meaning of sex.* New York: St. Martin's Press.

Reichert, T., & Lambiase, J. (Eds.). (2003). *Sex in advertising: Perspectives on erotic appeal.* Mahwah, NJ: Erlbaum.

Sabo, D., & Jansen, S. C. (1992). Images of men in sport media: The social reproduction of gender order. In S. Craig (Ed.), *Men, masculinity, and the media* (pp. 169–184). Thousand Oaks, CA: Sage.

Slater, M. D., Rouner, D., Domenech-Rodriguez, M., Beauvais, R., Murphy, K., & Van Leuven, J. K. (1997). Adolescent responses to TV beer ads and sports content/context: Gender and ethnic differences. *Journalism and Mass Communication Quarterly, 74,* 108–122.

Teinowitz, I. (1993, October 4). Days of "beer and babes" running out. *Advertising Age,* p. S8.

Tompkins, J. P. (Ed.). (1980). *Reader-response criticism: From formalism to post-structuralism.* Baltimore: John Hopkins University Press.

Wenner, L. A. (1991). One part alcohol, one part sport, one part dirt, stir gently: Beer commercials and television sports. In L. R. Vande Berg & L. A. Wenner (Eds.), *Television criticism: Approaches and applications* (pp. 388–407). New York: Longman.

Wenner, L. A. (1994). The dream team, communicative dirt, and the marketing of synergy: U.S.A. basketball and cross-merchandising in television commercials. *Journal of Sport and Social Issues, 18,* 27–47.

Wenner, L. A. (2004). Recovering (from) Janet Jackson's breast: Ethics and the nexus of media, sports, and management. *Journal of Sport Management, 18,* 315–334.

Wenner, L. A. (2006). Sports and media through the super glass mirror: Placing blame, breast-beating, and a gaze to the future. In J. Bryant & A. A. Raney (Eds.), *Handbook of sports media* (pp. 45–60). Hillsdale, NJ: Lawrence Erlbaum.

Wenner, L. A. (2007). Towards a dirty theory of narrative ethics. Prolegomenon on media, sport and commodity value. *International Journal of Media and Cultural Politics, 3,* 111–129.

What would Carlos do? [Television commercial]. (n.d.). Austin, TX: Latin Works Agency [for client Budweiser Light]. Retrieved June 29, 2007, from Ad Forum Web site: http://www.adforum.com

Zwarun, L., & Farrar, K. M. (2005). Doing what they say, saying what they mean: Self-regulatory compliance and depictions of drinking in alcohol commercials in televised sports. *Mass Communication & Society, 8,* 347–371.

Zylinska, J. (2005). *The ethics of cultural studies.* London: Continuum.

## ❖ NOTES

1. The proprietary video collections at http://www.adcritic.com and http://www.adforum.com primarily service the advertising industry in campaign development. The chief benefits are that these collections are substantial and void of "user-generated content" or "viral videos."

2. The public video collections at http://www.youtube.com and http://www.ifilm.com are considerably larger than those available at proprietary collections. This chief benefit is negated by the substantial presence of "user-generated content" and viral video that make it difficult to assess authenticity.

# 6

# Hegemonic Masculinity and the Rogue Warrior

*Lance Armstrong as (Symbolic) American*

Bryan E. Denham

Andrea Duke

L ike U.S. Olympian Carl Lewis, American cyclist Lance Armstrong found his retirement from sport disrupted by allegations of performance-enhancing drug use. Allegations that Lewis had failed a drug test prior to the 1988 U.S. Olympic trials surfaced in April 2003, just after the United States had launched a unilateral military assault on Iraq (Denham, 2004a), while charges that Armstrong had tested positive in 1999 for EPO, a red-blood-cell booster frequently used by competitive cyclists, appeared in August 2005. Reacting to the Lewis story, international journalists portrayed the sprinter and long-jump champion as arrogant and hypocritical, not unlike the Bush administration, which had largely ignored international opposition to the invasion of Iraq. Would journalists abroad characterize Armstrong in a similar fashion, criticizing the cyclist not only for the EPO allegations but for representing a nation that appeared to play by its own set of rules?

In this chapter, we examine U.S. and international media portrayals of Armstrong at a time when U.S. military operations in Iraq appeared to be worsening. Building on the earlier study by Denham (2004a), which found disparities across media portrayals of Lewis in the aftermath of the controversial report about his drug test, we anticipated that coverage patterns of Armstrong would also differ based on the nations in which news coverage of the EPO story originated. Because Armstrong had been regarded as a kind of "rogue warrior," taking on cancer and all who would challenge him in the Tour de France, we anticipated heavy criticism of the cyclist. Like Lewis, Armstrong had been somewhat pious in conversations about drugs in sports, and we thus expected international journalists to suggest hypocritical behavior by the self-assured American. As Burstyn (1999) suggested, the "masculinist ideological reflexes sport nurtures in its narrative of masculine heroics energize and inform other political identifications such as locality, ethnicity, and nationality" (p. 28). In the following section we establish a theoretical framework for anticipating differences in how U.S. and international media outlets portrayed Armstrong, a quintessentially heroic figure in America at a time when critics had accused the United States of continuing to operate unilaterally in Iraq, ignoring the concerns of leaders from other nations.

❖  THEORY AND RELATED LITERATURE

While scholars have assembled a large body of research addressing gendered media representations in the context of sport (see Billings, Halone, & Denham, 2002; Messner, Dunbar, & Hunt, 2000; Stempel, 2006; Whannel, 2002), as well as issues of nationalism in sporting environments (Allison, 2000; Billings & Tambosi, 2004; Sabo, Jansen, Tate, Duncan, & Leggett, 1996), relatively few studies have explored how gender portrayals stand to vary based on the nations in which content originates. As an example, scholars have described how mediated sport texts tend to reproduce dominant conceptions of masculinity, idealizing independence, physical strength, emotional stoicism, strict heterosexuality, and the capacity to overcome adversity and physical pain (see Connell & Messerschmidt, 2005; Denham, 2004b; Trujillo, 1991, 1995); however, little research has examined how idealized masculinities differ across cultures and nations (Jandt & Hundley, 2007), especially during periods of conflict that have been initiated unilaterally, such that media outlets may wish to emphasize differences instead of similarities. This chapter seeks to help fill that scholarly gap.

Mediated sport texts consistently reproduce traditional gender assumptions, idealizing a brand of masculinity grounded in strength and stamina, self-reliance, and sacrifice. This dominant conception of maleness—a conception generally referred to as *hegemonic masculinity*—rewards athletes who "hit like a man" and "withstand punishment" in sacrificing their physical well-being for the greater cause of a team or nation (Messner, Dunbar, & Hunt, 2000). As Koivula (2001) explained, sports characterized as masculine tend to involve danger, risk, violence, speed, and endurance; such sports include baseball, boxing, football, ice hockey, the martial arts, motor sports, rugby, and wrestling, among others (Klomsten, Marsh, & Skaalvik, 2005). Conversely, female athletes, as well as the sports in which female athletes compete, are expected to be aesthetically pleasing, full of grace and beauty; these pastimes include dance, figure skating, gymnastics, swimming, and tennis, among others (Coakley, 2004; Klomsten, Marsh, & Skaalvik, 2005).

Men and women who challenge socially constructed gender roles often find themselves stigmatized and labeled as different or abnormal (see Kane & Parks, 1992). Typically when an individual participates in a sport that runs contrary to his or her gender norm, the sexuality of that individual comes into question; a woman may be labeled a lesbian, and a man may be considered gay (see Caudwell, 1999). The gendered expectation for American male athletes in sport is largely one of hegemonic masculinity and "muscular mesomorphy," i.e., the body is characterized by a well-developed chest and arm muscles and wide shoulders tapering down to a narrow waist (Mishkind, Rodin, Silberstein, & Striegel-Moore, 1987). Such images of male perfection are reinforced when male athletes use their bodies for hitting, dunking, tackling, and running, receiving millions of dollars, media attention, and fan adoration for their efforts (see Trujillo, 1995). As Hearne and Morgan (1990) noted, "Many of the central concerns of men and masculinities are directly to do with bodies—war and sport are two obvious examples" (p. 10).

In recent research addressing the intersection between gender ideals and support for the war in Iraq, Stempel (2006) found a direct correlation between involvement in televised, "masculine" sports and support for the war. As Stempel suggested, "The invasion of Iraq went hand in hand with a major change in American foreign policy in the direction of asserting unilateral military hegemony for the United

States in the name of protecting American security and freedom and preventing the proliferation of weapons of mass destruction among terrorist groups and nations that support them" (p. 80). In the study, men who watched high levels of combative sport action on television lent the greatest amount of support to the war. Indeed, as Butterworth points out in Chapter 7 in this volume, athletes in traditionally masculine sports offer reassurance in times of uncertainty, their participation in combative action symbolizing the strength and determination of soldiers in the U.S. military.

One nation that did not support the U.S. military invasion of Iraq was France. As American forces mobilized, French Prime Minster Dominique de Villepin questioned the war and the intentions of the United States, prompting many Americans to boycott nearly everything French and to frequent restaurants that had altered the names of French fries and French toast to "freedom fries" and "freedom toast," respectively. Leaders from other nations apart from France also opposed the U.S. invasion of Iraq, and given the resulting international tensions, we grounded part of our study in social identity theory (Tajfel & Turner, 1986), which holds that members of "in groups" tend to exaggerate similarities and group cohesiveness when members of "out groups" pose a threat.

Bairner and Shirlow (2000) posited that sport stands to play a significant role in the construction and reconstruction of identity (see also Cooke, 2005; Whannel, 2002), especially concerning nationality. As support for that assertion, when Roger Bannister broke the four-minute-mile record in 1951, the runner noted that "the result had great significance for the British public. On this occasion, rightly or wrongly, I had become a symbol in athletics of British spirit against American and for the sake of national prestige I felt I had to win" (Crump, 1989, p. 58). As indicated in that quote, central to social identity theory is the notion that members of a collective self often gain a sense of empowerment from emphasizing not only who they *are* but also who they *are not*—real or imagined. To this end, Stempel (2006) opined that, "Sports are our most explicit and mythologized public spectacles of competition, power, and domination" (p. 82).

For purposes of the current chapter, if nations (a) viewed the United States as arrogant and irresponsible in its invasion of Iraq and (b) considered Lance Armstrong as the consummate American at a time when international tensions ran high, then one might expect international media characterizations of Armstrong to reflect a certain disdain, especially given a controversial news event about the cyclist, discussed below. One also might expect reports originating in the United States to be supportive of Armstrong, given the political economy of mass media and the nature of heroism. As Denham (2004a) explained, U.S. media tend to be ethnocentric in their reporting (see also Hachten & Scotton, 2002), especially during times of international uncertainty, and because U.S. media companies operate as part of the economic elite, they might be reluctant to expose alleged wrongdoings by a U.S. athlete regarded as a national hero and international athletic champion.

Whannel (2002) pointed out that sports often serve as a major signifier of national prowess (see also Hargreaves, 1992; Tomlinson, 1996), and as Kinkema and Harris (1998) explained:

> Mediated sport programs often reproduce dominant ideologies in the nations in which they originate, and world-wide transmission of sport programming from a few Western countries seems to have great potential to contribute to greater understanding of global, national, and local relations. (p. 34)

In this chapter, we thus operate within a conceptual framework grounded in the political economy of mass media as well as social identity theory, anticipating differences between U.S. and international media portrayals of Lance Armstrong given broader sociopolitical factors, namely the war in Iraq.

## Lance Armstrong and Mediated Identities

Seven times the winner of the prestigious Tour de France, Lance Armstrong is a cancer survivor and champion athlete in a sport that rewards individual excellence. Armstrong fought testicular cancer, which could be construed as both a physical and symbolic threat to masculinity, the same way he fought those who attempted to defeat him in cycling events, and the determination he showed in overcoming cancer as well as winning the most coveted race in cycling seven times—an all-time record—appears to have transcended sport and inspired millions. Butryn and Masucci (2003) characterized Armstrong as the "quintessential American hero, battling against all odds" (p. 124), and in studying the Armstrong autobiography *It's Not About the Bike* (Armstrong & Jenkins, 2000), Sparkes (2004) argued that the text served "to confirm and legitimize a number of dominant narratives that circulate within Western culture regarding what constitutes a good illness and self-story in relation to men, in general, and elite athletes, in particular" (p. 424).

In addition to overcoming physical adversity, Armstrong dated popular recording star Sheryl Crow, and his athletic successes landed him lucrative endorsement deals with companies such as Nike, Trek Bicycle, and Subaru. Indeed, the November 2006 cover of *Details* magazine dubbed Armstrong "America's New Playboy," with writer Bart Blasengame adding inside, "Compact in the chest, all wiry muscle and veins in his legs and arms, residually tanned from years of all-weather training, he still looks as if he could conquer a 2,000-mile road race and devour a couple of Frenchmen on his way up the hill" (p. 186).

Not everyone, including some of the Frenchmen against whom he raced, views Armstrong with such reverence. In fact, given allegations of performance-enhancing drug use and recent doping admissions by members of his own racing team,[1] Armstrong may be as unpopular in some parts of the world as he is popular in the United States; that is, he may have come to symbolize perceived U.S. arrogance, self-assuredness, and hypocrisy abroad. While many in the United States know Armstrong as a cycling champion and cancer survivor, many observers abroad have more intimate knowledge of the Tour de France and the nearly superhuman effort required to merely complete the race, let alone win it seven times (see Wieting, 2000).

In August 2005, a French newspaper, *L'Equipe*, reported that an Armstrong urine specimen from 1999 had tested positive for EPO, a red-blood-cell booster frequently used by competitive cyclists. As one might anticipate given the prominence of Armstrong as an international athlete and celebrity, the news traveled quickly, prompting journalists in both the United States and abroad to offer reports and analyses. Like Olympian Carl Lewis, Armstrong had consistently denied using performance-enhancing substances, and consequently international journalists may have accused Armstrong of arrogance and hypocrisy, just as they had accused U.S. President George W. Bush of playing by his own set of rules in deciding to invade Iraq (Denham, 2004a).

Denham (2004a) studied U.S. and international reaction to news in 2003 that Carl Lewis had failed a drug test prior to the 1988 U.S. Olympic trials. Despite the positive test for trace amounts of stimulants ephedrine, pseudoephedrine, and phenylpropanolamine, the U.S. Olympic Committee had allowed Lewis to compete, and after Canadian sprinter Ben Johnson tested positive for anabolic steroids at the 1988 Seoul Games, Lewis received the gold medal originally awarded to Johnson (see Jackson, 1998; Pound, 2004). The 2003 Lewis revelation occurred at a time when U.S. forces, acting on a unilateral command from Bush, had invaded Iraq, and to little surprise Denham (2004a) found not only a strong condemnation of Lewis in foreign nations but an indictment of the Bush administration for presuming to invade a sovereign nation without global support. The news about Lewis, in short, served as a metaphor for the Bush administration and its apparent unwillingness to hear arguments advanced by international leaders. In the Armstrong situation, a similar dynamic may have emerged.

Factors beyond allegations of performance-enhancing drug use also assist in explaining why international journalists may have shown little sympathy for Armstrong when the EPO story broke. As Cooke (2005) noted, riders who came before Armstrong, such as Irish competitor Seán Kelly, had approached every stage of the race in the same manner, essentially "gutting it out" to the finish line; in contrast, Armstrong and his teammates sometimes approached the race more strategically, peaking for just one stage. European observers also point out that Armstrong and his teammates brought to the Tour excessive commercialization, compromising its perceived intimacy and romance (see Reed, 2003; Wieting, 2000).

Still, as nostalgic as European cycling fans may be, the participation of Americans in the event has helped the Tour de France become one of the largest sporting competitions in the world, as Reed (2003) observed:

> During the 1980s, television emerged as the primary commercial engine of the Tour de France and of many professional sports throughout the western world. Race organizers employed the large war chest of capital generated by broadcast rights fees to mould the Tour into a televised sporting spectacle of global importance. (pp. 119–120)

A central concern of critics may be that further commercialization of the "televised sporting spectacle" effectively means further "Americanization" of the Tour (Marchetti, 2003).

### Evolution of—and American Influence on—the Tour de France

As an athletic event, the Tour de France began on July 1, 1903, created out of a rivalry between two French newspapers (see Reed, 2003). This early competition was shorter in distance and days, but it appears to have involved just as much drama and rider competition as the more recent races. Throughout the 20th century, the Tour saw its share of controversies, from on- and off-course deaths to a series of doping scandals, the most severe occurring in 1998 (Marchetti, 2003; Mignon, 2003; Schneider, 2006). As Schneider (2006) and others who have written about doping in the Tour have noted, there had long been a quiet tolerance of drug use due to the rigors of the course, but in 1998 discoveries concerning the magnitude of doping could not be ignored.

The World Anti-Doping Agency (WADA) appeared on the international sporting scene not long after the 1998 scandal, put in place to assist in "cleaning up" international sporting competitions (Pound, 2004, 2005). Yet, when it comes to doping and the Tour de France, the use of performance-enhancing drugs does not appear to offend fans as much as categorical denials of drug use do, because longtime observers understand the rigors of the Tour and seek champions they perceive as forthright. Dauncey (2003) explained:

> What precisely makes a sportsman or woman a star is often a mystery, but any level of popularity must depend on: admiration of sporting success; admiration of courageous behaviour in adversity; admiration of correct behaviour in adversity; "attractiveness" of personality. (p. 177)

"Overriding superiority or arrogant domination," Dauncey posited further, "can cause the public to withhold its support and affection." (p. 179)

In 1999, Lance Armstrong won his first of seven consecutive Tours, causing a degree of unrest among the French and in other European countries. Before Armstrong began dominating the event, Europeans reigned superior in both participation and fandom (Wieting, 2000), but each time Armstrong prevailed, more Americans appeared to take an interest in cycling—and by extension, in its media coverage. This newfound popularity of the Tour, based on the successes of a self-assured competitor from the United States, caused some friction in Europe, as Anderson (2003) described:

> Surely the last thing the French want[ed] to see . . . [was] the crowning of a Yank as Tour champ—especially one who hails from the same state as George W. Bush. What could be more galling to the Gauls, who have been the target of American jokes, boycotts, and diplomatic snubs because of their opposition to the Iraq war, than to see Lance Armstrong, whose record, cocksure manner and red-white-and-blue, government sponsored U.S. Postal Service team screams American domination, atop the podium on the Champs-Elysees . . . (p. A4)

In an interview with Jean-Marie Leblanc, organizer of the Tour de France, Marchetti (2003) shed light on how at least one European sport official found not only American athletes somewhat offensive but American media personnel as well. As Leblanc explained in the interview:

> One year the Americans—at the start of the 1990s—more or less asked us (I can't remember the exact details) that we have a time-trial on day four, and that on Sunday there should be a mountain stage (laughs). They

wanted us to design a Tour route that would fit perfectly with their schedules, needs and audiences. Obviously, we sent them packing, and they didn't ask again. (pp. 46–47)

That representatives of the American media would presume to request a rerouting of the Tour to accommodate American audiences appears to have incensed the Europeans charged with its organization, striking Tour officials as both arrogant and audacious. This is the type of situation in which social identity theory would predict an exaggeration of similarities and differences between "in groups" and "out groups," respectively.

In the present study, we examine how mediated characteristics of hegemonic masculinity, which assist in "heroifying" athletes in the United States, stand to interact with issues of national identity abroad, such that athletes who exhibit certain behaviors may be associated with public officials who show similar patterns. Characteristics such as strength and independence in one nation may be considered imperialistic and unilateral in another. In 2005, as international concern about U.S. involvement in Iraq continued to intensify, cyclist Lance Armstrong may have remained a quintessential American hero to his fans in the United States, but given the EPO report published in *L'Equipe*, journalists from other nations may have portrayed him with considerably less enthusiasm, linking him with George W. Bush, "The Decider," who large numbers of Europeans criticized for unilaterally invading Iraq (Denham, 2004a). Next we explain our approaches for examining potential differences in press coverage of Armstrong.

## ❖ METHODOLOGICAL APPROACH

Building on Denham's (2004a) earlier study, we examined U.S. and international newspaper reaction to a volatile news event involving American cyclist Lance Armstrong, given the broader backdrop of ongoing U.S. military involvement in Iraq. We anticipated differences in how newspapers published in the United States and in other nations would report the 2005 EPO story, with American reports defending Armstrong as an athletic hero and cancer survivor and international news stories criticizing Armstrong not only because of his perceived dishonesty about EPO, but as an American athlete who effectively sought to play by his own rules. We make no presumptions about whether Armstrong actually used EPO.

For the content analysis, we gathered newspaper articles from the LexisNexis Academic Universe database, with "Lance Armstrong" as a primary search term and "EPO" as a secondary term.[2] An examination of article distributions indicated that coverage of the EPO news story began on August 24, 2005, and concluded on October 29, 2005, and we therefore examined content published on or between August 24 and October 29. To be included in the study, an article had to focus specifically on the news about Armstrong and EPO and had to be published as either a news report or editorial comment. We did not include letters to the editor and articles with spurious mentions of Armstrong in the study.[3] Additionally, we coded wire reports (e.g., Associated Press stories) only once, based on the first one encountered. This approach yielded a total of 115 articles suitable for analysis, 54 (47%) from U.S. newspapers and 61 (53%) published internationally. Of the 54 articles published in U.S. outlets, 40 (74.1%) were basic news reports; in newspapers published internationally, 45 (73.8%) of 61 reported the EPO news, and thus news/commentary ratios were similar across the two categories of newspapers.

We coded newspaper articles by individual publication and total paragraphs per article, examining whether certain outlets tended to devote more coverage to the EPO story and whether article length tended to deviate significantly across national and international reports.[4] Additionally, consistent with Denham (2004a), we coded for the presence and prevalence of certain news sources. As Sigal (1973) discussed, sources define the news for mass audiences, and therefore the individuals with whom journalists communicate can affect the inferences audience members draw about news events. For a given article, we counted the number of paragraphs that quoted a certain news source (e.g., Lance Armstrong) and created a fraction in which that number appeared as the numerator and the total number of paragraphs in an article appeared as the denominator. Consistent with previous research (Denham, 2004a), we then rounded the resulting decimal value to the lesser of two whole numbers, thus developing an ordered value (i.e., a value between 0 and 9) for each source type in every article in the study.[5] This "source saturation" variable has proven instructive for identifying the sources who most frequently assist in defining a significant news event.

We coded for the presence of news quotes from (a) Lance Armstrong, (b) Richard Pound or other World Anti-Doping Agency (WADA) officials, (c) representatives of the U.S. Anti-Doping Agency (USADA), (d) representatives of the Lance Armstrong racing team, (e) officials with the Tour de France, (f) additional U.S. athletic officials, (g) additional international athletic officials, (h) active athletes, and (i) miscellaneous news sources. We also examined news content from a qualitative standpoint, extracting headlines and evaluating text material that appeared to inform the quantitative findings regarding news sources. In the following section, we report our quantitative content findings along with qualitative examples of news content in context.

### ❖ RESULTS

In this content study, articles averaged 14.9 paragraphs in length. Articles originating in the United States averaged 15.7 paragraphs, and articles published internationally averaged 14.2; these differences were not statistically significant. With respect to quotes, sourcing patterns in U.S. and international newspapers showed greater parity in this study than they did in the earlier analysis involving Olympian Carl Lewis.

Statistical analyses revealed that while 38 (70.4%) of 54 articles published in the United States contained at least one quote from Armstrong, 36 (59%) of 61 articles published internationally contained such a quote. Regarding "source saturation," U.S. and international reports showed similar patterns, and it thus appears that while slightly more articles published in the United States contained an Armstrong quote, the cyclist received relatively equal treatment (i.e., an opportunity to defend himself against EPO allegations) in U.S. and international news articles.[6] That pattern did not emerge with regard to Richard Pound and WADA, who had been overtly critical of Armstrong.

Approximately 3 in 10 articles from both U.S. and international newspapers quoted Richard Pound or another WADA official; however, among those that quoted Pound or one of his colleagues, 0 articles published in U.S. newspapers contained a "source saturation" value greater than 1. In contrast, 8 articles published internationally contained a source value of 2 or greater, meaning that 42% of the international articles containing at least one quote from Pound or WADA in fact included multiple quotes. This finding is important in that Pound and WADA have been highly suspicious of Lance Armstrong, as qualitative content examples below demonstrate.[7]

In our analyses, no articles contained a quote from a USADA representative; just 4 (3.5%) of all 115 articles contained a quote from an additional U.S. official; and 5 (4.3%) of 115 articles quoted another athlete. In U.S. newspapers, 9 (16.7%) of 54 articles contained a quote from the Armstrong team, compared to 6 (9.8%) of 61 articles published internationally. Interestingly, while 20 (37%) of 54 articles from U.S. newspapers referenced an official with the Tour de France, just 13 (21.3%) of 61 articles published internationally did so. Additional international officials were quoted in 17 (31.5%) of 54 articles published in U.S. newspapers, compared to 24 (39.3%) of 61 articles published internationally. Use of miscellaneous sources was both sparse and nearly identical across U.S. and international newspapers. Overall, then, sourcing patterns appeared consistent with the direction we expected, although the numbers were much closer than they were in the Carl Lewis study (Denham, 2004a). Dominant sources of information included Armstrong, Pound, and representatives of the Tour de France itself. We now examine news content in context, reviewing headlines and text material that inform quantitative sourcing patterns.

### U.S. Newspaper Coverage of Armstrong and EPO

In studying potential differences between U.S. and international press coverage of the EPO allegations, we observed that, overall, U.S. newspaper coverage tended to focus largely on France and the (in)stability of testing techniques, while international news coverage tended to focus largely on Armstrong and his perceived lack of truthfulness. Table 6.1 displays a series of headlines from U.S. newspapers, and collectively they appear to discount both the EPO tests and the nation responsible for conducting them, implying envy, perhaps jealousy, among the French. Terms such as "silly," "preposterous," "tampering," "politics," and "tirade" were evident in the headlines, and an inspection of news texts revealed similar patterns in addition to more favorable descriptions of Armstrong himself.

Writing in *The Washington Post*, Wilbon (2005) expressed admiration for Armstrong, commenting on the "doggedness" with which the cyclist had battled cancer. Wilbon wrote of the "dedication" Armstrong had shown in pursuing excellence in sport, and in the *San Francisco Chronicle*, Knapp (2005) wrote that Armstrong would remain "untouchable" as a cycling champion. In *USA TODAY*, Lopresti (2005) wrote of the "heroic" battle waged by Armstrong against cancer. In addition, Lopresti wrote:

> Also, it's the French doing most of the finger-pointing. Let's face facts. They don't mind us when we're buying their wine or storming German pillboxes. But aside from that, they don't really care for us. And they have never been able to accept their sporting jewel being dominated by an American, cancer survivor or otherwise. (p. 10C)

**Table 6.1**    U.S. Newspaper Headlines Addressing Lance Armstrong and the
2005 EPO News Report

| Headline | Newspaper | Date |
|---|---|---|
| Allegations fail to sway Lance's fans | Denver Post | August 25 |
| Lab test seems sound, but tampering can't be ruled out | San Francisco Chronicle | August 26 |
| USA Federation Chief: Accusations Against Armstrong: "Preposterous" | The Washington Post | August 27 |
| A top U.S. cycling group is standing by Armstrong | The New York Times | August 27 |
| Americans' faith in Lance Armstrong unshaken in wake of new allegations; Still champ | Cleveland Plain Dealer | August 28 |
| Case against Armstrong "France's latest tirade" | Houston Chronicle | August 29 |
| French pique at Lance just silly | Atlanta Journal Constitution | August 29 |
| Director of top lab questions findings | USA TODAY | August 31 |
| Tour de politics | The Washington Post | September 1 |
| Antidoping agency seeks test for EPO that is definitive | The New York Times | September 5 |
| Cycling authority says Lance was clean | St. Petersburg Times | September 10 |
| A combative Armstrong is committed to battling on | The New York Times | September 14 |
| Cycling body rips doping chief [Pound] | Chicago Sun-Times | September 20 |

In *The New York Times*, Abt (2005) questioned the protocol of freezing urine specimens, as well as the reliability of testing for EPO, in general. Abt also noted that the company that publishes *L'Equipe*, the newspaper that had accused Armstrong of doping, also owns the Tour de France (see also Rosenthal, 2005; Vecsey, 2005). Additionally, writing in the *Cleveland Plain Dealer*, Livingston (2005) asked:

> Why was the test on the 1999 sample not done as soon as EPO detection was perfected? Why did they hide the results? How valid is a six-year-old specimen? Since the testing laboratory has not identified it as Armstrong's, how can anyone be sure it's his? (p. C2)

Thus, in the days following the initial allegations of EPO use, several columnists in major U.S. newspapers questioned the legitimacy of the EPO tests, intimating that the French would almost certainly exploit the slightest possibility that Armstrong had doped in 1999. Columnists also described the determination Armstrong had showed in battling cancer—in overcoming the odds and maintaining strength and courage in the face of adversity—and a select few journalists positioned the story within the broader framework of foreign affairs and U.S. military action in Iraq. As an example, in *The Washington Post*, Hoagland (2005) posited that:

> Bitter disputes between Washington and Paris over the Iraq war and other foreign policy differences wind their surreptitious way through l'affaire Armstrong and help escalate it into a burgeoning test of popular wills. Behind the hard positions taken on each side of the Atlantic over a bicycle race there are lingering, across-the-board suspicions about motivation and credibility at the national level. (p. A29)

Indeed, while Armstrong may personify the term *hegemonic masculinity* before his many fans in the United States (and to many fans abroad), the same characteristics that make him a hero and a champion athlete—characteristics such as strength, determination, intensity, and internal drive—also stand to make him offensive to those who see arrogance and self-assuredness in place of focus and confidence. Those who do not hold Armstrong in the highest esteem may in fact consider the cyclist a metaphor for perceived U.S. arrogance, especially as it pertains to the unilateral invasion of Iraq.

### International Newspaper Coverage of Armstrong and EPO

International press reports focused largely on Armstrong, questioning his integrity and portraying him, in some instances, as a liar. A display of international headlines (shown in Table 6.2) indicates that some Canadian journalists tended to be especially harsh in their characterizations of the Armstrong EPO allegations, perhaps because they had not forgotten about sprinter Ben Johnson and the national embarrassment Johnson had caused Canada in 1988, after testing positive for anabolic steroids and returning an Olympic gold medal in disgrace

**Table 6.2** International Headlines Addressing Lance Armstrong and the 2005 EPO News Report

| Headline | Newspaper | Date |
|---|---|---|
| Pound: Onus is now on Lance | Toronto Sun | August 24 |
| "Ritual denial" no good: Pound | Toronto Star | August 24 |
| Armstrong faces fresh drug charges | Globe and Mail (Canada) | August 24 |
| Armstrong rides into Tour doping storm | Montreal Gazette | August 24 |
| US great positive to EPO: L'Equipe | The Australian | August 24 |
| Tour chief: "We were all fooled by Armstrong" | London Independent | August 25 |
| 'Circle tightening' around Armstrong | Globe and Mail | August 25 |
| Lance's myth takes a hit | Montreal Gazette | August 25 |
| Explain yourself, Armstrong urged | London Daily Telegraph | August 25 |
| Tour boss dumps on Lance | Sydney Daily Telegraph | August 26 |
| Say it ain't so, Lance | Globe and Mail | August 27 |
| Lance's poisoned legacy | The Scotsman | August 28 |
| Armstrong must show cards | London Observer | August 28 |
| Cycling great can't outride doping claims | New Zealand Herald | August 30 |
| We'll catch them eventually | Ottawa Citizen | August 31 |
| Lance used drugs, says sports chief | The Advertiser | September 7 |
| Doping denials | Toronto Sun | September 13 |
| Armstrong ignored | The Advertiser | October 29 |

(Christie, 2005c; Todd, 2005a). Lewis and the United States had asserted moral superiority in that situation, accepting the gold medal forfeited by Johnson. In 2005, some 17 years after the Johnson ordeal, an American athlete stood accused of doping with EPO, and select journalists seized the moment.

Richard Pound, head of WADA, which is located in Montreal, spoke of "ritual denial" on the part of Armstrong, suggesting that the "onus" had fallen on the cyclist to prove the allegations false. The *Globe and Mail*, a national newspaper in Canada, used the term "fresh drug charges" to indicate that Armstrong had been suspected of doping in other instances, and the newspaper suggested that the "circle" had begun "tightening" around the cyclist. The *Globe and Mail* also contained the headline "Say it ain't so, Lance," referring to a film in which a young boy asks the same of Shoeless Joe Jackson in reference to allegations that the Chicago White Sox had intentionally lost the 1919 World Series (see Tables 6.1 and 6.2 regarding quote fragments in this section).

Newspapers from other parts of the world used terms such as "poisoned legacy" and assertions that "Cycling great can't outride doping claims," "Lance used drugs," and "Armstrong must show cards" (see Table 6.2). Comparing the EPO story to that of Ben Johnson at the 1988 Olympics, *Montreal Gazette* columnist Jack Todd (2005a) wrote that "this is not about who is right and who is wrong. It is about the sports we watch, the heroes we worship—and the lies they tell" (p. C1). One day following that assertion, the *Montreal Gazette* published an editorial that also questioned the truthfulness of Armstrong in suggesting that "perhaps it is finally time to confront the reality that Armstrong the superhuman is not only a myth but, ultimately, a lie" (p. A18). If one considers such assertions against the backdrop of hegemonic masculinity, it becomes clear that Todd and the newspaper for which he worked characterized Armstrong as the antithesis of the honest, heroic figure whose integrity and fortitude cannot be compromised. Todd and the *Montreal Gazette* characterized Armstrong as a liar, and a probable cheat, and as an athlete whose apparent courage and resilience in overcoming cancer may have been largely the result of chemicals, not unlike his cycling successes.

Like Todd, journalist James Christie (2005c), writing in the *Globe and Mail*, recalled his disappointment following the 1988 Olympics, when Ben Johnson returned his gold medal and deprived the country of not only an international sporting success, but a moment of national pride. "There was symbolism attached to it," Christie wrote, "in that he vanquished rival Carl Lewis. It was a victory for a Canadian against an American, the silent humble underdog against the flamboyant popinjay" (p. F2). For journalists who experienced the bitterness of 1988, then, the Armstrong story served as a reminder that the United States (allegedly) plays by its own set of rules, forcing other nations to follow policies it largely ignores.

In a *Montreal Gazette* article published on August 29, 2005, Todd alleged that Armstrong had "bullied" cyclists who had "violate(d) the pro cyclist's code of omerta" (Todd, 2005b, p. C1). Again, if one considers the characteristics of hegemonic masculinity, a "man" protects the unsuspecting from the aggression of a bully, never abusing his strength and authority. A man also makes ethically sound choices, but as English (2005) opined in *The Scotsman*, "Armstrong has always had a confused morality in terms of cheating in cycling" (p. 24). Journalists such as Todd and English thus contrasted the characteristics of an idealized masculine hero with those of someone they suggested was not the individual he portrayed himself to be. Writing in the *New Zealand Herald*, Cleaver (2005) also made some frank statements about the Armstrong story:

> *L'Equipe* did what every newspaper worth its salt would have done. It worked a source, got a leak, checked its sources and had the balls—probably not the wisest choice of words considering the subject—to run with it. The US media now hold *L'Equipe* in the same regard as Arab television news service al Jazeera . . . *Time* magazine, a host of newspapers, sports network ESPN and even the supposedly neutral Associated Press have jingoistically implied that *L'Equipe* has an axe to grind; as if it's somehow acting as the guardian of a great French race which has been desecrated by a loathed American breaking all its records . . . The one good thing about *L'Equipe's* revelations is we finally have arguments based on science rather than innuendo. (12–14)

As indicated in the previous section, journalists in the United States questioned the science on which the allegations were based, but international reporters nevertheless used the laboratory findings as one approach for discrediting Armstrong.


❖  DISCUSSION

Commenting on the increasing politicization of the Tour de France, Wieting (2000) observed that "the potential exists, as the Tour enlarges its national representation of riders and certainly as it continues to extend its dissemination through television, radio, and print media, for groups to use the venues for political ends" (p. 358). In the case of Lance Armstrong and allegations of EPO use in 2005, that appears to have been the case among U.S. and international journalists. Newspaper reports in the United States portrayed Armstrong as a quintessentially heroic figure, while journalists in Canada and abroad questioned the Armstrong legacy. These reporting patterns were not as pronounced as they were in the Carl Lewis situation, but they nevertheless illustrate how a masculinized hero in one nation may appear far less heroic in others. In battling both cancer and other cyclists, Armstrong has appeared as a kind of lone or "rogue" warrior, fiercely competitive and confident in his capacity to defeat those who would challenge him.

As the current study has demonstrated, though, not everyone has been impressed; some even suggested that Armstrong lied and manipulated—even bullied—his way to the top of his sport, playing by his own set of rules, not unlike "rogue" U.S. President George W. Bush. As in the Carl Lewis situation, select journalists characterized Armstrong as symbolic of Bush and U.S. actions in Iraq, arguing that Americans presume to introduce self-serving rules when necessary, dismissing the concerns of other nations.

In sum, then, gendered media texts stand to vary based on the nations in which content originates, with sport participants standing to symbolize the countries for which they compete. International sport does not exist in a vacuum, nor do its competitors; we encourage continued scholarship on the intersection of gender ideals and nationalism given a backdrop in mediated sport.

## ❖ REFERENCES

Abt, S. (2005, August 24). Armstrong is accused of doping. *The New York Times*, p. D1.

Allison, L. (2000). Sport and nationalism. In J. Coakley & E. Dunning (Eds.), *Handbook of sports studies* (pp. 344–355). London: Sage.

Anderson, K. (2003, June 16). Will France take it out on Lance? Given the testy relations between the U.S. and France, will the French be harder than ever on Lance Armstrong? Au contraire. *Sports Illustrated, 98*(24), p. A4 [bonus section].

Andersson, A. (2005, August 25). Explain yourself, Armstrong urged. *London Daily Telegraph*, p. 3.

Armstrong, L., & Jenkins, S. (2000). *It's not about the bike: My journey back to life.* New York: Putnam.

Bairner, A., & Shirlow, P. (2000). Territory, politics and soccer fandom in Northern Ireland and Sweden. *Football Studies, 3*(1), 5–26.

Barron, D. (2005, August 29). Case against Armstrong "France's latest tirade." *Houston Chronicle*, p. 2.

Billings, A. C., Halone, K. K., & Denham, B. E. (2002). "Man, that was a pretty shot": An analysis of gendered broadcast commentary of the 2000 men's and women's NCAA Final Four basketball championships. *Mass Communication & Society, 5*(3), 295–315.

Billings, A. C., & Tambosi, F. (2004). Portraying the United States vs. portraying a champion: U.S. network bias in the 2002 World Cup. *International Review for the Sociology of Sport, 39*(2), 157–165.

Blasengame, B. (2006, November). Lance Armstrong. *Details,* pp. 184–189.

Buckley, W. (2005, August 28). Armstrong must show cards. *London Observer,* p. 5.

Burstyn, V. (1999). *The rites of men: Manhood, politics, and the culture of sport.* Toronto: University of Toronto Press.

Butryn, T. M., & Masucci, M. A. (2003). It's not about the book: A cyborg counternarrative of Lance Armstrong. *Journal of Sport & Social Issues, 7*(2), 124–144.

Caudwell, J. (1999). Women's football in the United Kingdom: Theorizing gender and unpacking the butch lesbian image. *Journal of Sport & Social Issues, 23,* 390–402.

Christie, J. (2005a, August 24). Armstrong faces fresh drug charges; French newspaper says 1999 testing shows EPO doping. *Globe and Mail,* p. S1.

Christie, J. (2005b, August 25). "Circle tightening" around Armstrong. *Globe and Mail,* p. S1.

Christie, J. (2005c, August 27). Say it ain't so, Lance. *Globe and Mail,* p. F2.

Cleaver, D. (2005, September 11). The strong arm of the media. *New Zealand Herald.* Retrieved September 23, 2008, from http://www.nzherald.co.nz/ sport/news/article.cfm?c_id=4&objectid=10344991

Coakley, J. (2004). *Sports in society: Issues and controversies* (8th ed.). Boston: McGraw-Hill.

Connell, R. W., & Messerschmidt, J. W. (2005). Hegemonic masculinity: Rethinking the concept. *Gender & Society, 19*(6), 829–859.

Cooke, R. (2005). The green fields of France: Ireland's sporting heroes and the Tour de France. *Sport in History, 25*(2), 206–220.

Crump, J. (1989). Athletics. In T. Mason (Ed.), *Sport in Britain: A social history* (pp. 44–77). Cambridge, UK: Cambridge University Press.

Cycling authority says Lance was clean (2005, September 10). *St. Petersburg Times,* p. 8C.

Cycling body rips doping chief (2005, September 20). *Chicago Sun-Times,* p. 107.

Dauncey, H. (2003). French cycling heroes of the tour: Winner and losers. *The International Journal of the History of Sport, 20*(2), 175–202.

Davis, J. (2005, October 29). Armstrong ignored. *The Advertiser,* p. 122.

Denham, B. E. (2004a). Hero or hypocrite? United States and international media portrayals of Carl Lewis amid revelations of a positive drug test. *International Review for the Sociology of Sport, 39*(2), 167–185.

Denham, B. E. (2004b). Toward an explication of media enjoyment: The synergy of social norms, viewing situations and program content. *Communication Theory, 14*(4), 370–387.

Doping denials (2005, September 13). *Toronto Sun,* p. S13.

Eligon, J. (2005, August 27). A top U.S. cycling group is standing by Armstrong. *The New York Times,* p. D2.

English, T. (2005, August 28). Lance's poisoned legacy. *The Scotsman,* p. 24.

Farrand, S. (2005, September 7). Lance used drugs, says sports chief. *The Advertiser*, p. 86.

Fotheringham, A. (2005, August 25). Tour chief: "We were all fooled by Armstrong." *London Independent*, p. 64.

Guinness, R. (2005, August 26). Tour boss dumps on Lance. *Sydney Daily Telegraph*, p. 104.

Hachten, W. A., & Scotton, J. F. (2002). *The world news prism: Global media in an era of terrorism* (6th ed.). Ames, IA: Iowa State Press.

Hall, C. T. (2005, August 26). The science: Lab test seems sound, but tampering can't be ruled out. *San Francisco Chronicle*, p. A1.

Hargreaves, J. (1992). Olympism and nationalism: Some preliminary considerations. *International Review for the Sociology of Sport, 27*, 119–137.

Hearne, J., & Morgan, D. (1990). *Men, masculinities, and social theory.* London: Unwin Hyman.

Henderson, J. (2005, August 25). Allegations fail to sway Lance's fans. *Denver Post*, p. D1.

Hoagland, J. (2005, September 1). Tour de politics. *The Washington Post*, p. A29.

Jackson, S. J. (1998). Life in the (mediated) fast lane: Ben Johnson, national affect and the 1988 crisis of Canadian identity. *International Review for the Sociology of Sport, 33*, 227–238.

Jandt, F., & Hundley, H. (2007). Intercultural dimensions of communicating masculinities. *Journal of Men's Studies, 15*, 216–231.

Kane, M. J., & Parks, J. B. (1992). The social construction of gender difference and hierarchy in sport journalism—a few twists on very old themes. *Women in Sport and Physical Activity Journal, 1*, 49–83.

Kinkema, K. M., & Harris, J. C. (1998). MediaSport studies: Key research and emerging issues. In L. A. Wenner (Ed.), *MediaSport* (pp. 27–54). London: Routledge.

Klomsten, A. T., Marsh, H. W., & Skaalvik, E. M. (2005). Adolescents' perceptions of masculine and feminine values in sport and physical education: A study of gender differences. *Sex Roles, 52*(9–10), 625–636.

Knapp, G. (2005, August 28). Lance fiasco calls for open testing system. *San Francisco Chronicle*, p. D2.

Koivula, N. (2001). Perceived characteristics of sports categorized as gender-neutral, feminine, and masculine. *Journal of Sport Behavior, 24*, 377–393.

Lance's myth takes a hit (2005, August 25). *Montreal Gazette*, p. A18.

Livingston, B. (2005, August 28). America's faith in Lance Armstrong unshaken in wake of new allegations; still champ. *Cleveland Plain Dealer*, p. C2.

Lopresti, M. (2005, August 24). All you can do is hope it's not true. *USA Today*, p. 10C.

Marchetti, D. (2003). The changing organization of the Tour de France and its media coverage: An interview with Jean-Marie Leblanc. *The International Journal of the History of Sport, 20*(2), 33–56.

Messner, M. A., Dunbar, M., & Hunt, D. (2000). The televised sports manhood formula. *Journal of Sport & Social Issues, 24*, 380–394.

Mignon, P. (2003). The Tour de France and the doping issue. *The International Journal of the History of Sport, 20*(2), 227–245.

Mishkind, M., Rodin, J., Silberstein, L., & Striegel-Moore, R. (1987). The embodiment of masculinity. *American Behavioral Scientist, 29*(5), 545–563.

Morris, J. (2005, August 24). "Ritual denial" no good: Pound. *Toronto Star,* p. D3.

Morris, J. (2005, August 24). Pound: Onus is now on Lance. *Toronto Sun,* p. S9.

Pound, R. W. (2004). *Inside the Olympics.* Toronto: Wiley.

Pound, R. W. (2005, August 31). We'll catch them eventually. *Ottawa Citizen,* p. A19.

Reed, E. (2003). The economics of the Tour, 1930–2003. *The International Journal of the History of Sport, 20*(2), 104–127.

Rosenthal, E. (2005, September 5). Antidoping agency seeks test for EPO that is definitive. *The New York Times,* p. D1.

Ruibal, S. (2005, August 31). Director of top lab questions findings. *USA Today,* p. 10C.

Sabo, D., Jansen, S. C., Tate, D., Duncan, M. C., & Leggett, S. (1996). Televising international sport: Race, ethnicity, and nationalistic bias. *Journal of Sport & Social Issues, 20,* 7–21.

Schneider, A. J. (2006). Cultural nuances: Doping, cycling and the Tour de France. *Sport in Society, 9*(2), 212–226.

Schultz, J. (2005, August 29). French pique at Lance just silly. *Atlanta Journal Constitution,* p. 1D.

Sigal, L. (1973). *Reporters and officials.* Lexington, MA: DC Heath & Co.

Sparkes, A. C. (2004). Bodies, narratives, selves, and autobiography: The example of Lance Armstrong. *Journal of Sport & Social Issues, 28*(4), 397–428.

Stempel, C. (2006). Televised sports, masculinist moral capital, and support for the U.S. invasion of Iraq. *Journal of Sport & Social Issues, 30*(1), 79–106.

Tajfel, H., & Turner, J. C. (1986). The social identity theory of intergroup behavior. In S. Worchel & W. Austin (Eds.), *Psychology of intergroup relations* (pp. 7–24). Chicago: Nelson-Hall.

Taylor, P. (2005, August 30). Cycling great can't outride dope claims. *New Zealand Herald.*

Todd, J. (2005a, August 24). Armstrong rides into Tour doping storm. *Montreal Gazette,* p. C1.

Todd, J. (2005b, August 29). Matthews up to his old tricks as Als fade. *Montreal Gazette,* p. C1.

Tomlinson, A. (1996). Olympic spectacle: Opening ceremonies and some paradoxes of globalization. *Media, Culture and Society, 18,* 583–602.

Trujillo, N. (1991). Hegemonic masculinity on the mound. Media representations of Nolan Ryan and American sports culture. *Critical Studies in Mass Communication, 8,* 290–308.

Trujillo, N. (1995). Machines, missiles and men: Images of the male body on ABC's *Monday Night Football. Sociology of Sport Journal, 12*(4), 403–423.

USA federation chief: Accusations against Armstrong "preposterous" (2005, August 27). *The Washington Post,* p. E2.

US great positive to EPO: L'Equipe (2005, August 24). *The Australian,* p. 18.

Vecsey, G. (2005, September 14). A combative Armstrong is committed to battling on. *The New York Times*, p. D1.

Whannel, G. (2002). *Media sport stars: Masculinities and modernities*. London: Routledge.

Wieting, S. G. (2000). Twilight of the hero in the Tour de France. *International Review for the Sociology of Sport, 35*(3), 348–363.

Wilbon, M. (2005, August 24). A very familiar accusation. *The Washington Post*, p. E01.

## ❖ NOTES

1. While professional cycling is largely about individual achievement, the team to which an individual belongs can impact overall success. Team members play important roles, from the domestiques who bring teammates water and food along the course to the climbers who help the team leader set the pace on a hill.

2. LexisNexis indexes content from major newspapers in the United States as well as those published internationally. For more on its contents, see http://www.lexisnexis.com/productsandservices/academic.asp

3. "Spurious" mentions might appear in articles about the music of Sheryl Crow or the movies of Armstrong's friend, actor Matthew McConaughey.

4. Following are the newspapers that reported on the EPO story, with the number of reports from each in parentheses. U.S. newspapers included the *Atlanta Journal Constitution* (2), *Boston Globe* (5), *Buffalo News* (1), *Chicago Sun Times* (4), *Christian Science Monitor* (1), *Cleveland Plain Dealer* (1), *Denver Post* (1), *Houston Chronicle* (8), *New Orleans Times Picayune* (1), *New York Daily News* (2), *The New York Times* (7), *Pittsburgh Post Gazette* (3), *San Diego Union Tribune* (1), *San Francisco Chronicle* (4), *Seattle Times* (2), *USA Today* (7), *St. Louis Post Dispatch* (1), *St. Petersburg Times* (1), and *The Washington Post* (2). International newspapers included the *Globe and Mail* of Canada (4), *Irish Times* (2), *London Daily Telegraph* (7), *London Independent* (5), *London Observer* (1), *Melbourne Herald Sun* (3), *Montreal Gazette* (5), *Ottawa Citizen* (2), *Queensland Sunday Mail* (2), *Sydney Daily Telegraph* (2), *The Advertiser* (8), *The Australian* (1), *The Guardian* of London (7), *The Herald* of New Zealand (2), *The Press* of New Zealand (1), *The Scotsman* (1), *The Tasmanian* of Australia (2), *Toronto Sun* (3), and *Toronto Star* (3).

5. As an example, if 4 paragraphs in an article with 12 total paragraphs contained quotes from Lance Armstrong, the resulting coefficient of .33 would be rounded down to 3. If that same article contained two paragraphs with quotes from Richard Pound or another official from WADA, the resulting coefficient of .167 would be rounded down to 1. The lowest value for any source quoted (even if the resulting decimal value yielded a whole number less than 1)

was 1, thus ensuring that every source quoted was accounted for in the study. In this analysis, we coded for the presence of direct quotes only.

6. Because several cells with a source value greater than 3 contained zero observations, we did not compute chi-square.

7. Richard Pound had so infuriated Armstrong with allegations regarding EPO that Armstrong publicly called for Pound to be dismissed by WADA once the EPO results were determined to be inconclusive.

# 7

# Do You Believe in Nationalism?

*American Patriotism in* Miracle

Michael L. Butterworth

*"Do you believe in miracles? Yes!"*

—*Al Michaels* (quoted in Curtright, 2002, p. E1)

The opening ceremony of any Olympic Games is certain to be a nationalistic affair. So it came as little surprise, coming only five months after the terrorist attacks of September 11, 2001, that the 2002 Winter Games in Salt Lake City provided a dramatic stage for the performance of American identity. In the words of Silk and Falcous (2005), the television broadcast of the Salt Lake opening ceremony "drew on narrative themes that redefined allies and foes and legitimated military intervention in Afghanistan (and subsequently Iraq) as a 'just response' to the attacks on September 11" (p. 457). Given the inclusion of U.S. military personnel, an appearance and speech by President George W. Bush, and NBC's splicing of images from New York City on 9/11, some worried that the 2002 Winter Games would become a "jingoistic, flag-waving convention" (Araton, 2002, p. D1).

In this context, the most potent symbol of American patriotism arguably came not from the literal references to terrorism or politics but from the metaphor ascribed to one of American sport's most enduring memories. As Rachel Nichols (2002) described the culmination of the opening ceremony:

> For more than 20 years, the members of the 1980 U.S. men's hockey team have been the standard-bearers of the improbable . . . [In 2002] they became the symbols of all that is possible when they lit the Olympic flame to open the Salt Lake City Games. (p. D13)

Indeed, when the American men defeated the Soviet Union 4–3 in the 1980 Olympic semifinal, it immediately became acknowledged as among the most stunning upsets in sports history. More importantly, the victory came at a time when American political culture was constituted by a loss of faith in a deteriorating economy at home and a fear of international threats made real by the Iran hostage crisis and the Soviet invasion of Afghanistan, as Chuck Finder (2004) notes:

> The perceived miracle of the 1980 Winter Olympics wasn't merely that a tremendous underdog overcame a juggernaut hockey team but rather that a downtrodden country could overcome its lines at the gasoline pumps, its hostages in Iran, its weak knees at the sight of the Soviets. (p. C2)

In addition, Farrell (1989) argues that the unlikely victory prompted a resurgence of Cold War fervor that "focused attention on Lake Placid's Olympics as a kind of symbolic confrontation with the Soviets" (p. 163).

That the 1980 Olympic hockey team could symbolize a profound triumph over moments of crisis found renewed rhetorical significance in the wake of 9/11. As a metaphor for American resolve and virtue during the Cold War, the team symbolized the superiority of democracy and freedom over communism and totalitarianism. Hogan (2003) argues that the team's appearance at the 2002 opening ceremony "evoked these cold war triumphs. The moment served as a symbolic assertion of American power, a promise to once again defeat its enemies in the 'war on terror'" (p. 108). The celebration of 1980's "miracle on ice" during the 2002 Winter Games is, then, emblematic of the relationship between the collective memory of sport and national identity. As Hayes (2001) suggests, "Sport, like no other cultural formation, mobilizes and heightens feelings of identification and collective belonging" (p. 164).

This renewed interest in the 1980 Olympic hockey team overlapped with other retrospective celebrations of the memorable upset. In 1999, *Sports Illustrated* named the "Miracle on Ice" the top sports moment of the 20th century ("The 20th Century Awards," 1999). In 2001, HBO (Home Box Office) produced a documentary titled *Do You Believe in Miracles*, a reference to the famous words of ABC television announcer Al Michaels. Then, in 2004, Disney released a feature-length dramatization of the Olympic triumph called, simply, *Miracle* (O'Connor, 2004). Although a 1981 made-for-television movie had previously chronicled the story, *Miracle* represented the first cinematic treatment of it. Released on February 6, 2004, the film generated a healthy $64 million in box office receipts in the United States ("Box Office," 2007). While there was no overt symbolism in this timing—it was the 24th anniversary of the 1980 Olympics, and the Summer Games were to take place later in the year—I argue that the release of *Miracle* must be understood in light of the heightened patriotism that was central to American identity after 9/11.

At first glance, it may seem relatively innocuous that a major motion picture would celebrate the patriotism aroused in the United States by the terrorist attacks. However, I contend that *Miracle* contributed to the construction of a form of nationalism that threatened the health of democratic politics. In the years following 9/11, U.S. foreign policy became increasingly belligerent, arrogant, and militant. The central problematic of this shift can be summarized in President Bush's now infamous declaration, "You are either with us, or you are with the terrorists" (Bush, 2001, ¶ 30). Such statements are about more than defining the enemy itself; they simultaneously construct allies and American citizens in ways that delimit the possibilities for democratic participation. As Mouffe (1993) insists, "A healthy democratic process calls for a vibrant clash of political positions and an open conflict of interests" (p. 6). Instead of political contestation, however, political discourse after 9/11 all too often was characterized by appeals to fear, rigid constructions of "us" and "them," and the suppression of democratic rights. Consequently, media representations of national identity are significant sites for rhetorical critique and intervention.

In this chapter, I view *Miracle* as a rhetorical text that uses the men's hockey victory of 1980 as a metaphor to reconstitute post-9/11 American national identity. As Jeffords (1994) argues, films are especially important vehicles for cultural production because nations exist "as something to be *seen*" (p. 6). Thus, *Miracle* presents a concrete image of the abstract "imagined community" (Anderson, 1991) that nations are often understood to be. In this sense, *Miracle* offers Americans a way of seeing political conflict in contemporary times, a vision that gives them what Burke (1973) terms "equipment for living." As I argue, however, this metaphor relies on familiar American mythologies that elevate individual heroism, trivialize pluralism, and extend the political divisions that constitute contemporary life. To make this argument, I first situate Olympic hockey within the political terrain. I then analyze four extended sequences from *Miracle* that make clear the connections between the cultural crises that prefaced the 1980 Winter Olympics and that followed the terrorist attacks of 9/11. Finally, I conclude that the critique of media texts such as *Miracle* is crucial if we are to understand national identity and envision a more productive form of democratic politics.

## ❖ THEORY AND RELATED LITERATURE: OLYMPIC HOCKEY AND THE POLITICAL

Despite claims to the contrary by the International Olympic Committee and the United States Olympic Committee, the Olympic Games have always been a stage for international politics. For Western democracies such as the United States, the "worth of the Olympics is their importance as a national and international symbol of encirclement of a kind of liberal idealism" (Bass, 2002, p. 12). Indeed, Olympic triumphs have routinely been upheld as demonstrations of national superiority. Historically, the *Summer* Games have provided the most visible moments of political contestation: Jesse Owens' performance at the 1936 Berlin Games; the Black Power protest of John Carlos and Tommie Smith in 1968; the violent terrorism in Munich in 1972. In the first Summer Games after 9/11, George W. Bush openly articulated the "war on terror" with the Athens Olympics when he took credit for the participation of Afghani and Iraqi athletes, particularly the Iraqi national soccer team. Yet the enduring memory of the 1980 men's hockey team, and its reinvention in 2004, reminds us that the *Winter* Games also should "be remembered as a crucial site in the context and transmogrification of Cold War politics" (Segrave, 2004, p. 228).

King (2007) argues that the Winter Olympics are an especially powerful reminder of the embedded mythologies of Western racial superiority. He notes, "The Olympics gave embodied expression to modern Europe's desire to project its shared values and vision as civilized nations, heirs to the institutions and ideals associated with the classical period in Greece and Rome" (p. 90). This is especially true of the Winter Games, where athletes compete in sports that find their origins almost exclusively in Europe and North America. Thus, the Olympic Games serve as an extension of a so-called "clash of civilizations" that constitutes the binaries between West and East, Democratic and Totalitarian, Christian and Godless, Good and Evil. Accordingly, international sporting events cannot be seen merely as athletic competitions; rather, they speak metaphorically for the state of the nation itself (Rowe, 2003).

In 1980, the state of the American nation was largely understood in negative terms. A sagging economy and rising fuel costs caused many Americans to question the direction of the country. President Jimmy Carter attempted to address those concerns in July 1979 but instead alienated many listeners through his "Crisis of Confidence" speech, which failed to affirm the American values of optimism and determination. When Iranian militants seized hostages at the American embassy in Tehran in November 1979, and the Soviet Union invaded Afghanistan in December, the combined weight of these crises constituted a culture of pessimism. Thus, when the men's hockey team took the ice against the Soviet Union in Lake Placid, New York, in 1980, it was easy to view the contest as a pivotal moment in the Cold War itself. *Miracle*'s co-producer, Gordon Gray, comments:

> It is important to understand the political and social environment in our nation a quarter-century ago. The Iran hostage crisis, the gas lines, President Carter's "crisis of confidence" speech and the Russians in Afghanistan. We were down on ourselves and looking for a spark. In many ways it was a genesis of a rebirth of our nation to start feeling good about ourselves. (quoted in Williams, 2006, p. 239)

This national rebirth depended on the relentless construction of the Soviet "other." If the Soviet Union was, as Ronald Reagan later stated, the "evil empire," then the Soviet hockey team was the visible sign of communist aggression and imperialism. Affiliated with the Russian Red Army, the national team thoroughly dominated Olympic competition by winning gold medals in 1964, 1968, 1972, and 1976. They were seen as methodical, mechanical—*inhuman*—in their dominance. In the words of Powers and Kaminsky (1984), "the Soviet National team was a marvelously tuned perpetual-motion machine, never out of synchrony, never running down . . . *Emotion never figured* [italics added]" (p. 19). Similarly, Coffey (2005) states, "The Soviets were . . . anonymous hockey assassins, robotic in their approach and unfaltering in their skating" (p. 33).

This rhetoric of dehumanization was commonplace in the United States throughout the 1980s. Sabo, Jansen, Tate, Duncan, and Leggett (1996) reveal that the "machine" metaphor was a prominent trope that constructed the Soviet other during international sports broadcasts. Consequently, American identity was asserted as much through the radical otherness of the Soviet Union as it was by affirming inherent principles. As Mouffe (2000) suggests, the construction of any "us" necessarily entails the construction of a "them." However, if we are to envision a *democratic* "us," Mouffe says we must aim to

> construct the "them" in such a way that it is no longer an enemy to be destroyed, but as an "adversary" that is, somebody whose ideas we combat but whose right to defend those ideas we do not put into question. (pp. 101–102)

In the years following 9/11, instead of maintaining a democratic respect for the plurality of identities and political positions, American political culture turned increasingly intolerant. Therefore, the national memory of the "miracle on ice" risks the "proclivity to marginalize or demonize difference to sanctify the identity you confess" (Connolly, 2002, p. xv).

It may seem odd that the most profound sporting memory in American history took place on the ice. After all, hockey in the United States lacks the "national pastime" mythology of baseball, and it has never enjoyed the popularity of sports such as football or basketball. Even professional hockey's status as one of the four "major" North American sports must be questioned in light of dwindling attendance and television ratings in the 21st century. However, it is precisely this marginal status that assures the enduring significance of the victory over the Soviets. To beat the "Russians" at their own game was far more powerful as a symbol of American superiority—i.e., it affirmed American convictions that "good" will always triumph over "evil." In addition, the U.S. status as underdogs played nicely alongside the American mythology of hard-working rugged individualists who are willing to face and overcome any obstacles placed in their way. This underdog mythology—preposterous, given the United State's economic and military influence—is consonant with a central principle of American nationalism: that the United States is always on the side of good and thus never shoots first (Marvin & Ingle, 1999).

Hockey also affirms a vision of masculinity that *Miracle* promotes as an antidote to a national crisis. As Meân (Chapter 4, in this volume) points out, international sport is a common site for rehearsals of masculine virtue and superiority. Hockey, specifically, valorizes "notions of rugged athletic masculinity" and "myths of nationhood" (MacNeill, 1996, p. 104). Because the Carter presidency was commonly seen as the embodiment of "weakness," the "miracle on ice" was a victory over the loss of masculine strength as much as it was a victory over the adversaries of America. When Ronald Reagan defeated Carter in the 1980 election, the longing for a mythic return to masculinity was validated. This became evident, Jeffords (1994) argues, in Hollywood cinema during the 1980s, when "the depiction of the indefatigable, muscular, and invincible masculine body became the linchpin of the Reagan imaginary" (p. 13). In celebrating the events of the 1980 Winter Olympics, therefore, *Miracle* hails an idealized performance of masculinity that uses historic events to negotiate a contemporary crisis.

❖  METHODOLOGICAL APPROACH:
    CLOSE RHETORICAL READING

While *Miracle* is a credible factual account of the hockey team's journey, it must be understood in its time and place as at least a partial reaction to the events of 9/11. In light of this, I proceed by integrating the theoretical framework outlined above with an approach to rhetorical criticism commonly called "close textual analysis." While close textual analysis was originally conceived as a response to the over-emphasis on theory (Burgchardt, 2005), I maintain that theory provides a critical context for interpreting the cultural and political dynamics of the film. Thus, by attending "to the elements contained within the text itself" (Leff, 1986, p. 378), I demonstrate the problematic logic of national identity constituted by the film. In particular, four segments of the film demonstrate this conflation of the political climates in 1980 and post-9/11: the opening credits; the multiple scenes during which team unity is fostered; the Christmas party juxtaposed with Carter's "Crisis of Confidence" speech; and the symbolic death and rebirth of Team USA in New York.

❖  RESULTS: NATIONAL IDENTITY IN *MIRACLE*

The action in *Miracle* centers around the sport of hockey, but it is not really a story about hockey. Rather, it is a story about the American Dream and the enduring victory of democracy over totalitarianism. Thus, the hockey team is merely the vehicle through which the metaphor of national identity is communicated. Significantly, the film's plot focuses almost exclusively on Team USA coach Herb Brooks, who is credited with orchestrating the improbable victory. This allows *Miracle* to follow a familiar trajectory in sports films, which "are especially fond of the idea that history is made by individuals" (Baker, 2003, p. 10).

Brooks was, in fact, a significant reason the team was able to defeat the Soviets. He had been the last player cut from the 1960 U.S. Olympic hockey team, which had been the last American team to win a gold medal. In the years between 1960 and 1980, Brooks became fascinated with the Soviet style of play; he studied game films and looked for ways to attack them. His plan in Lake Placid was to have Team USA play a hybrid style, combining the physical play of North American teams with the quick and fluid play of the Soviets. In the months leading up to the Winter Games, Brooks kept his distance from the players and relied on the unpredictability of his decisions and conditioning drills to create team unity (Powers & Kaminsky, 1984). In many ways he was stubborn, selfish, and uncommunicative (Coffey, 2005). Yet few could argue with the results: a 4–3 victory over the Soviets in the semifinal, and a 4–2 victory over Finland to secure the gold medal.

*Miracle* faithfully recreates the above narrative through the perspective of Brooks, portrayed by Kurt Russell. Russell's interpretation, guided by the screenplay, assures the audience that Brooks' behavior was motivated by what was best for the team. Even though the outcome is common knowledge, the film nevertheless presents multiple obstacles that threaten the team's success. Most of these obstacles— hovering U.S. Olympic officials, a nagging wife who wishes her husband was home more, a potential Soviet boycott of the Lake Placid Games as retaliation for Carter's boycott of the Moscow Summer Games—are filtered through Brooks so that they become obstacles to *his* success. The triumph at the end, therefore, is as much about Herb Brooks as it is about Team USA In addition to focusing on the individual heroism of Brooks, *Miracle* also presents the metaphorical link between the "miracle on ice" and national identity in such a way that it does far more than simply shed light on a particular moment in the nation's history. More than this, it reinvents the metaphor as a cultural resource for rehabilitating national identity in the wake of 9/11.

❖ OPENING CREDITS

Baker (2003) suggests that when sports films make claims about history they do so by looking "back in time through the lens of present concerns" (p. 7). From the opening credits of *Miracle*, it is clear that the film constitutes a sense of crisis. For viewers living through the uncertainty and anxiety characteristic of post-9/11 culture, the political crisis evoked by the opening credits likely has resonance. This sequence in *Miracle* does not begin in 1980 or even 1979. Instead, it presents a montage of newspaper headlines and video footage dating back to the start of the decade. As audio and video clips support the text, the following headlines move across the screen:

"U.S. Invades Cambodia"

"100,000 Anti-War Protestors Rally in Washington, DC"

"Munich Olympics Upset: Russia Takes Basketball Gold, Americans Refuse Silver"

"Watergate Break-In: 5 Arrested in Connection to GOP"

"NASA Budget Cuts Mean End of Era"

"Saigon Falls: U.S. Embassy Evacuated"

"America Catches Disco Fever"

"America Celebrates Bicentennial"

"Elvis is Dead: Long Live the King"

Each of these headlines is framed exclusively from the American point of view. It is no doubt memorable, for example, that the Soviets won the basketball gold medal in 1972 in controversial fashion. However, few would deny that the most lasting memory of those Summer Games was the death of 11 Israeli athletes who were murdered by terrorists. The effect of these headlines, then, is to constitute a political crisis of the 1970s that was distinctly American. This is most obvious in the final moments of the opening credits, when a video of President Carter reveals him stating, "It is a crisis of confidence. It is a crisis that strikes at the very heart and soul and spirit of our national will." As Carter speaks, the title "Miracle" comes together one letter at a time. At this moment of "crisis," therefore, it is clear that a national miracle is required.

More than hailing the familiar political problems of the 1970s merely as a plot device, the opening credits define national identity in opposition to moments of crisis in general, regardless of the era. To lose one's confidence, or to suffer embarrassment and defeat, is to risk one's status as an American. "Losing" the war in Vietnam, for example, disrupted the expectation held by many Americans that the United States would always emerge victorious. The subsequent "Vietnam Syndrome" affected national identity to the point that it influenced political campaigns, foreign policy, and national memory. As Ehrenhaus (2001) demonstrates, Hollywood films have been one of the primary sites for coming to terms with the "Vietnam Syndrome." *Saving Private Ryan,* he argues, reconstitutes the collective memory of World War II, partially as a means for overcoming the lingering memory of Vietnam. *Miracle,* by contrast, does not seek to overcome the unrest of the late 1970s. Rather, it features the inevitable triumph of the men's hockey team to imply that Americans can overcome the unrest of a post-9/11 world because they have done so in the past. The opening credits, therefore, are not a reminder of a crisis; they are a reminder that American resolve will always overcome a crisis.

### Building the Team

Most of the members of Team USA came from either Minnesota or Massachusetts. As a result, the rivalry between the University of Minnesota and Boston University presented an initial obstacle for Brooks, especially since he had coached Minnesota to three national championships during the 1970s. An early scene in *Miracle* illustrates the regionalism that threatened team unity. Jack O'Callahan, a former Boston defenseman, initiates a fight with Rob McClanahan as retribution for a confrontation during the 1976 national championship game. After the players spar and bloody each other, Brooks intervenes. Insisting that the Olympic team is not about "old rivalries," he demands, "We start becoming a team right now." He has each player introduce himself to his new teammates, asking, "Who do you play for?" The players state their names, hometowns, and college affiliations. This scene foreshadows the transcendental moment later in the film when team cohesion is assured.

Before unity can be achieved, *Miracle* establishes an analogy between hockey rivalries and international politics. Shortly after the fight scene detailed above, assistant coach Craig Patrick is seated in his car next to the team doctor, "Doc." When they hear a radio report about a nuclear test, Doc comments, "Ah, so much hate and fear . . . between the Soviets and the West." Nodding in agreement, Patrick responds, "Yeah, like hockey players from Boston and Minnesota." On the one hand, this moment trivializes the complexities of the Cold War by suggesting that the ideological disputes between the United States and Soviet Union were no more serious than a territorial battle for hockey supremacy. Yet on the other hand, the scene is more complicated, as

*Miracle* uses the analogy to set up an important contrast. Because we know the outcome of the 1980 Olympics in advance, we can assume that the players will transcend the Minnesota-Boston rivalry.

Subsequent scenes that show the players training and conditioning are interspersed with further player introductions. Each player continues to state his name, hometown, and affiliation. When Team USA travels to Norway for an exhibition, Brooks is incensed by their lack-luster play. They are complacent and distracted by attractive women in the stands, and they settle for a 3–3 tie against a team they should beat. When the game concludes, Brooks orders his players back on the ice. Demanding that they must understand how to compete at the highest level, he sends them up and down the ice in a brutal conditioning drill. Even as Patrick and Doc hesitate, and the ice arena's manager turns out the lights, Brooks is unrelenting. Finally, as players are doubled-over on the verge of collapse, team member (and later captain) Mike Eruzione shouts, "Mike Eruzione!" When Brooks replies, "Who do you play for?" Eruzione makes the transcendental leap. "I play for . . . the United States of America!" Recognizing that he has now molded this group of individuals into a team, Brooks allows them to leave the ice.

It is true that Brooks held his players after the Norway exhibition and skated them until they dropped (Coffey, 2005; Powers & Kaminsky, 1984). However, Eruzione's outburst is a moment of cinematic invention. It achieves an important narrative resolution, however, as the audience can now recognize that there is a purpose to Brooks' harsh treatment of the players and that being able to set aside differences is important if the team is to achieve its goal. Unlike the Soviets and the "West," who intimidate one another with nuclear tests, Team USA embodies the national fantasy of being able to assimilate differences into a coherent national identity. This, of course, is the chief illusion of the American Dream, a myth that depends on the metaphor of the "melting pot," where "people of all races commingle, and live and work together as a united citizenry" (Elias, 2001, p. 5). Modern sports provide one of the most visible arenas for witnessing the American Dream in action. Many assume that sports are based strictly on a meritocracy, that free and open competition will allow anyone to succeed, no matter their race, color, sex, or nationality. The fact that every player on the 1980 Olympic hockey team was a White male is unimportant to the myth, because they symbolized how Americans can and should live together.

The American Dream subtext is as relevant in the 21st century as it was in 1980. If anything, the contemporary moment is characterized by an even greater faith in the possibility that differences should be overcome. It is little wonder, then, that sports are often seen as exemplars of a democratic culture. However, as Mouffe (2000) contends, the belief that differences can be erased in the name of unity is an illusion. A political culture that overemphasizes unity and consensus, she argues, perpetuates the misconception that "antagonisms can be eradicated" (p. 8). Thus, the conflation of Cold War tensions with hockey regionalism threatens to minimize the degree to which legitimate conflicts are a part of our political culture. Moreover, a *democratic* culture requires that, far from erasing difference, we must acknowledge and respect difference, even when that demands "gritted-teeth tolerance of some things you hate" (Connolly, 2005, p. 43). Regrettably, the post-9/11 political climate is characterized by the villainization of difference and otherness. Anything but full-throated support from other nations for America's "war on terror" is deemed a threat to national security; anything but full-throated support for the president from U.S. citizens is deemed "un-American." In such a climate, the image of national identity symbolized by Team USA serves as a symbolic lesson for how Americans should behave during the "war on terror."

If the team provides a metaphor for the citizenry, then Brooks is a metaphor for the nation's leadership. As a coach, he is dedicated and innovative. He shapes and manipulates his players so he can mold the perfect team. In the process, the team becomes a "family," a theme that is overtly articulated when Brooks brings in an outside player late in the training process. When he asks a group of players why he should not keep the new addition, one responds, "Because we're a family." That satisfies Brooks and the intruder is sent home. "Family" is a relative term to Brooks, however, and *Miracle* shows a number of scenes where his dedication to hockey threatens the stability of his real family at home. These scenes are largely perfunctory, especially because Brooks' wife is depicted as a stereotypical nag who wishes her husband would just spend more time at home. In one crucial scene, Brooks asks his wife for her support, telling her that his obsessive approach is "the only way I know how" to coach. In these moments, Brooks is stoic and focused—a determined leader who knows he must go it alone in order to succeed. *Miracle*, then, promotes a vision of leadership grounded in rugged individualism, a characteristic often celebrated through sports.

Rugged individualism reminds us that "sports fit squarely within a traditional American mythology that champions the promise of a unified self through individual achievement" (Baker, 2003, p. 11). Central to this myth is the image of the frontiersman who is "characterized primarily by isolation and independence" (Harter, 2004, p. 93). As the embodiment of hegemonic masculinity, the frontiersman has long been a model of strong leadership in America, especially at times of crisis. The popularity of Ronald Reagan, for example, can be understood, partially at least, by his ability to situate himself as the romantic western hero of American mythology. Similarly, following the 9/11 terrorist attacks, George W. Bush deliberately capitalized on his Texas roots and Western image by framing issues of right and wrong in absolute terms and by viewing his actions as unambiguous and morally justified (Woodward, 2002). In this context, *Miracle* valorizes this vision of leadership and lends tacit consent to the current political regime.

### Christmas and Carter

When Brooks celebrates Christmas with Team USA instead of at home with his wife and kids, it is clear which "family" comes first for him. Moreover, the scene that shows the team at a holiday party constructs a vision of purity that depends on religious imagery and the strength of masculine youth. The Christmas scene is contextualized by the preceding moments, wherein Brooks and his wife discover that the hostages have been seized in Iran and the Soviet Union has invaded Afghanistan. When Brooks realizes that President Carter might boycott the Moscow Summer Games, he knows the Winter Games are in jeopardy if the Soviets boycott in retaliation. Without being able to compete against the world's best, any American achievement would be devalued. This certainly heightens the narrative tension, but it also provides an important contrast. In the clash of ideologies that defined the Cold War, religion was a central component. "In order to counteract the Soviet threat," Hughes (2004) points out, "Americans routinely juxtaposed their religion in general and their 'deeply felt religious faith' against 'godless' and 'atheistic' communism" (p. 172). Thus, as soon as the audience learns that the communists have invaded Afghanistan, *Miracle* shifts to the most optimistic symbol of Christian faith—Christmas.

The focus on Christmas is a subtle reminder that national identity in America is commonly linked to Christian faith. This is driven by the mythology of American exceptionalism, in which "citizens regard the American way of life as though it were somehow chosen by God, uniquely important to the history of the human race" (Novak, 1992, p. 35). Sports have long contributed to this mythology through the cultivation of "muscular Christianity," a doctrine that depends on "manliness, morality, and patriotism" (Ladd & Mathisen, 1999, p. 14). Sports and Christianity, therefore, are often discourses that mutually affirm the imagined community of America. The faith that is required to believe in "America," then, is ultimately what this Christmas scene is about.

As Brooks drives away from the Christmas party, he turns on the radio to hear a "best of 1979" segment featuring President Carter's "Crisis of Confidence" speech from July. In what follows, *Miracle* weaves the audio of the speech with images of the hockey players outside in the snow. Hearing Carter's words—"The erosion of our confidence in the future is threatening to destroy the social and political fabric of America"—recalls the opening credits. If a "miracle" is required, then the young men playing football in the snow are surely the ones to whom Americans can turn. Thus, the key to restoring confidence in the future, it is clear, lies with an idealized form of masculine youth. These players are young, they are naïve, and they are *pure.* Significantly, they are all White. As Dyer (1997) demonstrates, "whiteness" has long been associated with purity and innocence, and Christianity "has been thought and felt in distinctly white ways for most of its history" (p. 17). Within the context of sport, then, we must attend to McDonald's (Chapter 8, in this volume) contention that the "normative power of white masculinity" remains central to media representations and portrayals of athletes and games.

This combination of innocence, purity, Christianity, and masculinity provides an image of hope and faith for viewers. In these terms, calling the 1980 victory a *miracle* takes on an even greater significance. Further, the discourse of purity and innocence that has characterized American political rhetoric since 9/11 finds validation in the redemptive mission of the 1980 hockey team. Given the age of the players—all in their early 20s—it takes little work to imagine them as soldiers instead of athletes. Following 9/11, those same young men may well have attempted a "miracle" of a different sort by fighting in the "war on terror." President Bush framed the war in explicitly religious terms, regularly invoking themes that constitute America's enemies as the enemies of God. In this way, *Miracle* equates the threat of Soviet communism with the threat of Islamic terrorism. Moreover, if political conditions of 1980 called for a victory on the sports front, then the political conditions after 9/11 called for a victory on the war front. Thus, without making any such explicit claims, *Miracle* is nevertheless a subtle endorsement of the "war on terror."

### Rebirth and Renewal

On February 9, 1980, three days before the opening ceremonies in Lake Placid, Team USA played the Soviet Union in New York City. They were overwhelmed from the start, losing 10–3. *Miracle* uses this exhibition to reinforce how unlikely an American victory would be.

Predictably, the Soviets are portrayed as dehumanized machines. They are large and intimidating, they take cheap shots, and they never smile. Earlier in the film, an exchange between two players foreshadows this imagery. While watching game films of the Soviet team, one player asks, "Do those guys ever smile?" His teammate quickly responds, "They're Russian. They get shot if they smile." Such a stereotype is consistent with Hollywood representations of Russians and/or Soviets during that time period. In the words of Strada and Troper (1997), "Russians—whether friend or foe—tend to be flat and one-dimensional, lacking the depth and genuineness necessary to empathize with them" (p. 201). With the end of the Cold War, some of these images have changed. However, the Soviet demon has frequently been replaced by the Muslim demon. Again, *Miracle* provides the symbolic link between the two, thereby justifying a rhetoric of dehumanization against anyone deemed to be an "enemy" of the United States.

Additional symbolic work occurs during this segment. The establishing shot before the exhibition game shows the New York City skyline as it would have looked in 1980—brightly lit up by Manhattan buildings, the World Trade Center towers prominently rising from the ground. This is either stock footage or a computer-generated image, of course, since the towers had been destroyed more than two years before the film's release. The familiarity of that skyline, however, offers comfort and strength for a population still coping with the terror of 9/11, while simultaneously evoking the confusion of seeing New York without the twin towers. As Lakoff (2001) summarizes:

> The image of the Manhattan skyline is now unbalanced. We are used to seeing it with the towers there. Our mind imposes our old image of the towers, and the sight of them gone gives one the illusion of imbalance, as if Manhattan were sinking. Given the symbolism of Manhattan as standing for the promise of America, it appears metaphorically as if that promise were sinking. (¶ 15)

Upon seeing the World Trade Center in *Miracle*, it is impossible to ignore the knowledge of its destruction. Once inside the hockey arena that night, Team USA suffers a similar destruction. The team members are shaken, disoriented, and afraid. The Soviets clearly intimidate them, and Team USA is unable even to present a unified front. If the twin towers symbolize the fragility of the promise of America, then the superiority of the Soviets on the ice metaphorically stands in for that threat.

In the wake of 9/11, American culture faced new uncertainties about its future. The destruction of the World Trade Center, and the damage done to the Pentagon, are well beyond the scope of comparison to the defeat of a national hockey team. Nevertheless, *Miracle* offers a narrative of redemption, thereby renewing the promise of America. This rebirth, of course, occurs during the Olympic Games in Lake Placid. After advancing to the medal round, Team USA has a new-found sense of confidence. As Brooks insists before they play the Soviets, "Tonight, *we* are the greatest hockey team in the world!" When the American players take the ice, they are calm and self-assured. In *Miracle*, they now approach center ice *as a team*, refusing to back down against the mighty Soviets. Against the backdrop of the crowd chanting, "USA! USA," the Americans improbably win the game, 4–3. This 20-minute segment is followed by a remarkably brief voice-over, with Russell as Brooks reminding viewers that Team USA still needed to defeat Finland to win the gold medal. Regardless of that outcome, it was the victory over the Soviets that guaranteed a revitalization of national identity. As Mike Eruzione said about the victory, "By us winning the gold medal, the hostages weren't released and the Soviets didn't pull out of Afghanistan. But we did make Americans feel proud again" (quoted in Curtright, 2002, p. E1).

The image of a stronger nation rising from the ashes of disappointment is powerful within the political culture constituted by 9/11. In the immediate aftermath of the terrorist attacks, the nation witnessed public displays of patriotism not seen since World War II. Indeed, sports became one of the primary arenas for healing and patriotic celebration. Quite quickly, however, the discourse of sports, both at the games and through the media, affirmed a presidential rhetoric of war (Butterworth, 2005; Stempel, 2006). Embedded in this discourse was a belligerence and hostility toward dissent or difference, characterized by a rigid construction of "us" and "them." The patriotism that followed the "miracle on ice" rested as much on the villainization of the Soviet Union as it did on the valorization of the United States. In this way, it repeated the redemptive ritual of victimage that Burke (1984a) warns is the hallmark of the "tragic frame." Burke's fear is that the tragic motivates humans toward violence. When we require redemption, we may either look inwardly for a corrective, or we may seek a scapegoat, "a sacrificial receptacle for the ritual unburdening of one's sins" (Burke, 1984b, p. 16). By demonizing first the Soviets and now Islamic terrorists, Americans too often resort to the facile binary of good versus evil as a way to justify a range of actions seen by many around the world as unjust and undemocratic. Following 9/11, a time when careful reflection and deliberation was needed most, American politicians instead stoked fear and division by declaring a "war on terror." *Miracle* summons the familiar refrain of American exceptionalism through its depiction of America's triumph over totalitarianism. Much like the opening ceremony for the 2002 Salt Lake City Games, *Miracle* offers the promise of an American victory at a time of crisis.

❖  DISCUSSION: A NEW MIRACLE?

Media representations of sport are central to the "process of identity construction in American culture" (Baker & Boyd, 1997, p. xviii). In the case of *Miracle*, national identity is constructed in problematic ways that bolster the belligerence and militarism of contemporary America. Rather than viewing sport as a site of agonistic struggle, in which opponents are defeated but not destroyed, the narrative of the "miracle on ice" depends on the symbolic destruction of the enemy. The Soviets were godless communist machines, persistent threats to the American way of life. As so many have noted, the American victory in Lake Placid was a powerful metaphor for the superiority of the United States, which was made more powerful by the political conditions of the time.

With the release of *Miracle*, this metaphor found renewed life. Several critics who reviewed the film in 2004 noted the obvious parallels: The *Dallas Observer* called it "an unabashed flag-waver . . . authentic charmer does for its young hockey players what John Wayne used to do for the U.S. Marines, and it lifts us, too, onto the boys' cloud of belief." *ReelViews* commented, "*Miracle* is inspirational and uplifting— qualities we are as much in need of today as we were during the winter of 1980." The *Philadelphia Inquirer* added, "*Miracle* really isn't about the game. It's about the game as metaphor for united we stand" (all quotations found in "Miracle," 2004, Critics Reviews section). Finally, the *Christian Science Monitor* summed up the film appropriately:

> What the movie does demonstrate is that Hollywood still hasn't tired of refighting the cold war in every way it can think of. Based on the real 1980 Winter Olympics, the story shows Brooks' team, portrayed as a wholesome set of individualized American youths, preparing to beat the Soviet team. (The foes are portrayed as a faceless pack of "win at any cost" fanatics, whose excellence on the ice is somehow unfair to individualized American youths.) (Sterritt, 2004, ¶ 3)

Perhaps it is not the responsibility of a group of filmmakers to insist upon more robust democratic dialogue and a greater respect for political difference. Nevertheless, the ease with which *Miracle* reinvents familiar villains and presents them to an audience coming to terms with 9/11 is cause for concern. As Hall (1999) notes, Western nationalism is motivated by the quest to constitute the unity of "one people . . . backwards in an apparently seamless and unbroken continuity towards pure, mythic time" (p. 38). Like any other myth, nationalism is remarkably persuasive even as it fails to uphold its promise of a unified American people. Despite its obvious appeal, we would be wise to be skeptical of the nationalism promoted by a film such as *Miracle*. Surely, there must be ways to remember the beauty of that Olympic victory without resorting to predictable slogans and the continuation of a political culture defined by "us" versus "them." To do so, however, requires a different national miracle altogether.

## ❖ REFERENCES

Anderson, B. (1991). *Imagined communities: Reflections on the origin and spread of nationalism* (Rev. ed.). London: Verso.

Araton, H. (2002, February 7). Jingoism is the way of the Olympics. *The New York Times*, D1. Retrieved May 24, 2007, from http://web.lexis-nexis.com/universe

Baker, A. (2003). *Contesting identities: Sports in American film*. Urbana, IL: University of Illinois Press.

Baker, A., & Boyd, T. (1997). Introduction: Sports and the popular. In A. Baker & T. Boyd (Eds.), *Out of bounds: Sports, media, and the politics of identity* (pp. xiii–xviii). Bloomington, IN: Indiana University Press.

Bass, A. (2002). *Not the triumph but the struggle: The 1968 Olympics and the making of the black athlete*. Minneapolis: University of Minnesota Press.

Box office/business for Miracle. (2004). Retrieved June 30, 2007, from the Internet Movie Database, http://www.imdb.com/title/tt0349825/business

Burgchardt, C. R. (Ed.). (2005). *Readings in rhetorical criticism* (3rd ed.). State College, PA: Strata Publishing.

Burke, K. (1973). *The philosophy of literary form: Studies in symbolic action* (3rd ed.) Berkeley: University of California Press.

Burke, K. (1984a). *Attitudes toward history* (3rd ed.). Berkeley: University of California Press.

Burke, K. (1984b). *Permanence and change: An anatomy of purpose* (3rd ed.). Berkeley: University of California Press.

Bush, G. W. (2001, September 20). Address to a joint session of Congress and the American people. White House press release. Retrieved August 31, 2007, from http://www.whitehouse.gov/news/releases/2001/09/20010920-8.html

Butterworth, M. L. (2005). Ritual in the "church of baseball": Suppressing the discourse of democracy after 9/11. *Communication and Critical/Cultural Studies*, 2, 107–129.

Coffey, W. (2005). *The boys of winter: The untold story of a coach, a dream, and the 1980 U.S. Olympic hockey team*. New York: Crown.

Connolly, W. E. (2002). *Identity\difference: Democratic negotiations of political paradox* (Exp. ed.). Minneapolis: University of Minnesota Press.

Connolly, W. E. (2005). *Pluralism*. Durham, NC: Duke University Press.

Curtright, G. (2002, February 10). Hockey miracle of 1980 endures. *Atlanta Journal-Constitution*, E1. Retrieved May 24, 2007, from http://web.lexis nexis.com/universe

Dyer, R. (1997). *White*. London: Routledge.

Ehrenhaus, P. (2001). Why we fought: Holocaust memory in Spielberg's *Saving Private Ryan*. *Critical Studies in Media Communication, 18*, 321–337.

Elias, R. (2001). Introduction: A fractured fit for a fractured society. In R. Elias (Ed.), *Baseball and the American dream: Race, class, gender and the national pastime* (pp. 3–33). Armonk, NY: M. E. Sharpe.

Farrell, T. B. (1989). Media rhetoric as social drama: The winter Olympics of 1984. *Critical Studies in Mass Communication, 6*, 158–182.

Finder, C. (2004, January 20). "Miracle" lacking only man who brought it to life. *Pittsburgh Post-Gazzette*, C2. Retrieved May 24, 2007, from http://web .lexis-nexis/academic

Hall, S. (1999). Culture, community, nation. In D. Boswell & J. Evans (Eds.), *Representing the nation: A reader* (pp. 33–44). London: Routledge.

Harter, L. (2004). Masculinity(s), the agrarian frontier myth, and cooperative ways of organizing: Contradictions and tensions in the experience and enactment of democracy. *Journal of Applied Communication Research, 32*, 89–118.

Hayes, S. (2001). America's national pastime and Canadian nationalism. In S. G. Wieting (Ed.), *Sport and memory in North America* (pp. 157–184). London: Frank Cass.

Hogan, J. (2003). Staging the nation: Gendered and ethnicized discourses of national identity in Olympic opening ceremonies. *Journal of Sport & Social Issues, 27*, 100–123.

Hughes, R. T. (2004). *Myths America lives by*. Urbana, IL: University of Illinois Press.

Jeffords, S. (1994). *Hard bodies: Hollywood masculinity in the Reagan era*. New Brunswick, NJ: Rutgers University Press.

King, C. R. (2007). Staging the winter white Olympics: Or, why sport matters to white power. *Journal of Sport & Social Issues, 31*, 89–94.

Ladd, T., & Mathisen, J. A. (1999). *Muscular Christianity: Evangelical protestants and the development of American sport*. Grand Rapids, MI: BridgePoint Books.

Lakoff, G. (2001, September 16). *Metaphors of terror. The days after*. Retrieved June 30, 2007, from University of Chicago Press Web site: http://www .press.uchicago.edu/News/911lakoff.html

Leff, M. (1986). Textual criticism: The legacy of G. P. Mohrmann. *Quarterly Journal of Speech, 72*, 377–389.

MacNeill, M. (1996). Networks: Producing Olympic ice hockey for a national television audience. *Sociology of Sport Journal, 13*, 103–124.

Marvin, C., & Ingle, D. W. (1999). *Blood sacrifice and the nation: Totem rituals and the American flag.* Cambridge, UK: Cambridge University Press.

Miracle. (2004). Retrieved June 28, 2007, from Metacritic Web site: http://www.metacritic.com/print/video/titles/miracle

Mouffe, C. (1993). *The return of the political.* London: Verso.

Mouffe, C. (2000). *The democratic paradox.* London: Verso.

Nichols, R. (2002, February 10). "Miracle men" get fired up. *The Washington Post,* D13. Retrieved May 24, 2007, from http://web.lexis-nexis.com/universe

Novak, M. (1992). The natural religion. In S. J. Hoffman (Ed.), *Sport and religion* (pp. 35–42). Champaign, IL: Human Kinetics Books.

O'Connor, G. (Director). (2004). *Miracle* [Motion picture]. Burbank, CA: Disney/Buena Vista.

Powers, J., & Kaminsky, A. C. (1984). *One goal: A chronicle of the 1980 Olympic hockey team.* New York: Harper & Row.

Rowe, D. (2003). Sport and the repudiation of the global. *International Review for the Sociology of Sport, 38,* 281–294.

Sabo, D., Jansen, S. C., Tate, D., Duncan, M. C., & Leggett, S. (1996). Televising international sport: Race, ethnicity, and nationalistic bias. *Journal of Sport & Social Issues, 21,* 7–21.

Segrave, J. (2004). Toward a cosmopolitics of the winter Olympic games. In L. R. Gerlach (Ed.), *The winter Olympics: From Chamonix to Salt Lake City* (pp. 225–251). Salt Lake City: University of Utah Press.

Silk, M., & Falcous, M. (2005). One day in September/a week in February: Mobilizing American (sporting) nationalisms. *Sociology of Sport Journal, 22,* 447–471.

Stempel, C. (2006). Televised sports, masculinist moral capital, and support for the U.S. invasion of Iraq. *Journal of Sport & Social Issues, 30,* 79–106.

Sterrit, D. (2004, February 6). "Miracle" is a hit and miss affair. *Christian Science Monitor.* Retrieved June 28, 2007, from http://www.csmonitor.com/2004/0206/p18s02-almo.htm

Strada, M. J., & Troper, H. R. (1997). *Friend or foe? Russians in American film and foreign policy.* Lanham, MD: The Scarecrow Press.

The twentieth century awards. (1999, December 3). *Sports Illustrated.* Retrieved December 7, 2008, from http://sportsillustrated.cnn.com/features/cover/news/1999/12/02/awards

Williams, R. (2006). *Sports cinema 100 movies: The best of Hollywood's athletic heroes, losers, myths, and misfits.* Pompton Plains, NJ: Limelight Editions.

Woodward, B. (2002). *Bush at war.* New York: Simon & Schuster.

# 8

# The Whiteness of Sport Media/Scholarship

## Mary G. McDonald

I t is now fairly standard in critical academic circles to conceive of race as a highly meaningful social construction. Read from this perspective, "race" exists as a human invention that seriously impacts quality of life and access to valued social rewards (Dyson, 2004; Nakayama & Martin, 1999). Among the notable works that promote this position is Michael Omi and Howard Winant's (1986) *Racial Formation in the United States*, which eschews commonsense understandings of race as a static biological identity to trace the historical and shifting constructions of racial identifications, formations, projects, and meanings within the United States. Omi and Winant argue that skin color held great import for Europeans who questioned whether the indigenous people they encountered in the "new world" were fully human, civilized, and children of God. During slavery, race served as one means to monitor who would be enslaved and who would be free. According to the pervasive binary ethos of slavery to have light skin meant—in more contemporary terminology—to be not "Black." Importantly, to have light skin in this era, especially for "White" men of status, also meant access to sovereignty.

Historically, sport and the sport media have served as important sites for the production and contestation of competing narratives of race and ethnicity. For example, early 20th century athletic contests between Whites and Native Americans, such as when Harvard played the Carlisle Indian School, generated great box-office appeal (Lipsyte & Levine, 1995). Turn of the century newspaper sport reporters contributed to this interest by hyping Indians as crafty, while White successes were characterized as evidence of White superiority. Matchups between White ethnic boxers provided recent immigrants sources of identification with their home nations while promoting solidarity within German, Irish, and Italian communities. In a similar way, Black versus White fisticuffs offered symbolic entry into broader struggles over segregation, equity, and definitions of manhood (Lipsyte & Levine, 1995).

In the post–civil rights era, liberal narratives of pride, tolerance, and multiculturalism are offered through the contemporary sport media as are lingering articulations of White supremacy where Black athletic bodies are frequently equated with inherent physical prowess and Whites are presumed to be culturally superior. As social constructionists suggest and these brief examples illustrate, the significance of race extends beyond superficial understandings of identity and categorization in that this human invention is implicated in power relations that continue to impact life chances and freedom itself (Dyson, 2004; Omi & Winant, 1986).

The media plays a significant role in encouraging the processes of racism, racialization, and racial formation. Omi and Winant (1986) note that "film and television, for example, have been notorious in disseminating images of racial minorities which establish for audiences what people from these groups look like, how they behave, and 'who they are'" (p. 63). Thus the representational "power of the media," including the sport media, "lies not only in their capacity to reflect the dominant racial ideology, but in their capacity to shape that ideology in the first place" (Omi & Winant, 1986, p. 63).

Increasingly scholars have focused attention on the (sport) media's role in promoting White hegemony. These critics have drawn from divergent theoretical and methodological assumptions to reveal the multiple ways in which sporting representations too frequently advance the power of whiteness via attempts to secure social, cultural, economic, and political advantages for Whites over people of color. This chapter provides an overview of this topic and begins by briefly discussing some related theories, concepts, and literature, including those that note the increasing visibility and potentially troubling character of whiteness and sport scholarship. It moves on to review a variety of studies that document both the overrepresentation of Whites—especially White males—as media producers and the stereotypical ways White athletes and coaches are frequently framed as hard workers who allegedly possess intellectual advantages in comparison to Black bodies. This section is followed by a review of emerging interdisciplinary scholarship, which reveals both the normalizing and contradictory power of the media in promoting White social, cultural, and political advantage. I conclude the chapter by briefly discussing the implications of this sport media scholarship for future research and action.

## ❖ THEORY AND RELATED LITERATURE

Since the 1970s a growing body of North American scholars and journalists has documented the sport media's key role in promoting demeaning stereotypical images of racial minorities in relation to Whites (see especially Davis & Harris, 1998; Grainger, Newman, & Andrews, 2006). This scholarship has consistently demonstrated the media's role in perpetuating and legitimating sport and cultural inequities via crude images of Latino athletes as "hot blooded," emotional firecrackers (Hoose, 1989); Native Americans as colorful caricatures and violent sport mascots (King & Springwood, 2001b); and Asian American sport figures as unemotional but highly disciplined performers (Feder-Kane, 2000).

The majority of critical race scholarship produced since the 1990s has focused on representations of Black masculinity demonstrating the powerful ability of television, newspapers, magazines, advertising, and the Internet to repeatedly construct Black male athletes as inherently physically orientated and within binary visions as either the "good Black" or "bad Black" (Abdel-Shehid, 2005; Andrews, 1996; Cole, 1996; McDonald, 1996). That is, mediated narratives offer narrow notions of Black males sporting physicality on the playing fields while also characterizing Black sport figures as either affable, engaging, and safe, àl la such sporting superstars as golfer Tiger Woods and basketball player Michael Jordan, or as inherently suspect, dangerously deviant, and violent as with track athlete Ben Johnson, boxer Mike Tyson, and football star O. J. Simpson (Abdel-Shehid, 2005; Houck, 2006). Despite the presence of competing narratives, the sport media help legitimate inequitable social conditions by focusing attention on the alleged physical and "personal" attributes of Black bodies while largely ignoring social structural disparities that continue to disproportionately impact people of color more broadly.

Building upon critical race theory, social constructionist critiques, and a legacy of criticism historically written and enacted by racially marginalized and colonized subjects, since the 1990s a growing body of media scholarship has begun to shift analytic attention from a preoccupation with the representational plight of people of color toward greater scrutiny of whiteness (Nakayama & Krizek, 1995). Collectively these writings expose the exclusionary tactics and political workings, practices, and institutions of the dominant culture, thereby challenging popular ideas that suggest that only people of color are raced. In this way, many media scholars are following Toni Morrison's (1992, p. 90) charge to move the critical focus "from the racial object to the racial subject; from the described and imagined to the describers and imaginers."

Increasingly sport media scholars have supplemented preexisting scholarship on the media's role in promoting racial differences by bringing White identities and White power under greater scrutiny, thus explicitly outlining the particular, temporal, spatial, and relational character of whiteness. However, much as with "whiteness studies" scholarship more broadly, this scholarship also continues to provoke several concerns, hesitations, and cautions. Chief among these concerns is confusion over what the concept of whiteness encompasses. In some sense, this is partially the result of studies where the concept is not defined or is reduced to essentialist notions of a homogenized White identity (Doane & Bonilla-Silva, 2003). Much of the analytic confusion also may be due to the fact that this growing body of scholarship draws from a diverse array of paradigmatic and political assumptions, which are in turn "implicated in contemporary racial formations and struggles over meaning" (McDonald, 2005, p. 247).

According to numerous critical race scholars, much like the concept of race itself, whiteness does not refer to an essential biological identity nor a fixed set of characteristics but rather a shifting set of racial meanings and practices seeking to legitimate cultural, structural, psychic, and economic advantages for the culturally created category of "White" people over "people of color" (McDonald, 2005). In this way, whiteness is "a dynamic of cultural production and interrelation" (Ellsworth, 1997, p. 260) that nevertheless works much differently in particular contexts—globally, nationally, and locally. Whiteness additionally works by colonizing other discourses of class, sexuality, gender, and nationality (McDonald, 2006); thus scholarship that focuses exclusively on either class or sexuality or gender or nationality often reproduces "White" norms. That whiteness frequently operates invisibly as an unexamined normative discourse is also powerfully evident in the taken-for-granted assumptions that "race" is equated with people of color and that Whites somehow exist as raceless beings outside the processes of racialization. Dominant notions of "racelessness" encourage Whites to view race relations and racial disparities as something that is not nor should not be part of their everyday concerns (McDonald, 2008).

Working alongside invisibility and cultural embeddedness is the persistence of "white racial unconsciousness" which marshals visions of White identity as victimized by progressive racial gains in an effort to deny White culpability in perpetuating inequalities (Doane & Bonilla-Silva, 2003, p. 8). Claims of victimization and subsequent denial of racism are most apparent historically and in contemporary times "when Whites felt threatened by social changes, immigration and challenges from subordinate groups" (Doane & Bonilla-Silva, 2003, p. 8).

These and other insights, taken as a whole, reveal whiteness to be unstable, hybrid, contingent, and contestable (Dyson, 2004; Gabriel, 1998). Thus efforts continue to critique the complex and myriad ways that whiteness performs both within sport scholarship and within cultural institutions including the media (McDonald, 2005). In this spirit, Cynthia Levine-Rasky (2002) argues that critical attention must be directed toward working "against the inequalities that whiteness arranges" (p. 18) via investigation of a broad array of issues including

> the denial and legitimation of white hegemony; the texts in which whiteness is read, how whiteness is constructed and practiced: how it structures social relations: how it is produced and is produced by power; the problem and contradiction of white pluralism; how it converges with other social categories that modify and fortify white privilege; and the diffuse tensions attending the questions of how to prompt whites to challenge the social order from which they benefit. (p. 18); (also cited in McDonald, 2005, p. 249)

Shannon Winnubst (2006, p. 9) cautions that "the project of critically examining whiteness" is a "dangerous one." That is, given the powerful universalizing pull of whiteness culturally, politically, and psychically, the risks of interrogation potentially run "the gamut from playing into cultural discourses of white supremacy, to uncritically fixing white superiority, to reinscribing whiteness at the center of concern and focus" (Winnubst, 2006, p. 9; also see McDonald, 2008). King (2005) is particularly wary about the efficacy of White sport scholars critiquing whiteness given the White-dominated status of higher education in North America. King fears that this line of inquiry runs the danger of becoming a White-dominated endeavor where "white perspectives and practices (ways of thinking and learning) shape the organization and dissemination of knowledge" (King, 2005, p. 403; also see McDonald, 2008). Such a position serves as an illusionary set of political practices in potentially substituting self-serving writings about whiteness for a more active agenda where Whites join the efforts of people of color to eradicate racism and White privilege.

## ❖ METHODOLOGICAL APPROACHES

Sport media scholars have interrogated representations of White identities and White power using a variety of methods, including the use of interviews, ethnographies, and content analysis. These methods have been useful in establishing the racialized character of media content and production practices. Emerging scholarship embedded in post-structuralist and interdisciplinary sensibilities provides an explicit discussion of the discourses and consequences of particular formations of whiteness and sport within popular visual culture. While each of these approaches carries with it different sets of assumption about identity, social life, and power, in sum these approaches assist in illuminating the complicated workings of whiteness.

Methodologically, this chapter offers a review of the existing scholarship on media constructions of White identities and the broader workings of whiteness. As is the case when the review method is employed, a central aim of this chapter is to promote both critique and a broader understanding of existing scholarship, which will in turn encourage greater discussion about whiteness and the sport media. Another related aim is to encourage wider conversations about the efficacy and whiteness of sport media scholarship itself in the quest for more equitable and just social conditions for all.

## ❖ RESULTS

Long before the advent of so-called "whiteness studies" in the 1990s, scholars have demonstrated the ways in which popular assumptions about sport, race, and the sport sciences themselves—with the assistance of the media—have contributed to the naturalization of the long-standing U.S. Black-White racial binary through an excessive preoccupation with the athletic performance of Black, mostly male sporting bodies. In the following section I review some key ideas from social constructionist perspectives related to the historical writings about sport and race; delineate important content analyses that demonstrate the media's role in perpetuating racial stereotypes, especially in elite football and basketball; theorize about the role of media producers in this process; and discuss the power of these mediated constructions of White identities. In addition, I review the emerging poststructuralist and interdisciplinary scholarship that treats media content as texts that must be read and analyzed against a variety of changing contexts.

### Narratives in Black and White: The Media's Historical Role in Promoting Mind-Body Dualisms

Early 20th century racist science greatly impacted dominant interpretations of athletic performances in peculiar ways. At this time African Americans were excluded by Whites from widespread participation in sport and thus when Blacks and Whites did compete, the events proved to be spectacular symbols of contemporary race relations. Think only of the narratives used to explain the successes of the early 20th century heavyweight Black boxing champion Jack Johnson. As the specter of Black boxing success became more widely publicized in the burgeoning print sport media, theories of White supremacy promoted by racist science still held that Whites were both physically superior and intellectually advanced and that Blacks possessed weak minds and flawed physical constituencies. The White sporting press helped to further fuel White fears and defensiveness at the thought of Black masculine boxing success or what Charles Dana, then editor of the *New York Sun*, referred to in 1895 as the "growing menace." When Jack Johnson beat Tommy Burns in 1908 in Sydney for the heavyweight title, the White press called for the "The Great White Hope" (also known as Jim Jeffries) to return from retirement to reassert White control and entitlement. As Johnson's success continued, Jeffries, who had refused to fight Black men during his previous tenure as champion, stated "that portion of the white race that has been looking to me to defend its athletic superiority may feel assured that I am fit to do my very best" (cited in Levine, 1977, p. 430).

Jeffries may have been widely characterized as the "Great White Hope," but Johnson defeated him, spawning rioting by Whites in many U.S. cities while also destroying Black inferiority storylines rooted in the mythologies used to justify slavery and Jim Crow segregation laws. However, due to the pervasiveness of racist science and the White-dominated media, these myths were retooled and widely disseminated into the 21st century so that Black athletic performance became equated with physical superiority while White athletes were presumed to be inherently culturally and emotionally superior (Bass, 2002).

## Promoting Racial Stereotypes Via Media
## Constructions of Basketball and Football

A considerable number of content analyses have established that sport journalists and broadcasters continue to promote essentialistic thinking by disproportionately praising White athletes as possessing outstanding intellect and industriousness and Black athletes as possessing the presumed "natural" talents of quickness, physical strength, speed, jumping ability, and force (Davis & Harris, 1998; Goss, Tyler, & Billings, Chapter 9, in this volume; Grainger, Newman, & Andrews, 2006; Smith, 1990). While critics contend that content analyses have limitations in reifying existing racial categories and in merely describing attributes associated with particular bodies, such inquiries are also frequently grounded in social constructionist theories of race and theories of the media power. Often analyses of sport commentary conceive of the media as powerful gatekeepers with the ability to frame events and promote stereotypes, which help shape public perception and agendas (Billings, 2004). This means that sport announcers and journalists help to promote racial meanings via coded language and formulaic storylines, which construct Black athletes as inherently different and as "other" in relationship to their White counterparts (Billings, 2004).

For instance, Jackson (1989) noted that over the course of two seasons in the late 1980s profession add "al" to end of word football and college basketball television announcers more frequently made "brawn" comments about Black players in highlighting their apparent size, strength, quickness, etc., while characterizing White athletes as lacking such exceptional physical traits but possessing intelligence and leadership capabilities. A more recent study of men's and women's college basketball commentary found that the "traditional prejudices against black players and the concomitant flatter of white players persist," so much so that the study's authors suggest that "stereotypes seem to be the language of sport, at least in college basketball, and few sportscasters make an effort to break out of the patterns of speech used by their predecessors" (Eastman & Billings, 2001, p. 198). An additional dynamic related to the intersections of race and gender was also detected in the study. White women received a disproportionate number of commentaries from announcers in relation to their Black female counterparts thus "revealing a kind of favoritism not exhibited nowadays in men's basketball announcing" (Eastman & Billings, 2001, p. 198).

James Rada and K. Time Wulfemeyer's (2005) analysis of college football and men's basketball commentary found that the pattern of promoting Black physicality and White intelligence still persists. Their study also explored positive and negative characterizations offered by announcers about the players as people beyond the playing fields. All of the negative statements made about personal character, "off-the-field" intelligence, and human interest were directed toward African Americans, while White players were praised within each of these categories. Thus, not only do announcers portray Blacks and Whites as different types of athletes, they also infer that Black behavior is at odds with cherished social expectations and values.

There is some evidence that in particular cases announcers may be making more positive assertions in regards to Black male leadership and intellect perhaps partially thanks to the coaching that these broadcasters now receive in order to provide more equitable commentary (Denham, Billings, & Halone, 2002). It should be noted that this change was accompanied by a concurrent overemphasis on Black physicality and was initially detected during a study of the 2000 Men's and Women's Basketball Final Four Tournament commentary. The study's authors speculated that a component of this change may also be attributed to the disproportionate number of comments offered about the leadership abilities of one Black athlete, Michigan State point guard Mateen Cleaves (Denham, Billings, & Halone, 2002).

Commentary about Black quarterbacks seems to be undergoing yet another shift in that some announcers are now providing more enlightened characterizations regarding the growing presence and intellectual capabilities of Black National Football League (NFL) quarterbacks (Billings, 2004; Buffington, 2005). While media personnel do acknowledge the historical barriers that limit Black access to the quarterback position, they often do so with rhetoric that champions the new need for race-neutral understandings of social life (Buffington, 2005). In a similar way the movement by some announcers to characterize Black quarterbacks as intellectually competent is often muted by the persistent characterization of Black quarterbacks as athletically superior to their White counterparts (Billings, 2004; Buffington, 2005).

❖ SPORT MEDIA PRODUCERS

While most of the scholarship on race and the media focuses on media content, especially televised content, a few scholars have documented the White-dominated structure of the sport media by delineating the demographic makeup of those producing media sport. Despite some notable exceptions particularly with television sideline reporters and with announcers in the sports of baseball, basketball, and football, White males are overrepresented as producers of mainstream media (Coventry, 2004). Sport equity activist Richard Lapchick (2006) argues that this numerical overrepresentation among newspaper producers is troubling:

> It is important to have voices from different backgrounds in the media. When 94.7 percent of the sports editors, 86.7 percent of the assistant sports editors, 89.9 percent of our columnists, 87.4 percent of our reporters and 89.7 percent of our copy editors/designers are white, and those same positions are 95, 87, 93, 90 and 87 percent male, we clearly do not have a group that reflects America's workforce. And in the world of sports, they are covering a disproportionate number of athletes in basketball, football and baseball who are African-American or Latino. On the high school and college levels, more than 40 percent of the student-athletes are girls and women. (Lapchick, Brenden, & Wright, 2006, p. 1)

While a diverse labor force may potentially "provide a different perspective" (Lapchick, Brenden, & Wright, 2006, p. 4) as currently organized, the White-owned and controlled commercial sport media mainly continue to perform a gatekeeping role while White male broadcasters and journalists serve in important positions as the "voices of authority" (Messner, Dunbar, & Hunt, 2000).

## The Power of Racialized Media Narratives

In sum, despite notable counterexamples, much as with the racist assertions of early 20th century White press and racist science, White-dominated media characterizations frequently infer that White bodies inherently excel in the culturally valued status positions as leaders, hard workers, and authoritative experts. Despite some recent trends to laud intellectual capabilities, a sizable portion of sport commentary infers that Black bodies possess natural athleticism. The overall and persistent emphasis on Black physicality undercuts progressive gains in subtly inferring that Blacks generally lack the intellectual necessities and discipline necessary to succeed in the wider society (Harris, 1991). In this way, the contemporary sport media deploy whiteness as an essentializing strategy by "reproducing one of the most pervasive stereotypes of African Americans: They have the physical tools, but their intellect is questionable. On the other hand the real praise is reserved for white players" for their inherent ability to persevere and prevail despite their "modest athletic endowment" (Harris, 2000, p. 69).

Given these insights, the process of media stereotyping must be understood "as an effect of power—as a discursive strategy that attempts to establish particular subject positions as fixed, often degenerate types, as a way of legitimating social hierarchies and inequalities" that, as exemplified in the cases cited here, seek to secure White privilege (Carrington, 2002, p. 5). Thus the sport media's preoccupation with promoting racial stereotypes often serves to naturalize "the categories of 'black' and 'white,'" thereby inferring that these cultural constructions are "fixed, unambiguous and dichotomous" instead of arbitrary distinctions historically forged under the illusion of immutability (Davis, 1990, p. 180). Understood from this perspective, contemporary sport announcers' comments, sport journalist characterizations, and other forms of media representation serve as important sites "for the construction and constitution of identities, collective and individual, rather than merely being a secondary reflection of already formed social identities" (Carrington, 2002, p. 5). Importantly this perspective also suggests that the legacies of White supremacy must be constantly struggled over and negotiated in the interest of social justice and in order to challenge the essentializing power of whiteness (Carrington, 2002).

## ❖ WHITENESS, SPORT MEDIA TEXTS, AND CONTEXTS

Indebted to theoretical movements within interdisciplinary scholarship, especially within critical race theory, ethnic studies, communication studies, cultural studies, and gender and women's studies, since the 1990s there has been a rise in scholarly writings that delineate the historically and contextually specific workings of White power in a variety of realms, including sport (McDonald, 2005). Unlike previous studies embedded in agenda setting or framing theories, these accounts focus on media representations as one crucial element of discursive regimes. These analyses assume race and racialized bodies to be effects of a powerful set of shifting political relations. Among the most valuable insights from this interdisciplinary work is the contention that the 20th and 21st century technologies of film, television, advertising, video, and the Internet have also produced a different visual economy than that promoting whiteness through 19th century structures of slavery (Wiegman, 1995).

In North America, contemporary capitalist consumer and sport cultures are composed of an array of signs, texts, images, and commodifed bodies seemingly promoting freedom and transcendence even though social structures, discourses, and practices still seek to maintain White hegemony. Thus among the most powerful force of whiteness in this contemporary moment "is the visual and verbal masking and trivializing of deep economic, cultural and psychic disparities and inequities on the one hand, and the rigid maintenance of naïve individualism and rhetorical democracy on the other" (Wiegman, 1995, p. 42).

This scholarship focuses on several overlapping themes, three of which I briefly introduce and characterize below: sport spectacles and the sanitizing and normalizing power of whiteness; media assertions of heroic White masculinity in the face of cultural change, backlash, and uncertainty; and the contradictions and paradoxes of whiteness and sport.

## Sport Spectacles and the Sanitizing and Normalizing Power of Whiteness

This trivializing and masking process is powerfully demonstrated in the representational spectacles that surround the use, promotion, and celebration of Native American mascots in sport. According to Staurowsky (2007), fans attending athletic contests featuring their favorite college teams such as the North Dakota Fighting Sioux and the Florida State University Seminoles are encouraged by both cheerleaders and tradition to perform a longstanding White script in self-identifying with and even "becoming" American Indians. In some instances this "identification with" has intensified as a form of backlash against the NCAA's recently imposed policy banning American Indian mascots from their tournaments. This continuing desire and elevated quest to "play Indian" is additionally problematic as Native American sport mascots are White caricatures of indigenous people and of the past.

One case in point is the strange spectacle of painted White faces, the "Tomahawk chop," and fans chanting in unison that are frequently broadcasted on radio and television locally, nationally, and globally, thus normalizing White fantasies of American Indians. Importantly, the uncritical proliferation of this type of fictional imagery renders "invisible the ignominious history of American Indian genocide by the U.S. government replacing it with the comfortable and comforting myth of the 'American Indian warrior'" (Staurowsky, 2007, p. 62). The result is a mythological version of the past—a metaphoric and literal "white out" (King & Springwood, 2001a, p. 39) where a history of White imperialism is erased and replaced by sanitized performances of White identification with fairy tales of "Indianness."

A similar dynamic can be seen in other sporting contexts. For example, while the considerable accomplishments of tennis players Venus and Serena Williams have been celebrated by fans and the media, at other times the sisters have been treated with ambivalence, and in the case of the tournament at Indian Wells, California, in 2001, with overt hostility and distain as Douglas (2005) demonstrates. Shifting the analytic gaze unto the fans and media's reaction to the players demonstrates that Whites lead racially structured lives with the cultural power to construct dominant understandings of events, which also ensure that White actions, advantages, and interpretations largely escape scrutiny. In this incident, fan, player, and media accounts dismissively intimated that Venus's withdrawal from the Indian Wells tournament due to injury was actually directed by her father William in an effort to "fix matches," ensuring an easier route for sister Serena. In actuality, the chorus of boos designed to humiliate Serena Williams in the finals of the tournament and the media narratives that maligned her family's character represent displaced fears and anxieties over the presence of successful Black women in the normative space of women's professional tennis, which previously lauded middle-class White femininity (Douglas 2005). The relentless focus on the family's character additionally serves as a "sincere fiction," a normalizing and rationalizing process whereby Whites make sense of their attitudes and behaviors without acknowledging complicity in the perpetuation of racism (Spencer, 2004, p. 116).

## Media Assertions of Heroic White Masculinity in the Face of Cultural Change, Backlash, and Uncertainty

A number of scholars have examined the ways in which the media promotion of normative visions of such sport celebrities as baseball player Cal Ripken, Jr. (Nathan & McDonald, 2001); cyclist Lance Armstrong (Kusz, 2001); tennis player Andre Agassi (Kusz, 2001); America's Cup sailor Sir Peter Blake (Cosgrove & Bruce, 2005); professional basketball player Susie McConnell-Serio (McDonald, 2002); and within long distance running (Walton & Butryn, 2006) and extreme sports (Kusz, 2001) also serve to reassert white hegemony. This work is consistent with recent post-structuralist scholarship which conceives of sport celebrities and sporting events as texts or as analytic entry points into broader social relations within particular salient contexts (Birrell & McDonald, 2000).

While each analysis details particular local social formations, a sizable portion of these works delineate the varied ways in which iconic images of White sporting masculinity are made to serve as comforting figures amidst the confusion, backlash, and ambiguity brought on by cultural and economic changes. For instance, as Cal Ripken, Jr. was chasing and beating Lou Gehrig's Major League Baseball record 2,130 consecutive game streak, he was discussed in the media as "an ideal role model," a "throwback player," and as a symbol of reliability and durability—qualities allegedly representative of the bygone era of Gehrig. Yet, such accounts offered highly selective versions of the past devoid of any controversy or sordid details from the 1920s and 1930s, including the stock market crash and the subsequent Great Depression, the end of the first wave feminist movement, and the entrenchment of Jim Crow segregation. Instead, back in contemporary times and amidst lingering fan discontent over a settled Major League Baseball strike, rising major league baseball contracts, discourses admonishing Black players for selfish styles of play, and of broader changes brought on by deindustrialization and globalization, Ripken was nostalgically mediated as a workmanlike persona committed to the simple joys of baseball and his own nuclear family (Nathan & McDonald, 2001). In short, representations of Ripken offered Whites an imaginary image of heroic White masculinity and nostalgic White innocence as antidotes to rapidly changing times (Nathan & McDonald, 2001).

In New Zealand the death of adventurer and sailor Sir Edward Blake offers a comparable opportunity to understand the role that narratives of heroic White masculinity play in reestablishing particular national imaginings (Cosgrove & Bruce, 2005). Media discussions surrounding Blake's death lauded the America's Cup sailor as emblematic of the authentic character of New Zealand as "truly a Kiwi" in being successful but modest, inspirationally uncompromising, committed to egalitarian values, and dedicated to preserving the beauty of nature. In death, Blake "served as a symbol of whiteness and a sense of identity that has been challenged by growing indigenous political power, an increasingly diverse population and radical shifts in the social values underpinning New Zealand society" (Cosgrove & Bruce, 2005, p. 349).

The ubiquitous circulation of sporting images lauding heroic White masculinity not only seek to reassert particular visions of social life but, at times, also articulate local struggles in important ways. This is certainly the case when allegations of domestic violence or charges of rape are made by women against White middle-class sporting figures. Given the articulating structures of White, masculine, and class privilege, in these instances the accused White men "are often endowed with an unacknowledged cultural capital that makes claims of individualism, innocence and redeemable character seem far more plausible then when men of color are accused of violent actions" (McDonald, 1999, p. 125).

Closer inspection of the public and media reactions to rape accusations made against three Duke University lacrosse players helps illustrate this point (Leonard, 2007). While the players were eventually cleared of all the charges, the initial public and media reaction to the allegations suggested shock and disbelief that students from such a prestigious and privileged university and athletic department could have ever committed such a crime. Ignoring the legacy of sexual violence perpetrated by White men of means against Black women, media and cyberspace accounts drew upon the increasingly common trope and backlash strategy of proclaiming White victimhood (also see Kusz, 2001) in order to dismiss the seriousness of the allegations made against the players. In a time of increased scrutiny and visibility in regard to discourses of domestic and sexual violence committed by male college and professional athletes, defensive media and cyberspace responses suggested that the players' athletic identities were either meaningless or proof of their innocence. Thanks to the normative power of White masculinity, this rush to innocence stands in stark contrast to a frequent rush to judgment, which too often demonizes Black men when similar allegations of rape are made (Leonard, 2007).

## Contradictions and Paradoxes of Whiteness and Sport

A growing number of essays have revealed the ways that whiteness frequently operates through contradictory, competing discourses. For example, according to Brayton (2005), commercialized skateboarding is not only about White victimhood and White backlash where Whites use the sport to reassert their cultural dominance. Rather, advertisers frequently market skateboarding as the epitome of White countercultural resistance to the repressive uniformity of White corporate culture. Skate magazines, movies, advertisements, and the packaging for the skate products themselves celebrate the rebellious White skater, much like the Bohemian "Beat" culture of the 1950s. These images offer progressive elements in challenging the normativity of middle-class White masculinity. Yet they frequently do so by promoting the rebellious skater and skate products through stereotypical signs of urban blackness and style, including the use of Rap music, baggy skate clothing, graffiti, gang symbols, and the marketing of such products as skateboards under the brand name of "Ghetto Child."

The signs of blackness co-opted in order to associate skateboarding with coolness are problematic on several fronts. First they represent the appropriation of a fantasized other in the form of stereotypical representations of urban blackness that only exist in the White imagination. Second, those White skaters who "take up" and perform this urban Black persona have the ability to do so without the fear of oppressive elements, such as police harassment that frequently greet urban Black youth. Finally, the images of rebellious masculinity are offered through capitalist commodity culture as styles further limiting the resistant possibilities of the skater-rebel. Brayton (2005) concludes that while the whiteness of skate culture cannot be simply equated with backlash politics, any effective progressive agenda must begin by fully engaging the daily material struggles over White privilege.

Contradictory sensibilities are also evident in the 2003 controversy created by conservative radio commentator and then ESPN *NFL Countdown* analyst Rush Limbaugh in relationship to then Philadelphia Eagles quarterback Donovan McNabb. A few weeks into his brief 2003 ESPN stint, Limbaugh claimed that McNabb had not been "that good from the get-go . . . what we have here is a little social concern in the NFL." He continued that the "media has been very desirous that a black quarterback" do well, thus McNabb received "credit for the performance of his team that he didn't deserve. The defense [has] carried this team" (Hartmann, 2007, p. 46).

When critics challenged his remarks, Limbaugh denied any racial intent. Instead he argued his comments were solely about McNabb's football performance, whereas the mainstream media was overly sympathetic to McNabb. Despite this color-blind defense, Limbaugh's logic served racist ends by failing to acknowledge the persistent institutional barriers and discrimination that Black athletes still face in sport (Hartmann, 2007).

An enlightened, some might say, progressive public response saw Limbaugh routinely critiqued in popular and media commentaries, and he subsequently resigned from his ESPN stint. While the story seems like a straightforward case, a close reading of the media narratives generated around the event reveals the subtle, complicated, and contradictory ways that whiteness works. Similar "sanctity of sport" and color-blind narratives that Limbaugh used were also mobilized by many of his critics to censure him. Only a minority of commentators surveyed actually condemned the comments as racist, while others denied the salience of this charge by instead using color-evasive language to suggest that Limbaugh was inexperienced and out of his element in commenting about professional sport. Still others claimed that sport exists as an apolitical arena, and these commentators chastised Limbaugh for allegedly bringing race and racism into the pure space of sport. Hartmann (2007) suggests that to these critics Limbaugh's biggest offense was ignoring the White mandate of pretending that sport is racially neutral as Limbaugh's comments potentially brought the persistence of racism in the NFL into clearer view.

## ❖ DISCUSSION

This chapter demonstrates that whiteness is insinuated throughout cultural formations and everyday practices. It is apparent in the contemporary media's preoccupation with promoting racialized mind-body dualisms within sport and the wider U.S. culture (Davis, 1990). This preoccupation has grown from the classic U.S. Black-White racial binary and can be seen most vividly in the coverage of the visible spectacles of professional and college basketball and football where African American men are numerically overrepresented in relationship to their White counterpart. While there are some content analyses that offer insight into media representations outside of the White-Black binary, the majority of the scholarship frequently fails to illuminate the construction of whiteness vis-à-vis other "races" and in relation to media coverage of women's sports. Such a sustained focus still awaits further scholarly attention.

Still, the numerous examples cited here all illustrate the contradictory, normative, often insidiousness of whiteness that interested scholars of the sport media must continue to carefully discuss, delineate, and challenge. As increasing numbers of scholars shift the analytic gaze to focus on the ways in which whiteness operates via sporting discourses, they will also encounter the enabling and constraining challenges—the progressive and dangerous elements of such investigations. Future care, dialogue, and work are needed to resist the power of whiteness to reassert normativity even within critical media scholarship. Care must also be taken to broaden the analytic focus to more fully delineate the workings of whiteness within women's sports and contemporary relations of gender and sexuality as well as among a variety of sporting communities of color, including but not limited to Latina/os, Asian Americans, and Native Americans. More scholarship is needed to explore the complex intersections of sport, whiteness, gender, nationality, ability, and sexuality both within and beyond local North American contexts. Such a focus will no doubt require different analytic tools and the deployment of emerging theoretical perspectives in order to map the complex global performances of whiteness and sport.

## ❖ REFERENCES

Abdel-Shehid, G. (2005). *Who da man? Black masculinities and sporting cultures.* Toronto: Canadian Scholars.

Andrews, D. L. (1996). The fact(s) of Michael Jordan's blackness: Excavating a floating racial signifier. *Sociology of Sport Journal, 13*(4), 315–318.

Bass, A. (2002). *Not the triumph but the struggle: The 1968 Olympics and the making of the black athlete.* Minneapolis: University of Minnesota Press.

Billings, A. C. (2004). Depicting the quarterback in black and white: A content analysis of college and professional football broadcast commentary. *The Howard Journal of Communications, 15*(4), 201–210.

Birrell, S., & McDonald, M. G. (2000). Reading sport, articulating power lines: An introduction. In S. Birrell & M. G. McDonald (Eds.), *Reading sport: Critical essays on power and representation* (pp. 3–13). Boston: Northeastern University Press.

Brayton, S. (2005). "Blacklash": Revisiting the "white negro" through skateboarding [Special issue, Whiteness and Sport]. *Sociology of Sport Journal, 22*(3), 256–372.

Buffington, D. (2005). Contesting race on Sundays: Making meaning out of the rise in the number of black quarterbacks. *Sociology of Sport Journal, 21,* 19–37.

Carrington, B. (2002). *"Race," representation and the sporting body.* CUCR's Occasional Paper Series. London: Goldsmith College.

Cole, C. L. (1996). American Jordan: P.L.A.Y., consensus and punishment. *Sociology of Sport Journal, 13*(4), 366–397.

Cosgrove, A., & Bruce, T. (2005). "The way New Zealanders would like to see themselves": Reading white masculinity via media coverage of the death of Sir Peter Blake [Special issue, Whiteness and Sport]. *Sociology of Sport Journal, 22*(3), 236–255.

Coventry, B. (2004). On the sidelines: Sex and racial segregation in televised sports broadcasting. *Sociology of Sport Journal, 21*(4), 322–341.

Davis, L. R. (1990). The articulation of difference: White preoccupation with the question of racially linked genetic difference among athletes. *Sociology of Sport Journal, 7*(3), 179–187.

Davis, L. R., & Harris, O. (1998). Race and ethnicity in U.S. sport media. In L. A. Wenner (Ed.), *MediaSport* (pp. 154–169). London: Routledge.

Denham, B. E., Billings, A. C., & Halone, K. K. (2002). Differential accounts of race in broadcast commentary of the 2000 NCAA Men's and Women's Final Four basketball tournaments. *Sociology of Sport Journal 19*(3), 315–332.

Doane, W., & Bonilla-Silva, E. (Eds.). (2003). *White out: The continuing significance of racism.* New York: Routledge.

Douglas, D. (2005). Venus, Serena, and the Women's Tennis Association (WTA): When and where "race" enters [Special issue, Whiteness and Sport]. *Sociology of Sport Journal, 2*(3), 256–282.

Dyson, M. E. (2004). *The Michael Eric Dyson reader.* New York: Basic Civitas.

Eastman, S. T., & Billings, A. C. (2001). Biased voices of sports: Racial and gender stereotyping in college basketball announcing. *The Howard Journal of Communications, 12,* 183–201.

Ellsworth, E. (1997). Double binds of whiteness. In M. Fine, L. Weis, L. C. Powell, & L. Wong (Eds.), *Off white: Readings on race, power and society* (pp. 259–269). New York: Routledge.

Feder-Kane, A. (2000). "A radiant smile from the lovely lady": Overdetermined femininity in ladies figure skating. In S. Birrell & M. G. McDonald (Eds.),

*Reading sport: Critical essays on power and representation* (pp. 206–233). Boston: Northeastern University.

Gabriel, J. (1998). *Whitewash: Racialized politics and the media.* London: Routledge.

Grainger, A., Newman, J., & Andrews, D. (2006). Sport, the media and the construction of race. In A. Raney & B. Jennings (Eds.), *Handbook of sports and media* (pp. 447–467). Mahwah, NJ: Lawrence Erlbaum.

Harris, O. (1991). The image of the African American in psychological journals, 1825–1923. *The Black Scholar, 21*(4), 25–29.

Harris, O. (2000). African-American predominance in college sport. In D. Brooks & R. Althouse (Eds.), *Racism in college sport: The African American athlete's experience* (pp. 51–74). Morgantown, WV: Fitness Information Technology.

Hartmann, D. (2007). Rush Limbaugh, Donovan McNabb, and "a little social concern": Reflections on the problems of whiteness in contemporary American sport [Special issue, White Power and Sport]. *Journal of Sport and Social Issues, 33*(1), 45–60.

Hoose, P. (1989). *Necessities: Racial barriers in American sport.* New York: Random House.

Houck, D. (2006). Crouching Tiger, hidden blackness: Tiger Woods and the disappearance of race. In A. Raney & J. Bryant (Eds.), *The handbook of sports and media* (pp. 469–484). Mahwah, NJ: Lawrence Erlbaum.

Jackson, D. (1989, January 22). Calling the plays in black and white: Will today's Super Bowl be black brawn versus white brains? *The Boston Globe,* p. A25.

Jackson, S. J. (1998). A twist of race: Ben Johnson and the Canadian crises of racial and national identity. *Sociology of Sport Journal, 15*(1), 21–40.

King, C. R. (2005). Cautionary notes on whiteness and sport studies [Special issue, Whiteness and Sport]. *Sociology of Sport Journal, 22*(3), 397–408.

King, C. R., & Springwood, C. F. (2001a). *Beyond the cheers: Race as spectacle in college sport.* Albany: SUNY Press.

King, C. R., & Springwood, C. F. (Eds.). (2001b). *Team spirits: The Native American mascot controversy.* Lincoln: University of Nebraska Press.

Kusz, K. (2001). "I want to be the minority": The cultural politics of young white males in sport and popular culture. *Journal of Sport and Social Issues, 25*(4), 390–416.

Lapchick, R., Brenden, J., & Wright, B. (2006). *The 2006 racial and gender report card of the Associated Press sports editors: Executive summary.* PDF retrieved July 25, 2007, from http://www.bus.ucf.edu

Leonard, D. (2007). Innocent until proven innocent: In defense of Duke lacrosse and white power (and against menacing black student-athletes, a black stripper, activists and the Jewish media) [Special issue, White Power and Sport]. *Journal of Sport and Social Issues, 33*(1), 25–45.

Levine, L. (1977). *Black culture and black consciousness: Afro-American folk thought from slavery to freedom.* New York: Oxford University Press.

Levine-Rasky, C. (Ed.). (2002). *Working through whiteness: International perspectives.* Albany, NY: SUNY Press.

Lipsyte, R., & Levine, P. (1995). *Idols of the game: A sporting history of the American Century.* Atlanta: Turner.

McDonald, M. G. (1996). Michael Jordan's family values: Marketing, meaning and post Reagan America. *Sociology of Sport Journal, 13*(4), 344–365.

McDonald, M. G. (1999). Unnecessary roughness: Gender and racial politics in domestic violence media events. *Sociology of Sport Journal, 16*(2), 111–133.

McDonald, M. G. (2002). Queering whiteness: The peculiar case of the Women's National Basketball Association. *Sociological Perspectives, 45*(4), 379–396.

McDonald, M. G. (2005). Mapping whiteness and sport: An introduction [Special issue, Whiteness and Sport]. *Sociology of Sport Journal, 22*(3), 245–255.

McDonald, M. G. (2006). Beyond the pale: The whiteness of queer and sport studies scholarship. In J. C. Caudwell (Ed.), *Sport, sexualities, and queer theory* (pp. 33– 45). London: Routledge.

McDonald, M. G. (2008). *Dialogues on whiteness, leisure, and (anti)racism.* George Butler Lecture presented at the Leisure Research Symposium during the 2008 National Recreation and Park Association Congress and Exhibition, Baltimore, MD.

Messner, M., Dunbar, M., & Hunt, D. (2000). The television sports manhood formula. *Journal of Sport and Social Issues, 24*(4), 380–394.

Morrison, T. (1992). *Playing in the dark: Whiteness and the literary imagination.* Cambridge, MA: Harvard University Press.

Nakayama, T., & Krizek, R. (1995). Whiteness: A strategic rhetoric. *Quarterly Journal of Speech, 81,* 291–309.

Nakayama, T. K., & Martin, J. N. (Eds.). (1999). *Whiteness: The communication of social identity.* Thousand Oaks, CA: Sage.

Nathan, D., & McDonald, M. G. (2001). Yearning for yesteryear: Cal Ripken, Jr., the streak and the politics of nostalgia. *American Studies, 42*(1), 99–123.

Omi, M., & Winant, H. (1986). *Racial formation in the United States: From the 1960s to the 1980s.* New York: Routledge.

Rada, J., & Wulfemeyer, K. T. (2005). Color coded: Racial descriptors in television coverage of intercollegiate sport. *Journal of Broadcasting & Electronic Media, 49*(1), 65–85.

Smith, E. (1990). The genetically superior athlete: Myth or reality? In T. Anderson (Ed.), *Black studies: Theory, method and cultural perspective* (pp. 120–131). Pullman, WA: Washington State University Press.

Spencer, N. (2004). Sister act IV: Venus and Serena Williams at Indian Wells: "Sincere fictions" and white racism. *Journal of Sport and Social Issues, 28*(2), 115–135.

Staurowsky, E. (2007). "You know we are all Indian": Exploring white power and privilege in reaction to the NCAA Native American mascot policy [Special issue, White Power and Sport]. *Journal of Sport and Social Issues, 33*(1), 61–76.

Walton, T., & Butryn, T. (2006). Policing the race: U.S. men's distance running and the crises of whiteness. *Sociology of Sport Journal, 23*(1), 1–28.

Wiegman, R. (1995). *American anatomies: Theorizing race and gender.* Durham, NC: Duke University Press.

Winnubst, S. (2006). *Queering freedom.* Bloomington: Indiana University Press.

# 9

# A Content Analysis of Racial Representations of NBA Athletes on *Sports Illustrated* Magazine Covers, 1970–2003

Benjamin D. Goss

Andrew L. Tyler

Andrew C. Billings

Researchers have suggested that issues of recognition and equality are continually negotiated for Black Americans, specifically within mediasport (Billings, 2004; Entine, 2000; Rada, 1996; Rada & Wulfemeyer, 2005). Dufur (1998) and Eitzen and Sage (2003) observe that all forms of print and broadcast journalism, movies, books, and other scholarly works have contributed to the current nebulous state of racial discussion within our country. As a result, popular beliefs (often in the form of stereotypes) articulated about race have had a major impact on sport as people perpetuate ideas and beliefs about skin color within society (Coakley, 2007; Sage, 2005). For instance, a White high school football and basketball star was asked by a sportswriter what sport he intended to pursue in college. He responded: "I guess, right now, I'd take football because it's more unique to be a 6' 6" quarterback than a 6' 6" *White* forward" (Coakley, 1998, p. 249). A common explanation for the high percentage of Blacks in professional sport is that they are presumed to be naturally better athletes (Berlow, 1994; King, 2007) and excel because of perceived physical supremacy (Eitzen & Sage, 2003).

However, the essentialist function of the problem is not the assumption that Black basketball players can jump higher and run faster than White players. Rather, Carlston (1986) contends that broadcasters' commentaries often portray the differences between the styles of play of Blacks and Whites to be so stark that they appear to be playing two entirely different versions of the same game. Denham, Billings, and Halone (2002) analyzed some of these notions empirically within an examination of the NCAA Final Four; while some deviations persisted (e.g., Blacks [primarily Mateen Cleaves of Michigan State] received bountiful comments about leadership), the authors concluded that substantial dialogic differences can be unearthed within sports commentary.

Representation within mass media becomes a primary correlate of these types of ethnic differences, with studies finding underrepresentation of Blacks in many other aspects of modern society (Tomaskovic-Devey, 1994). Black Americans have, however, achieved marked representational progress in professional sport, though appropriate credit given by mass media for such accomplishments is debated (Dewar, 1993; Edwards, 1969). Since Jackie Robinson broke baseball's modern-era color barrier in 1947 (Beller, Lumpkin, & Stoll, 1999), the participation of Black athletes in professional sport has increased drastically (Coakley, 2007; Dufur, 1998; Eitzen & Sage, 2003). For example, Black Americans currently make up approximately 12% of the U.S. population but comprise 73% of the players in the National Basketball Association (Lapchick, 2006).

As the participation of Black athletes in professional sport has grown, the opportunity for these athletes to become public figures is propagated within the media, with sport becoming the world's broadest cultural common denominator (Coakley, 2007; Lapchick, 1986). For instance, the proportion of column inches devoted to sport in newspapers and magazines far exceeds those devoted to politics, national affairs, and education (Lapchick, 1986; Moretti, 2005). As a result, this deluge of sport-related print media has created an increase in photographic portrayals of professional athletes in magazines, advertisements, and other forms of mass media.

Sport is a massive commercial enterprise with markets in 2005 valued at $30 billion in the United States ("Changing sponsorship," 2006) and $80 billion globally ("Sports," 2006), and, in many cases, these photographic portrayals are designed to sell or endorse a product (Berry, 2006; Dufur, 1998). The most prominent and consistent print media within the sports nation has been *Sports Illustrated* (*SI*), a magazine with tremendous reach and a circulation of millions. *Sports Illustrated* has been popularizing athletes for decades by placing them on the front cover of issues, making them the showpieces for one of the most prominent sports magazines in the United States. However, questions percolate as to whether these portrayals differ greatly by type of pose, sport, content, and—most pertinent for this study—race.

Past research on racial portrayals has been conducted to develop knowledge concerning issues surrounding the portrayals of athletes in media, but while scholars have analyzed racial differences in radio and television broadcast commentary (Eastman & Billings, 2001; Denham, Billings, & Halone, 2002; Dewar, 1993; Rainville & McCormick, 1977), magazine advertisements (Dufur, 1998), and portrayals of Blacks in media (Andrews, 1996; Eastman & Billings, 2001; Carlston, 1986; Dufur, 1998; Hawkins, 1998; Kellner, 1996; Uchacz, 1998), little research has focused on the racialization of photographic sport images created for magazine covers. Some studies of *Sports Illustrated* have focused on gender representations (e.g., Cuneen & Sidwell, 1998; Fink & Kensicki, 2002), yet these studies only focused upon that singular identity-oriented variable. Further, little data have been collected in an attempt to discover any longitudinal changes that may have occurred in the photographic portrayals of Black and White athletes.

This study examines NBA (National Basketball Association) players as represented through the lenses of *SI* photographers. In doing so, one can determine whether White and Black NBA players have been portrayed in similar and/or dissimilar ways over time as well as pinpoint whether such trends are escalating or diminishing. Such scholarly interrogations aid in uncovering whether stereotypical traits (Blacks being naturally athletic; Whites being hardworking team players) hold true. Using content analytic methodology, this research will help to determine whether, for instance, Black NBA players are portrayed as violent, angry, sexualized, entertaining, or amusing athletes who are successful because of natural physical skills. Analysis of such stereotypical portrayals over multiple decades is clearly needed to aid the unmasking of modern-day race issues within mediasport (Wenner, 1989).

## ❖ THEORY AND RELATED LITERATURE

### Theoretical Understandings of Race

Both social learning (Bussey & Bandura, 1999) and cognitive developmental (Warin, 2000) theories offer explanations for the learning of culturally appropriate roles, ideologies, practices, and behaviors via both social reinforcement and modeling. According to these socialization theories, children learn about their expected roles in the world and strive to enact these expectations, which bring specific intrinsic and extrinsic rewards. Conversely, violations of these roles or ideologies can be met with punishment, denigration, and even, in extreme cases, violence. Social psychologists have demonstrated that many attitudes and beliefs operate at least partially on implicit/unconscious and automatic levels (Bargh & Ferguson, 2000; Greenwald & Banaji, 1995). For example, in numerous studies, most White participants show an automatic association between African Americans' names or faces and negative adjectives (Cunningham, Preacher, & Banaji, 2001).

Combining these social theories to those postulated within sport scholarship, sporting generalizations suggest that Black athletes are smooth, flashy, independent, and naturally gifted in playing styles (Coakley, 1998). In contrast, Carlston (1986) suggests that, because of supposed limited natural athletic ability, White athletes are known for possessing skills such as leadership, hard work, and heart. However, Dewar (1993) believes that these assumptions downplay the success of Black athletes and the lack of success by White athletes in professional sport. Social identity theory, referring to an individual's belief that he/she belongs to a specific group, as well as the emotional attachment that he/she feels for the group membership (Tajfel, 1972), seems particularly pertinent to this discussion of media representation because, when individuals become socially aware of their membership to a specific group, they will begin to find justification in keeping social distance from other out-groups (Suzuki, 1998). This argument may be applied to young athletes who choose to participate in sport primarily played by athletes of their same race. Coakley (1998) told the story of a young White athlete who starred on his middle school basketball team before deciding that he would participate in soccer and track in high school because he believed that Black students would likely make the basketball team. This young athlete used principles of Suzuki's (1998) argument about social identity in determining that he would not pursue future endeavors in basketball. Photographic portrayals of athletes help shape this identity-laden negotiation, as media prompts can cue people as to what they might or might not consider pursuing within sport based on social expectations.

In addition, agenda-setting theory (McCombs & Shaw, 1972) suggests that mass media do not necessarily tell the public what to think, but the media can be quite effective in telling people what to think about when pressing issues are not otherwise present in their lives. This is also highly applicable to the study of media representation as mass media spotlight certain issues that may be less visible by creating greater public awareness and shaping public perception (Dewar, 1993; Edwards, 1969). Magazines such as *Sports Illustrated* serve as powerful gatekeepers in this regard, as the cover of *SI* informs people as to what athletes and teams are considered prominent for a given week. Examples of agenda-setting in sport are present throughout mass media. Though studied and found to be freer than any other country's media from economic and government influences on its media content (Cooper-Chen, 2005), agenda-setting in American mass media is both widely acknowledged and debated, based on two assumptions: (1) that media filter and shape reality, not reflect it, and (2) that media's concentration on relatively few issues leads the public to accept those issues as more important than others.

Several photographic images that appear on the cover of *Sports Illustrated* could be interpreted as standard stereotypes of Black and White professional basketball players. For example, one cover portraying Kenyon Martin describes him as "Bad Boy: Nets Flagrant Flyer" and displays a photograph of Martin tearing off his jersey to reveal his tattoo covered body (*SI Classic Cover Collection*, 2004). Coupled with the word "flagrant," the image of Martin might lead readers to believe that he is an angry and violent player. Also, the term "flyer" creates the perception that Martin maintains an incredible natural jumping ability.

In contrast, one of the more recent covers that featured a White NBA basketball player came in 1998 when John Stockton was pictured converting a lay-up shot. Below the picture was this caption: "Wipeout! John Stockton and the *unhip* Jazz embarrass the *happenin'* [italics added] Lakers" (*SI Classic Cover Collection*, 2004). Several factors must be considered for proper contextualization of the elements on this cover to properly compare it to the Martin cover. Coupled with Stockton's role as a White point guard known more for his skillful passing than foot speed, his propensity for wearing high-rising uniform shorts that were staples of pre-1990s basketball uniforms, and his signature execution of the strategy-laden primordial pick-and-roll play with teammate Karl Malone that frequently led to efficient lay-ups instead of showy dunks, the term "unhip" might well lead readers to believe that, because of (so-called) intelligent play, Stockton's Utah Jazz squad (a team domiciled in a city situated in a noted socially conservative state) was a hard-working team that defeated the "happenin'" Los Angeles Lakers squad (a team perpetually laden with marquee players that is domiciled in America's glamorous entertainment capital and was known during the 1980s for an exciting up-tempo brand of basketball dubbed "Showtime"). Since the photographs and written text captions lead readers to think about less visible issues in the NBA, agenda-setting theory could reasonably be applied to both aforementioned covers.

## Sports Scholarship and the Intersection of Race

Researchers have conducted several studies to explain differences in the portrayals of Black and White athletes by mass media. Scholars have analyzed racial differences in magazine advertisements (Dufur, 1998), radio and television broadcast commentary (Billings, Angelini, & Eastman, 2007; Billings & Eastman, 2002, 2003; Rainville & McCormick, 1977), and contextual portrayals of Blacks in various media (Byrd & Utsler, 2007; Wonsek, 1992). Studies such as these raise important issues surrounding racial portrayals in mass media and invite further examination of portrayals of Black athletes in professional sport.

Dufur (1998) investigated advertisements with products endorsed by NBA players to determine whether Black players were more likely to be portrayed as successful because of natural abilities and if White players were portrayed as successful because of hard work, leadership, and intelligence. A content analysis of 210 advertisements featuring White (N = 119) and Black (N = 91) NBA players was performed to determine if common stereotypes could be accurately applied to media advertising coding for implied reasons for an athlete's success. Dufur (1998) concluded that Black and White athletes were equally likely to be in a posed position or pictured in color. However, a large majority of Black athletes were found to be portrayed as successful because of physical skills, while White athletes were more often portrayed as successful because of intellectual traits. Further, few ads containing White athletes emphasized their bodies, and more than one-third of the ads containing Black athletes portrayed them as violent or angry. Such findings correlate with Bass (2002), who argued, "Sport exists as a realm where Black masculinity and physicality are visually represented. When applied to the athlete, the appellation 'Black' implies a variety of inherent or, more directly, *inherited* [italics added] traits and abilities" (p. 47).

Explaining the polar extremes often used to describe Blacks in the media, Hawkins (1998) believes that Black men are portrayed as either super-athletes, super-entertainers, or super-criminals, arguing the exemplar of O. J. Simpson, who was variably offered within mediated contexts as all three at various points of his life. Similar assertions to the Black athlete as simultaneously uber-athlete and uber-criminal are made by Uchacz (1998), who maintains that mass media characterize the Black body as being violent but then argues that Tiger Woods has made a reversing impact on media representations, claiming that Woods' Cablinasian background has been used by the mass media as a change agent for racial stereotyping in American society.

Such contentions are tested in content analyses such as the one performed by Eastman and Billings (2001) in which the treatment of race and gender by sports announcers was analyzed to determine if standard racial and gender stereotypes continued to exist despite an increase in Black and female announcers. The researchers found that the number of comments made about Black and White athletes was proportional to the percentages of Black and White athletes playing college basketball. However, the study did conclude that comments by Black announcers did not contain significant differences between Black and White athletes, while White announcers emphasized White players as shooters. Overall, White announcers tended to enhance the skills of White players, while Black announcers did not exaggerate the racial portrayals of Black players (Eastman & Billings, 2001).

Entine (2000) adopts a different tack, noting that exceptional physical ability (an attribute of the usual Black stereotype) and intellectual superiority (stereotypically attributed to Whites) have historically been linked as key positive attributes of strong athletes, and that no scientific support exists for the belief that athleticism and intelligence are not inherently related. He also indicated that the dumb-jock stereotype has only recently emerged within sports telecasts and modern social beliefs. Carlston (1986) took still another angle of examining racial differences, focusing on uncovering differences between inner-city and non-city basketball. Final analysis determined that individual skills, styles, and attitudes were directly tied to the environmental surroundings in which the athlete learned to play basketball.

According to Edwards (1973), four reasons exist as to why sports have a tendency to be more prominent within the Black culture. First, Black males spend large amounts of time honing their athletic abilities while believing they will become professional athletes. Second, Black families and communities tend to over-reward achievement in athletics as compared to other areas of accomplishment. Third, Black males more likely view sports participation as a way of proving their manhood. Fourth, Blacks are afforded few role models outside the fields of sport and entertainment. While not directly mentioned in these postulations, media permeates each of these four negotiations/discussions of racial identity.

### Research Questions

Past research on racial portrayals has uncovered issues (and subsequent divergent discourses and representations) surrounding the media portrayals of athletes. While scholars have analyzed racial differences in mass media, little research has focused on comparing race portrayals in photographic images created for magazine covers. Given the prominence of the covers within mass media outlets, the importance of racial representation within the fabric of modern sport, and the relative dearth of studies examining racial images in mediasport, this study provides important longitudinal heuristics stemming from the following research questions:

> *Research Question 1a* (RQ-1a): Will photographs on *Sports Illustrated* magazine covers (1970–2003) be more likely to portray Black NBA players than White NBA players as successful because of natural physical abilities?

> *Research Question 1b* (RQ-1b): Will photographs on *Sports Illustrated* magazine covers (1970–2003) be more likely to portray White NBA players than Black NBA players as successful because of hard work and intelligence?

> *Research Question 2* (RQ-2): Will written text on *Sports Illustrated* magazine covers (1970–2003) be more likely to characterize Black NBA players than White NBA players as angry, violent, or sexualized?

> *Research Question 3* (RQ-3): Will written text on *Sports Illustrated* magazine covers (1970–2003) utilize negative qualifiers and descriptors more often to characterize Black NBA players than White players?

*Research Question 4* (RQ-4): In what ways have racialized trends regarding the portrayals of NBA athletes on *Sports Illustrated* magazine covers changed from 1970 to 2003?

## ❖ METHODOLOGICAL APPROACH

In this study, the term *race* refers to a category of people considered socially distinct because of shared genetic traits believed to be important within the group (Coakley, 1998). Using this operationalization, a content analysis of 216 *Sports Illustrated* covers featuring Black and White NBA players from January 1970 through November 2003 was used to determine differences in portrayals of Black and White athletes and whether these differences have changed over the course of time. This time period was incorporated mostly because of convenience, as *Sports Illustrated* had nostalgically printed all of these covers from this time period at the end of 2003. This sample represents just 8.4% of all *Sports Illustrated* magazine covers ever printed but 100% of all covers featuring NBA players from 1970 to 2003. Only *Sports Illustrated* covers portraying NBA players during their playing careers were coded (e.g., a retired Michael Jordan was not included within the database), but a count of covers not containing NBA players was also taken to obtain percentages. Finally, covers that featured multiple NBA players were coded individually by each athlete (unit of analysis = athlete, not cover) and for the overall message/caption on each cover.

To complete the study, the only necessary material was a collection of all 216 covers. On November 10, 2003, *Sports Illustrated* published a special edition magazine that contained pictures of every cover (Cover Index, 2003; *SI* Classic Cover Collection, 2004), with this resource providing a singular universe of investigation in which NBA-specific covers were extracted. Pictures of *Sports Illustrated* covers were also available at www.SI.com and were utilized when items from printed images needed further clarification or enhancement.

All the covers featuring NBA players during the specified time period were then coded by a single author in multiple ways. First, the athlete's race and the decade in which the cover appeared were recorded. All covers were then coded based on two attributions for athletic success in accordance with coding schemes constructed and operationalized by Billings and Eastman (2002): *natural/physical abilities* [speed, strength, physicality] and *intellectual/cognitive abilities* [leadership, intelligence, work ethic, cognitive skill]. Other visual cues within the photographs were also coded to understand differences between the portrayals of races. First, the cover photograph setting (*sport* or *non-sport*) and the overall direction of the content (*positive* or *negative*) were recorded (Lee, 1992). Next, the visual cues of apparel, exposure of body parts, and positioning of the athlete in relation to the camera were recorded. For instance, apparel was coded based on whether the athlete was in uniform, casual dress, formal dress, or a costume. Next, *facial expression, clothing, body position, actions of others* in the picture, and *messages* within the written text were coded for violence/anger and activity/passivity. For instance, *body position* involved coding for whether the athlete was standing/face toward camera, standing/face away from camera, posed below camera, or posed above camera, in addition to examinations involving active or posed positions, black-and-white or color prints, and use of special effects. Finally, written lines of text within the covers were coded for issues such as the use of the athlete's first or last name, descriptions of the athlete, and the presence of qualifying statements about the athlete (e.g., "Scoring Champ").

After the covers were coded, collected data were used to develop three tables that compare percentages using expected and anticipated frequencies analyzed within chi-square ( 2) calculations. Given the disparate sample sizes between Black and White basketball players present on *Sports Illustrated* magazine covers, this form of analysis was the most worthy choice to unearth meaningful differences in the racial depictions.

❖   RESULTS

A total of 216 *Sports Illustrated* magazine covers featured NBA players between January 1970 and November 2003. On these covers were 186 Black players, 37 White players, and two players who fit other racial classifications. Because multiple players were featured on some covers, a total of 225 NBA players were analyzed. Since only two covers contained athletes of other origins, these covers were included in the statistics but excluded from the final analysis of the topic. The 1990s was the decade with the most covers featuring NBA players, with 81 separate covers, while the 1970s had only 51 separate covers featuring NBA players. From 2000 to 2003, covers featuring NBA players accelerated in frequency, with 33 separate covers portraying 38 NBA players during that time span. Although White NBA players have appeared on the cover of *Sports Illustrated* 37 times, the vast majority (81%) of those covers appeared before 1990. In fact, since 1990, of the 114 covers featuring NBA players, only 7 have portrayed White NBA players.

To code the covers, 40 categories were developed to determine the nature of the visual and written textual portrayals of the athletes. Table 9.1 shows the percentages of *Sports Illustrated* covers featuring Black and White NBA players that contained differential portrayals regarding layout characteristics. In some situations, differences between the portrayals of Black and White players were relatively small. For example, both groups are equally likely to be pictured in color, in a posed position, and in uniform. However, Table 9.1 also supported several predictions.

As Table 9.1 shows, differences were found in answering RQ-1. Overall, 30% of the Black NBA players were portrayed as successful because of speed (74% because of strength; 78% because of body composition). In comparison, only 19% of White players were portrayed as successful because of speed, 30% because of strength, and 19% because of body composition. Results indicated that the body composition of Black NBA players was emphasized significantly more than that of White players ($2 = 49.733$; $p < .05$). The findings clearly answer RQ-1 by supporting the idea that Black NBA players are more often portrayed as successful because of natural physical abilities.

In answering RQ-1b, however, fewer differences were found. For example, a slightly greater percentage of Black players (63%) than White players (57%) were portrayed as leaders, and a nearly equal percentage of Black (10%) and White (11%) players were portrayed as hard workers. However, a greater percentage of White players (22%) than Black players (15%) were portrayed as intelligent, and a significantly greater percentage of White players than Black players ($2 = 10.160$; $p < .05$) were portrayed as mentally skilled. Overall, White players were more often portrayed as successful because of intelligence than Black players but not to the extent that might have been hypothesized.

The second aspect of analyzing the *Sports Illustrated* covers was to determine the nature of the written text passages accompanying the photographs. Table 9.2 shows the percentages of the written text content of *Sports Illustrated* covers featuring Black and White NBA players.

Overall, Table 9.2 demonstrates that the written text passages about White and Black players were not significantly different. For example, White and Black players were equally likely to have their first or last name used and to be described with a positive qualifier or positive descriptor. The written text content was also equally likely to discuss the achievement or struggle of White and Black players in their particular sport of basketball. In fact, the only significant difference found in the written text was the use of descriptors in messages about Black NBA players ($2 = 27.708$; $p < .05$).

**Table 9.1**    Layout Characteristics of Black and White NBA *SI* Covers

| Characteristic | Black NBA Players (N = 186) | | White NBA Players (N = 37) | | Other NBA Players (N = 2) | | Total NBA Players (N = 225) | |
|---|---|---|---|---|---|---|---|---|
| | N | % | N | % | N | % | N | % |
| **Portrayals** | | | | | | | | |
| Overall Positive | 149 | (80%) | 34 | (92%) | 2 | (100%) | 185 | (82%) |
| In Uniform | 169 | (91%) | 35 | (95%) | 2 | (100%) | 206 | (92%) |
| Body Exposure | 6 | (3%) | 0 | (0%) | 0 | (0%) | 6 | (3%) |
| Overall Violent | 20 | (11%) | 1 | (3%) | 0 | (0%) | 21 | (9%) |
| Overall Angry | 17 | (9%) | 1 | (3%) | 0 | (0%) | 18 | (8%) |
| Overall Sexual | 2 | (1%) | 0 | (0%) | 0 | (0%) | 2 | (1%) |
| Serious | 145 | (78%) | 30 | (81%) | 1 | (50%) | 176 | (78%) |
| Smiling/Laughing | 35 | (19%) | 6 | (16%) | 1 | (50%) | 42 | (19%) |
| **Physical Success** | | | | | | | | |
| Speed | 56 | (30%) | 7 | (19%) | 0 | (0%) | 63 | (28%) |
| Strength | 138 | (74%) | 11 | (30%) | 1 | (50%) | 150 | (67%) |
| Body Composition | 145 | (78%) | 7 | (19%) | 1 | (50%) | 153 | (68%) |
| **Intellectual Success** | | | | | | | | |
| Leader | 118 | (63%) | 21 | (57%) | 1 | (50%) | 140 | (62%) |
| Intelligence | 28 | (15%) | 8 | (22%) | 1 | (50%) | 37 | (16%) |
| Work Ethics | 19 | (10%) | 4 | (11%) | 1 | (50%) | 24 | (11%) |
| Mental Skill | 15 | (8%) | 8 | (22%) | 1 | (50%) | 24 | (11%) |
| **Layout Characteristics** | | | | | | | | |
| Posed | 47 | (25%) | 10 | (27%) | 2 | (100%) | 59 | (26%) |
| Action | 140 | (75%) | 27 | (73%) | 0 | (0%) | 167 | (74%) |
| Color | 182 | (98%) | 37 | (100%) | 2 | (100%) | 221 | (98%) |
| Special Effects | 19 | (10%) | 4 | (11%) | 0 | (0%) | 23 | (10%) |
| Others in Picture | 119 | (64%) | 27 | (73%) | 0 | (0%) | 146 | (65%) |
| Facing Away | 86 | (46%) | 15 | (41%) | 0 | (0%) | 101 | (45%) |
| Posed Above | 106 | (57%) | 16 | (43%) | 1 | (50%) | 123 | (55%) |

**Table 9.2**    Written Text Passage Characteristics of Black and White NBA *SI* Covers

| Characteristic | Black NBA Players (N = 186) | | White NBA Players (N = 37) | | Other NBA Players (N = 2) | | Total NBA Players (N = 225) | |
|---|---|---|---|---|---|---|---|---|
| | N | % | N | % | N | % | N | % |
| **Written Text Passage** | | | | | | | | |
| Name Used | 156 | (84%) | 31 | (84%) | 2 | (100%) | 189 | (84%) |
| Qualifier Used | 100 | (54%) | 17 | (46%) | 1 | (50%) | 118 | (52%) |
| Positive Qualifier | 86 | (46%) | 16 | (43%) | 1 | (50%) | 103 | (46%) |
| Negative Qualifier | 15 | (8%) | 1 | (3%) | 0 | (0%) | 16 | (7%) |
| Descriptor Used | 104 | (56%) | 18 | (49%) | 1 | (50%) | 123 | (55%) |
| Positive Descriptor | 78 | (42%) | 17 | (46%) | 1 | (50%) | 96 | (43%) |
| Negative Descriptor | 24 | (13%) | 1 | (3%) | 0 | (00%) | 25 | (11%) |
| **Written Text Content** | | | | | | | | |
| Personal Life | 17 | (5%) | 2 | (5%) | 0 | (0%) | 19 | (8%) |
| Victim | 4 | (0%) | 0 | (0%) | 0 | (0%) | 4 | (2%) |
| Athlete in Sport | 169 | (91%) | 35 | (95%) | 2 | (100%) | 206 | (92%) |
| Struggle in Sport | 19 | (10%) | 5 | (14%) | 0 | (0%) | 24 | (11%) |
| Achievement in Sport | 128 | (69%) | 24 | (65%) | 1 | (50%) | 153 | (68%) |
| Personal Health | 2 | (1) | 0 | (0%) | 0 | (0%) | 2 | (1%) |
| Overall Violent | 20 | (11) | 1 | (3%) | 0 | (0%) | 21 | (9%) |
| Overall Angry | 17 | (0%) | 1 | (3%) | 0 | (0%) | 18 | (8%) |
| Overall Sexual | 2 | (1%) | 0 | (0%) | 0 | (0%) | 2 | (1%) |

In answering RQ-2, the findings of overall violent, angry, or sexual written text passages aligned with the findings of the overall visual portrayals. Approximately 11% of Black players were referred to as violent, 9% as angry, and 1% as sexual. In contrast, only one cover (3%) referred to a White player as violent and angry; no covers portrayed a White player as sexual.

The use of qualifiers and descriptors provided more evidence in supporting the claim that Black players are portrayed negatively more often than White players. Overall, 54% of the written text passages accompanying Black players used qualifiers, and 56% used descriptors. Similarly, 46% of the messages referring to White players used qualifiers and 49% used descriptors. Most important in answering RQ-3 is the use of negative qualifiers and descriptors. While 8% of the messages accompanying Black players used negative qualifiers, only one cover (3%) portraying a White player used a negative qualifier. Likewise, 13% of messages used a negative descriptor when referring to Black players, while only one cover used a negative descriptor with a White player.

The most telling findings from this study are evident in Table 9.3. Table 9.3 shows changes in the percentages of the overall portrayals of Black and White NBA players on *Sports Illustrated* covers by decade.

As Table 9.3 shows, significant changes were found in answering RQ-4. Overall, the negative portrayal of Black NBA players increased drastically, while the portrayal of White players remained fairly consistent. For example, the overall violent portrayal of Black players (see Figure 9.1) increased from 3% in the 1970s to 31% from 2000 to 2003. Similarly, the overall angry portrayal of Black players (see Figure 9.2) increased from 3% to 28%. In contrast, one cover during the entire sample period portrayed a White player as angry and violent. Further data that answers RQ-4 stems from the decrease in overall positive portrayals of Black players (see Figure 9.3). In the 1970s, approximately 91% of the covers portraying Black players were positive. By the 1990s, 74% of the covers were positive, while from 2000 to 2003, 59% of the covers were positive. Furthermore, while the number of White players featured on covers decreased (94% in the 1970s to 80% in the 1990s), the number of positive portrayals was greater than that of Black players.

❖  DISCUSSION

**Critical Findings**

Overall, this study uncovers both physical and written textual differences used by *Sports Illustrated* magazine when portraying Black and White NBA players. While many of the results mirrored findings of other empirical investigations of race in sports media, analysis did find surprising contradictions as well. For example, one commonly existing belief is that White athletes are more often touted for their intellectual abilities than Black players. However, findings show that Black players were almost equally likely as White players to be portrayed for their intellectual skills. In fact, a larger percentage of Black players than White players received salient mention of their leadership abilities.

**Table 9.3**    Anger/Violence Characteristics of Black and White NBA *SI* Covers

| Characteristic | Black NBA Players (N = 186) | | White NBA Players (N = 37) | | Other NBA Players (N = 2) | | Total NBA Players (N = 225) | |
|---|---|---|---|---|---|---|---|---|
| | N | % | N | % | N | % | N | % |
| **1970s** | (N = 35) | | (N = 16) | | | | (N = 51) | |
| Overall Positive | 32 | (91%) | 15 | (94%) | | | 47 | (29%) |
| Overall Violent | 1 | (03%) | 0 | (00%) | | | 1 | (02%) |
| Overall Angry | 1 | (03%) | 0 | (00%) | | | 1 | (02%) |
| **1980s** | (N = 46) | | (N = 14) | | | | (N = 60) | |
| Overall Positive | 44 | (96%) | 13 | (93%) | | | 57 | (95%) |
| Overall Violent | 3 | (07%) | 0 | (00%) | | | 3 | (05%) |
| Overall Angry | 0 | (00%) | 0 | (00%) | | | 0 | (00%) |
| **1990s** | (N = 76) | | (N = 5) | | | | (N = 81) | |
| Overall Positive | 56 | (74%) | 4 | (80%) | | | 60 | (74%) |
| Overall Violent | 8 | (11%) | 0 | (00%) | | | 8 | (10%) |
| Overall Angry | 7 | (09%) | 1 | (20%) | | | 8 | (10%) |
| **2000–2003** | (N = 29) | | (N = 2) | | (N = 2) | | (N = 33) | |
| Overall Positive | 17 | (59%) | 2 | (100%) | 2 | (100%) | 21 | (64%) |
| Overall Violent | 9 | (31%) | 0 | (00%) | 0 | (0%) | 9 | (27%) |
| Overall Angry | 8 | (28%) | 0 | (00%) | 0 | (0%) | 8 | (24%) |

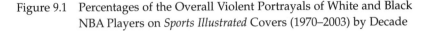

Figure 9.1    Percentages of the Overall Violent Portrayals of White and Black
             NBA Players on *Sports Illustrated* Covers (1970–2003) by Decade

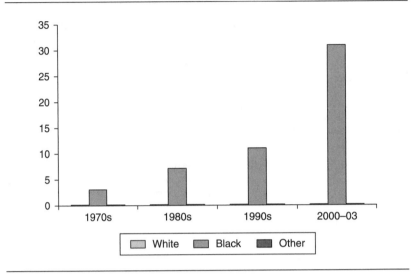

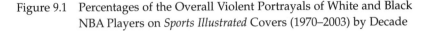

**Figure 9.2**    Percentages of the Overall Angry Portrayals of White and Black
             NBA Players on *Sports Illustrated* Covers (1970–2003) by Decade

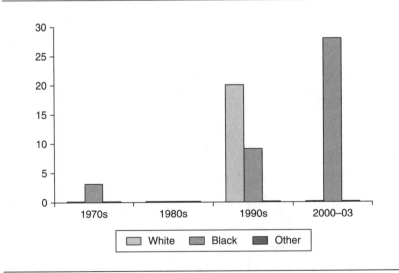

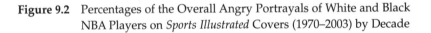

Unlike advertisements that are designed to sell products, magazine
cover photos are usually made to celebrate an athlete's accomplishments, and the covers analyzed seemed to uniformly spotlight team

**Figure 9.3**    Percentages of the Overall Positive Portrayals of White and Black
NBA Players on *Sports Illustrated* Covers (1970–2003) by Decade

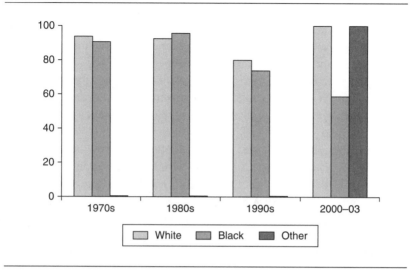

leaders regardless of race, a finding that correlates with Denham, Billings, and Halone's (2002) report of a large number of leadership comments now being attributed to Black basketball players.

Changes in the portrayals of White and Black NBA players over time also prove interesting. Since 1990, a vast decline in covers featuring White NBA players occurred. Logically, the assumption may be made that this phenomenon might be because of the decline in White NBA stars and the influx of Black and foreign-born players into the NBA. Also notable over time was the decrease in positive portrayals of Black NBA players, alongside the relative stability in positive portrayals of White NBA players. This change is perhaps a direct result of the generally increasing level of scandal surrounding the NBA (e.g., allegations of rape against Kobe Bryant; Ron Artest's on-court fighting, alleged mistreatment of animals, and arrest for domestic abuse; the November 2004 Pacers/Pistons brawl; referee Tim Donaghy's alleged bets on NBA games) and professional sport as a whole (e.g., Pete Rose's alleged bets on Major League Baseball, O.J. Simpson's trial for two murders, Barry Bonds' alleged steroid use, Michael Vick's involvement with dog fighting).

### Implications

Results of this study directly examine the alleged propagations of race through mass media and found evidence to support several of them. For example, the continued stereotyping of Black athletes as violent individuals who are successful because of their "natural abilities" more than their intellectual abilities can directly influence Black youths. Youths of all races still regard media outlets like *Sports Illustrated* as purveyors of "truth" in some form, meaning that any racialized inequities in perhaps the most salient of all sports magazine portrayals (i.e., the cover of *SI*) could result in skewed understandings of American culture. As might be expected, research indicates that youths and other individuals take mass media messages to heart and apply them to their everyday lives (Harrison, 1995). In time, these assumptions about Black and White athletes may grow and evolve in form throughout society, particularly when one considers the segregated nature of many communities in which some viewers may not interact with people of different races on a daily basis but watch people of different races play basketball for hours at a time.

Future studies should increase the scope of sports scholarship by examining more sports magazines and athletes from a variety of sports. By examining athletes from other sports, empirical results will yield more comprehensive data regarding the portrayal of Black and White athletes (and hopefully move beyond mere Black/White distinctions as American sports become increasingly racially diverse). Further examination of other sports magazines should also be coupled with examinations of all media, including movies, music videos, music lyrics, video games, blogs, and Internet sites. Of particular noteworthiness for consideration would be Web-based media images as this format becomes increasingly ubiquitous, particularly for younger consumers. Studies of this variety should also take note of access to and usage patterns of various media formats among various racial groups to further comprehend the possible ramifications of racially distorted images in media. Such cross-comparisons may include print versus electronic media, traditional media versus new media, and visually based media versus aurally based media.

Subsequent studies should also attempt to examine the vague but increasingly fascinating world of media effects, identifying how racialized sport images may influence consumers. When combined with content-analytic work, effects studies offer a much more complete view of the ebb and flow that occurs within modern mediasport and the people who interact with it. Such comprehension encourages media consumers to notice the messages inherent in media, to think about who is sending those messages and why, and to challenge the realism of such messages (Potter, 2004).

Finally, the global appeal and nature of sport offers the opportunity for the investigation of relationships between international issues such as immigration and globalization, potentially yielding racially distorted images in worldwide media outlets, such as the influx of global talent into traditionally culturally heterogeneous sport entities such as NBA franchises (Lombardo, 2004) and European professional soccer clubs (Wingfield, n.d.). This line of inquiry could document the global prevalence of race as negotiated within sport, noting differences by countries or regions. It may further determine whether effects of racialized sport portrayals are moderated (and/or mitigated) by country of origin, age at immigration, and level of acculturation.

Ultimately, some long-held notions and stereotypes of Black and White professional athletes were detected in this study of *Sports Illustrated* covers featuring NBA players. However, results did find that Black players were portrayed as successful because of intellectual traits such as leadership, intelligence, work ethic, and mental skill almost as often as White athletes. Such findings may indicate a shift in racial perceptions in American sports, as suggested by Billings (2004). While this study represents empirical investigation of only a very stratified element of a global issue, the findings merit consideration because of the perpetuity of racial portrayals as part of human existence, the global appeal of sport spectatorship, and the considerable scope of the commercial aspects of sports media and sport as a major industry within the global economy.

## ❖ REFERENCES

Andrews, D. L. (1996). The facts of Michael Jordan's blackness: Excavating a floating racial signifier. *Sociology of Sport Journal, 13*(1), 125–158.

Bargh, J. A., & Ferguson, M. J. (2000). Beyond behaviorism: On the automaticity of higher mental processes. *Psychological Bulletin, 126*, 925–945.

Bass, A. (2002). *Not the triumph but the struggle: The 1968 Olympics and the making of the black athlete.* Minneapolis: University of Minnesota Press.

Beller, J. M., Lumpkin, A., & Stoll, S. K. (1999). *Sport ethics: Applications for fair play.* Boston, MA: McGraw-Hill.

Berlow, L. H. (1994). *Sports ethics: A Reference Handbook.* Santa Barbara, CA: ABC-CLIO.

Berry, S. (2006, February 15). Sportscaster's comments take a Turin for the worse. *The Columbus Dispatch*, p. 8C.

Billings, A. C. (2004). Depicting the quarterback in black and white: A content analysis of college and professional football broadcast commentary. *The Howard Journal of Communications, 15*(4), 201–210.

Billings, A. C., Angelini, J. R., & Eastman, S. T. (2007). Wie shock: Television commentary about playing on the PGA and LPGA tours. *The Howard Journal of Communications, 18*(3), 64–84.

Billings, A. C., & Eastman, S. T. (2002). Nationality, gender, and ethnicity: Formation of identity in NBC's 2000 Olympic coverage. *International Review for the Sociology of Sport, 37*(3), 349–368.

Billings, A. C., & Eastman, S. T. (2003). Framing identities: Gender, ethnic, and national parity in network announcing of the 2002 Winter Olympics. *Journal of Communication, 53*(4), 369–386.

Bussey, K., & Bandura, A. (1999). Social cognitive theory of gender development and differentiation. *Psychological Review, 106,* 676–713.

Byrd, J., & Utsler, M. (2007). Is stereotypical coverage of African-American athletes as "dead as disco"? An analysis of NFL quarterbacks in the pages of *Sports Illustrated. Journal of Sports Media, 2*(1), 1–28.

Carlston, D. E. (1986). An environmental explanation for race differences in basketball performance. In R. E. Lapchick (Ed.), *Fractured focus: Sport as a reflection of society* (pp. 87–108). Lexington, MA: Lexington Books.

Changing sponsorship, advertising, and marketing model. (2006, March 27–April 2). *Sports Business Journal, 8*(46), 36.

Coakley, J. J. (1998). *Sport in society: Issues and controversies* (5th ed.). Boston: Irwin/McGraw-Hill.

Coakley, J. J. (2007). *Sport in society: Issues and controversies* (9th ed.). Boston: Irwin/McGraw-Hill.

Cooper-Chen, A. (2005). The world of television. In A. Cooper-Chen (Ed.), *Global entertainment media* (pp. 221–236). Mahwah, NJ: Lawrence Erlbaum.

Cover index. (2003, November 10). *Sports Illustrated, 99*(18), 114–150.

Cuneen, J., & Sidwell, M. J. (1998). Gender portrayals in *Sports Illustrated for Kids* advertisements: A content analysis of prominent and supporting models. *Journal of Sport Management, 12*(1), 39–50.

Cunningham, W. A., Preacher, K. J., & Banaji, M. R. (2001). Implicit attitude measures: Consistency, stability, and convergent validity. *Psychological Science, 12,* 163–170.

Denham, B. E., Billings, A. C., & Halone, K. K. (2002). Differential accounts of race in broadcast commentary of the 2000 NCAA Men's and Women's Final Four basketball tournaments. *Sociology of Sport Journal, 19,* 315–332.

Dewar, A. (1993). Sexual oppression in sport: Past, present and future alternatives. In A. G. Ingram & J. W. Loy (Eds.), *Sport in social development* (pp. 147–165). Champaign, IL: Human Kinetics Books.

Dufur, M. (1998). Race logic and "being like Mike": Representations of athletes in advertising, 1985–1994. In G. A. Sailes (Ed.), *African Americans in sport* (pp. 67–81). New Brunswick, NJ: Transaction Publishers.

Eastman, S. T., & Billings, A. C. (2001). Biased voices of sports: Racial and gender stereotyping in college basketball announcing. *The Howard Journal of Communications, 12*(4), 183–202.

Edwards, H. (1969). *Revolt of the Black athlete.* New York: Free Press.

Edwards, H. (1973). *Sociology of sport*. Homewood, IL: Dorsey Press.

Eitzen, D. S., & Sage, G. H. (2003). *Sociology of North American sport*. New York: McGraw-Hill.

Entine, J. (2000). *Taboo: Why Black athletes dominate sports and why we're afraid to talk about it*. New York: PublicAffairs.

Fink, J. S., & Kensicki, L. J. (2002). An imperceptible difference: Visual and textual constructions of femininity in *Sports Illustrated* and *Sports Illustrated for Women*. *Mass Communication & Society, 5*(3), 317–340.

Greenwald, A. G., & Banaji, M. R. (1995). Implicit social cognition: Attitudes, self-esteem, and stereotypes. *Psychological Review, 102*, 4–27.

Harrison, L. (1995). African-Americans: Race as a self-schema affecting physical activity choices. *Quest, 47*(1), 7–18.

Hawkins, B. (1998). The dominant images of black men in America: The representation of O. J. Simpson. In G. A. Sailes (Ed.), *African Americans in sport* (pp. 39–51). New Brunswick, NJ: Transaction Publishers.

Kellner, D. (1996). Sports, media culture, and race—some reflections on Michael Jordan. *Sociology of Sport Journal, 13*(4), 458–467.

King, C. R. (2007). Staging the Winter Olympics, or why sport matters to white power. *Journal of Sport & Social Issues, 31*, 89–94.

Lapchick, R. E. (1986). *Fractured focus: Sport as a reflection of society*. Lexington, MA: Lexington Books.

Lapchick, R. E. (2006). *The 2005–06 season racial and gender report card: National Basketball Association*. Orlando: DeVos Sport Business Management Program.

Lee, J. (1992). Media portrayals of male and female Olympic athletes: Analyses of newspaper accounts of the 1984 and the 1988 Summer Games. *International Review for Sociology of Sport, 27*(3), 197–219.

Lombardo, J. (2004, October 25). Global trade: NBA imports talent and exports the game. *Sports Business Journal*, p. 21.

McCombs, M. E., & Shaw, D. L. (1972). The agenda-setting function of mass media. *Public Opinion Quarterly, 36*, 176–187.

Moretti, A. (2005). The Olympics. In A. Cooper-Chen (Ed.), *Global entertainment media* (pp. 221–236). Mahwah, NJ: Lawrence Erlbaum.

Potter, W. J. (2004). Argument for the need for a cognitive theory of media literacy. *American Behavioral Scientist, 48*, 266–272.

Rada, J. (1996). Color blind-sided: Racial bias in network television's coverage of professional football games. *The Howard Journal of Communications, 7*, 231–240.

Rada, J., & Wulfemeyer, K. T. (2005). Color coded: Racial descriptors in television coverage of intercollegiate sports. *Journal of Broadcasting & Electronic Media, 49*, 65–85.

Rainville, R., & McCormick, E. (1977). Extent of covert racial prejudice in pro football announcers' speech. *Journalism Quarterly, 54*(1), 20–26.

Sage, G. H. (2005). Racial inequality and sport. In D. S. Eitzen (Ed.), *Sport in contemporary society: An anthology* (pp. 266–275). Boulder, CO: Paradigm Publishers.

SI Classic cover collection. (2004, January 24). *Sports Illustrated*. Retrieved September 24, 2008, from: http://www.sicovers.com

Sports as a global language. (2006, March 27–April 2). *Sports Business Journal, 8*(46), 44.

Suzuki, S. (1998). In-group and out-group communication patterns in international organizations: Implications for social identity theory. *Communication Research, 25*(2), 154–183.

Tajfel, H. (1972). Experiments in a vacuum. In J. Israel & H. Tajfel (Eds.), *The context of social psychology: A critical assessment* (pp. 69–119). London: Academic Press.

Tomaskovic-Devey, D. (1994). *Gender and racial inequality at work: The sources and consequences of job segregation*. Ithaca, NY: ILR Press.

Uchacz, C. P. (1998). Black sports images in transition: The impact of tiger's roar. In G. A. Sailes (Ed.), *African Americans in sport* (pp. 53–65). New Brunswick, NJ: Transaction Publishers.

Warin, J. (2000). The attainment of self-consistency through gender in young children. *Sex Roles, 42*, 209–231.

Wenner, L. A. (1989). Media, sports, and society: The research agenda. In L. A. Wenner (Ed.), *Media, sports, & society* (pp. 13–48). Thousand Oaks, CA: Sage.

Wingfield, M. (n.d.). Why we need a return of the local football economy. *Voice of Freedom, 81*, p. 10.

Wonsek, P. L. (1992). College basketball on television: A study of racial portrayals in the media. *Media, Culture & Society, 14*, 449–461.

# 10

# Sporting Images of Disability

## Murderball *and the Rehabilitation of Masculine Identity*

### James L. Cherney

### Kurt Lindemann

❖  ❖  ❖

From the Special Olympics to the Paralympics, sport segregated for people with disabilities is often viewed as therapeutic. Sport provides camaraderie (Brasile, 1992), a sense of inclusion (Martin & Smith, 2002), and physical benefits, including increased strength and agility (Guthrie & Castelnuovo, 2001). Participation in sport is also believed to help repair damage to an individual's identity that occurs when one transitions from an ablebodied to a disabled condition (Taub, Blinde, & Greer, 1999), encouraging an empowered sense of self (Brittain, 2004) and enhancing social networks (Ashton-Shaeffer, Gibson, Autry, & Hanson, 2001). Disability sport, then, is used as much to rehabilitate identity as to rehabilitate muscular impairments.

However, it is difficult for sport to reduce the stigma our ableist culture assigns to disability if the activities are themselves stigmatized. In our ableist culture, images of disability have long been associated with negative connotations and stigma. Historically, the American cinema has perpetuated an ableist gaze that variously ignores, exploits, rejects, obscures, and isolates disabled bodies and privileges the able-bodied viewer (Norden, 1994). The images of disability sport perpetuated in mainstream media can often have detrimental effects on the way disabled athletes view themselves (Brittain, 2004), undercutting the potential benefits of sport participation. Disability sport needs a positive public image if participating in it is to have a positive impact on the self identity of the participants.

In this chapter, we examine Jeffrey Mandel, Henry Alex Rubin, and Dana Adam Shapiro's 2005 documentary *Murderball* as a film that works to present a positive image of disability sport. The film focuses on one of the most visible and fastest growing wheelchair sports: quadriplegic rugby, or quad rugby, originally called "Murderball." The sport is a combination of ice hockey, basketball, and ablebodied rugby, in which players must carry a ball across one end of a basketball court, passing to teammates while avoiding getting hit by opposing players. The film achieved popularity through critical accolades and word-of-mouth praise about its humorous and energetic take on disability sport. Claudia Puig (2005) of *USA Today* wrote that the film "brilliantly captures the intensity of the little-known athletic competition, offering more intimacy and drama than most Hollywood sports movies" (¶ 4). Similarly, Desson Thompson (2005) of *The Washington Post* called it "one of the most powerful films of the year" (¶ 1). The influential film critic Roger Ebert (2005) of the *Chicago Sun-Times* compared *Murderball* to the 1994 hit *Hoop Dreams*, as both successfully used "sport as a way to see into lives, hopes, and fears" (¶ 2). Several critics emphasized the documentary's departure from conventional displays of disability. Peter Travers (2005) wrote in *Rolling Stone* that *Murderball* is "not depressing . . . not sappy . . . it's not like something you've ever seen" (¶ 1). In the *San Francisco Chronicle* Peter Hartlaub (2005) likewise observed that the film "is a great movie not because of the feelings it invokes, but because of the ones it avoids" (¶ 3). Finally, the film was praised in disability activist publications such as *Ragged Edge Online*, where Ed Hooper (2005) proclaimed that "*Murderball* is quite simply the best film ever made on disability" (¶ 3).

In addition to overwhelmingly positive reviews, *Murderball* received many awards and honors including the Audience Award and a Special Jury Prize at the prestigious Sundance Film Festival. Its Oscar nomination for Best Documentary in 2005 further catapulted it into the popular consciousness. Given both the popularity of the film and its groundbreaking presentation of disabled sport participants as serious athletes, the film deserves critical examination of its portrayal of disability. In doing so, we examine the potential for sport media to promote the identity of people with disabilities and to evaluate disability sport's potential to operate as a therapeutic system that can rehabilitate one's sense of self.

## ❖ THEORY AND RELATED LITERATURE: DISABILITY SPORT AND REHABILITATION

Disability sport participation is often used for rehabilitation from spinal cord injury, and quadriplegic rugby plays a prominent role in this process. Physically impaired people—especially those who were ablebodied athletes—may have difficulty coming to terms with their "new" bodies. Sparkes and Smith (2002) discovered in the narratives of disabled athletes an irresolvable anxiety over the loss of the athletic ability they had when ablebodied. That athletic identities are tied to this notion of ability is not surprising, as Messner (1992) explains that ablebodied sport prioritizes the body's role as a tool to accomplish competitive goals. For some disabled athletes who previously competed in ablebodied sport, the desire for a "restored" athletic self is unachievable, and they have limited narrative resources for coping with this "dilemma" (Sparkes & Smith, 2002). Organized sport participation provides both mental and physical benefits that help manage this situation. Unfortunately, much coverage of therapeutic sport primarily frames these benefits as compensatory and as helping those with spinal cord injuries "overcome" their disability (Schell & Duncan, 1999). Among others, Linton (1998) argues that framing disability this way undermines an empowering perspective by placing undue emphasis on compensating for one's injury instead of on living a meaningful life.

Furthermore, much therapeutic recreation literature invokes not just the overcoming of one's disability but the interpretation of disability as "stigma." Stigma, or the "spoiling" of an otherwise "normal" social identity (Goffman, 1963), figures prominently into scholarly discussions of how physical recreation functions in the rehabilitation process. Through their participation, wheelchair athletes resist stereotypical notions of the disabled as weak, helpless, or passive (Guthrie & Castelnuovo, 2001). Yet disability studies literature widely criticizes associating disability with stigma as affirming an ableist orientation

(Murphy, 1990), which suggests potential problems with this perspective of disability sport. Physical activity also allows participants to take pride in showing the ablebodied world that they can still "do things" (Ashton-Shaeffer, Gibson, Autry, & Hanson, 2001, p. 107). In this way participants emulate an idealized athletic physique (Taub, Blinde, & Greer, 1999), which is typically imagined as ablebodied. Disabled athletes proving that they are just as "good" as ablebodied athletes may ultimately reinforce the traditional privilege accorded to the "normal" body; in other words, disabled athletes may adopt some of the very standards by which society marginalizes them as "abnormal" (Guthrie & Castelnuovo, 2001).

Historically, images have played a crucial role in such ableist evaluation and discrimination, and the social meaning of disability is deeply connected to how it is viewed (DePauw, 1997). Yet the therapeutic literature generally examines disability sport itself rather than the way it is portrayed, just as studies of the images associated with disability sport have focused on their contribution to discrimination rather than examining the role of such images in rehabilitation. Our project brings these two areas together and draws from both to investigate how images of disability sport impact its ability to rehabilitate. Specifically, we address the ways that *Murderball* challenges us to see disability sport anew.

Conventional images of disability are widespread in popular media, but they typically promote discernable stereotypes like the "monster" and the "criminal," easily recognized as dehumanizing because of their close association with evil and social ostracization (Longmore, 1987). Other stereotypes permeate contemporary popular media as well: the person with a disability who escapes through suicide, the one who adjusts to ableist expectations, and the "supercrip" who dramatically overcomes disability through some extraordinary physical feat (Longmore, 1987). These also degrade by positioning disability as an individual problem, requiring acceptance of his or her "natural inferiority" to the ablebodied community. In general, when media—from films to magazines—contain images of disability, they overwhelmingly portray it in a negative and ableist light (Nelson, 1994; Smit & Enns, 2001). In this context, it comes as no surprise that images of disability are relatively rare in traditional media outlets associated with sport.

Sport media focuses on ablebodied athletes and provides comparatively little coverage of sport involving disabled athletes. The Paralympic Games—the international competition of athletes with disabilities that has followed the Olympic Games since 1960—receives more attention than any other disability sport event, yet media coverage demonstrates severe disparities in the amount of disability sport featured and the time and duration of such segments (Hardin & Hardin, 2003). In 1996—the first time the games were aired on a major American network—CBS *sold* four hours of coverage to Paralympic officials; in contrast, NBC *paid* $456 million for the rights to broadcast the 1996 Olympics and aired 171.5 hours of coverage—55 of which were in prime time (Eastman & Billings, 1999; Lainson, 1996). This pattern extends well beyond coverage of the Paralympics into the rare sport magazine articles that feature disabled athletes, which typically omit visible evidence of a disability, tend to reinforce negative stereotypes and reinforce ableist values, and do not show disabled athletes as team players or in a leadership position (Hardin, Hardin, Lynn, & Walsdorf, 2004).

Negative images of disabled athletes potentially undermine the capacity of disability sport participation to rehabilitate one's self-image. While participating in disability sport promotes the rehabilitation of recently disabled individuals on a number of levels, only 23% of individuals with disabilities engage in regular physical activity (Kosma, Cardinal, & Rintala, 2002). Kosma et al. (2002) attribute this disparity to the presence of "cultural stereotypes" in such socializing agents as the media, which promote negative attitudes that "may result in low success expectations and physical activity salience leading to sports attrition" (p. 122). In short, negative perceptions of disability, particularly those perpetuated by media coverage of disability sport, "combine to inhibit involvement in sporting activities" (Brittain, 2004, p. 450).

❖   METHODOLOGICAL APPROACH: GAZE AND THE
      RHETORICAL CONSTRUCTION OF BODIES IN FILM

In this analysis, we perform a close textual reading of *Murderball* to examine the ways it rhetorically rehabilitates the image of disability sport and to suggest the implications of its approach. By "close textual reading" we refer to the method of using a variety of analytical tools to expose and direct attention to the way(s) a text works. By "analytical tools" we mean the concepts or devices on which we focus our attention to explain how the text generates meaning. We chose our tools based on their appropriateness for the text examined; since the rhetoric we examine appears in a film, we integrated techniques associated with both film and rhetorical criticism. From the field of film criticism we adopt the concepts of gaze, voyeur, image, and stereotype. From rhetorical criticism we obtain theories of identity and narrative. All of these tools are connected by the idea of perspective or orientation so that our study emphasizes the way disability is viewed in and because of the film. We value this approach because it allows us to read *Murderball* in the context of cultural views of disability and its meaning, and to illustrate the implications of the text in a predominantly ableist culture.

Film theory has long recognized the camera's "gaze" as an important cinematic element, because it teaches the audience to see from a particular perspective that "focus[es] attention on the human form," and gaze often perpetuates discriminatory assumptions about the appropriateness of looking at other people's bodies (Mulvey, 1989, p. 17). Looking and being looked at are important activities in our culture that are extensively regulated by social norms and expectations—especially when the act involves disability (Murphy, 1990; Norden, 1994). Particularly relevant are the codes that govern the voyeur who derives pleasure from power associated with controlling the experience of looking. In face-to-face contact, the power dynamics of viewer and viewed are unstable, as both participants simultaneously view each other and regulate each other's gaze through verbal and nonverbal devices. In contrast, the power relations become relatively fixed when choosing to look is entirely up to the viewer. Once captured by the camera and rendered replicable and unchanging, the viewed becomes relatively powerless and the audience becomes voyeurs who enjoy the ability to look at will. Yet the audience's control is in no way absolute, as the camera, director, editor, and other elements that created the film mediate this interaction. The experience of watching a film encourages the audience to adopt its way of seeing its material, which it frames—intentionally or not—through such devices as focus, lighting, background, foreground, proximity, and other elements of the *mise-en-scène*. Thus, the film invites and encourages the audience to gaze at its subject from a particular perspective, which has the potential to re-constitute bodies and subjectivity in surprising, jarring, and empowering ways that counter traditional discourses.

At the same time, the presentation of disability in film potentially reifies traditional discourses when audiences make sense of what they see by relying on conventional images of disability that reinforce its position in ableist society. Norden (1994) charts the history of the "impoverished" image of disability in American cinema and shows how it traditionally exploits such stereotypes as the "Sweet Innocent"—e.g., Tiny Tim or the blind flower-seller of Chaplin's *City Lights*—and the "Obsessive Avenger"—e.g., Captain Hook from *Peter Pan* or Captain Ahab of *Moby Dick*. These conventional characters render inferior the person with a disability as either the proper object of pity or the appropriately excluded pariah. Such depictions pervade the visual scene, and this tradition of discriminatory cinematic conventions might undermine the emancipatory potential of unconventional images. Even when portrayed positively, physically disabled characters presented on film in more-or-less conventional film "language" may do little to change ableist stereotypes and may lack the potential to prompt a radical reappraisal on the part of spectators.

We join elements of rhetorical criticism to the tools addressed above because we view disability as a social construction whose meaning is established, contested, and negotiated through texts (DePauw, 1997). Values associated with disability, including the very definition of the word, change over time. At any point in time, texts both communicate this meaning and have the potential to alter it as such texts are the materials out of which people craft identities as ablebodied or disabled. The narratives that society uses to make sense out of disability are the same stories individuals use to make sense of who they are when they become disabled. Simply put, labeling a physical condition "a disability" and labeling a person "an athlete"—and the significance of those labels—are rhetorical products, so the rhetoric contesting cultural conventions can challenge the social meaning of disability. In *Murderball*, the interplay of gaze, social position, and the conventions of ableist cinema enacts this dynamic. Its narratives, images, and cinematic devices engage the notion of rehabilitation through sport, challenging and correcting the traditional image of disability sport while simultaneously reifying other ableist notions of disability and athletic ability.

❖  RESULTS: *MURDERBALL*
    AND THE IMAGE OF REHABILITATION

*Murderball* weaves together three main narratives that display the complex relationship of disability, sport, and rehabilitation. The primary plot line tells the familiar story of a classic sport rivalry. Starring Mark Zupan, a leader of Team USA's quad rugby team, and featuring his fellow teammates, Scott Hogsett, Bob Lujano, and Andy Cohn, the first story details their clashes with Team Canada as they work to reach the 2004 Paralympics in Athens, Greece. The second story extends the drama of the first by depicting Joe Soares, a former outstanding U.S. Paralympian who has "defected" to become new head coach for the Canadian national team. In his narrative, Soares learns to balance his personal life and life on the rugby court, coping with his disappointment in his son for not being athletically inclined and with a heart attack, partially induced by his obsession with beating the U.S. team. The third interwoven narrative tells of Keith Cavill, a newly injured quadriplegic person who learns to cope with his disability and develops an interest in quad rugby as part of his rehabilitation.

In depicting a typical sport rivalry, the film satisfies many aspects of the sport film genre, including heroes, villains, conflict, and redemption (Baker, 2003). The players are presented as serious athletes who train, compete, and engage in demanding contests that require mental and physical strength and stamina. The rivalry between Canada and the United States attracts any sport enthusiast, and the dramatic footage of the games gives the sport an exciting, frenetic feel. The presence of the Cavill narrative brings the subtext of rehabilitation into focus and magnifies this theme in the other two narratives. While Cavill's story blatantly *portrays* the sport as a form of physical rehabilitation, the players' rivalry story works to *enact* rehabilitation by redeeming the image of disability sport. Additionally, Soares' story *requires* rehabilitation for a man whose obsession with the game has taken control of his life, marriage, and family. In short, *Murderball* engages rehabilitation on different levels and in different ways, and reading the images it displays in this context reveals the techniques and complications involved with rehabilitating identity.

### *Murderball's* Positive Images of Disability

*Murderball* presents a very different image of disability than is generally found in the contemporary media of Western culture. The difference is apparent even at the very beginning of the film, where spliced with the opening credits are several statements by players. Featuring Hogsett, Lujano, Cohn, and Zupan, these shots directly challenge ableist assumptions and make ableism seem utterly ridiculous. Hogsett tells of people shaking his hand and saying, "It's good to see you *out*," when he visits clubs. He wonders aloud: "It's good to see me out? What am I supposed to be *in*? A closet hanging out?" (Mandel, 2005). His tone is humorous but exasperated, encouraging the audience to question its own assumptions about what it means to live with a disability. Cohn jokes about people asking if he needs help as he loads groceries into his car after a visit to the store. He smiles as he sarcastically exposes the thoughtlessness of these "well meaning" offers: "And I'll go to get into my car and people will go, 'Well, do you need help in your car?' Well, I wouldn't have come to the grocery store if I couldn't get back in my car" (Mandel, 2005). These vignettes counter ableist stereotypes and thinking, but they also display the players' sense of humor. Hogsett appears more bemused than angry, and Cohn tempers his sarcasm with a smile.

Although they have been mistreated in these stories—like the stereo-types Norden calls the "Obsessive Avenger" and the "Sweet Innocent"—they are neither bitter and angry nor passive and accepting. Their response is complex—it is offended yet patient, insulted yet laughing—and it resists being stereotyped and dismissed easily.

This image of disabled athletes as people comfortable with their lives dominates the film. In addition to the game sequences, viewers observe players engaging in a number of everyday behaviors. They play cards, go swimming, have conversations, go to bars, and have cookouts. Some of these images probably astound ableist audiences, such as when Lujano—who has no legs or forearms—demonstrates how he gets around his kitchen, eats pizza, and types on his computer at work. Many of these glimpses are rather intimate, as when the characters describe in detail how they became disabled, talk about their sex lives, party to celebrate their wins, and cry as they lament their losses. Their willingness to self-disclose such personal information shows how self-assured they are; insecure people could not be so frank, open, and forthcoming. Except for some of the early shots of Cavill and other newly disabled people, the characters with disabilities appear dressed in conventional clothes that express their individual personality—just like all the ablebodied people around them. Like anyone else they have their flaws, but even when at their worst, audiences see them as multi-dimensional people not defined solely by their disability. These images are rehabilitative in that they help these athletes (re)claim a place in mainstream society. These images are also resistant, challenging ableist assumptions about disability.

Along with the improved image of athletes with disabilities, *Murderball* provides extensive images that present disability sport in a positive light. The athletes train extensively, display their awards, are cheered by emotional fans, and pump themselves up in pre-game rituals. Repeatedly the film directs the audience to see past the athletes' disabilities to enjoy this exciting drama and recognize it as very serious competition. On the whole, the images and drama of the film work together to make disability sport fast-paced and electrifying, present-ing the activity with as positive an image as it offers for the athletes. This is accomplished in large part by the camera shots and editing tech-niques used by the filmmakers.

## (Re)Viewing Disability

Historically, the American cinema has perpetuated an ableist gaze privileging the ablebodied viewer (Norden, 1994). For example, often the bodies of people with disabilities (especially those in wheelchairs) are displayed as below the vantage point of the ablebodied viewer so that the audience literally "looks down" on them from a "superior" position. Not only does *Murderball* conspicuously avoid this convention by usually putting the camera on level with the wheelchair athletes, the film occasionally reverses this orientation by adopting a "chair's eye view" that visually "looks up" at the Paralympians. Viewers are primed for these untraditional displays immediately, as shots cut into the opening credits employ both innovations before a single line of dialogue is uttered.

The opening sequence depicts Mark Zupan in a wheelchair preparing for a workout. In the first shot he removes his jeans, pulls his paralyzed legs onto his footrests, and throws the jeans carelessly on the floor as he rolls toward the camera and out of the visual field. Zupan is in a bedroom—presumably his—with plain white walls, a wooden chest of drawers, and a suggestively unmade bed. The room is marked by the disarray expected of a "bachelor pad," as clothes are strewn about haphazardly as a baseball and a not-quite-empty bottle of beer graces the nightstand. His movements may be unusual to those unfamiliar with life in a chair, but what one might interpret as physical contortions do not appear painful or even stressed. Zupan's face is calm, his movements unhurried, his attitude that of anyone going through the everyday ritual of dressing. Similar characteristics appear in the second shot where he puts on a pair of athletic shorts. He is again in the bedroom, and this slightly wider shot taken from the same basic angle reveals more of the same clutter, including yet another beer bottle on the floor. All of this encourages the audience to see Zupan as "just another guy" whose most remarkable features are his elaborate tattoos, his trademark goatee, and his fashionable triangular sideburns. The gaze of the camera reinforces this perspective in two ways. First, in both shots the camera is placed precisely on level with Zupan, so that he is looked upon as an equal. Second, in these shots the camera moves very little—except for the brief moments described below, it is nearly static and unmoving—so that Zupan himself provides the motion in the scene. In effect, audiences see only what he shows. Like the first shot, Zupan is active while the camera generally remains stable. Indeed, his exit at the end of the shot places him firmly in control of the gaze, as he moves out of the stilled and passive camera frame and out of view. These images of his life cannot fit into any neat stereotypes that position him as "other"; the only stereotype that fits is that of untidy bachelor.

The second unconventional gaze previewed in this opening scene places viewers nearly at floor level and looks out from the point of view of the wheel. It appears here in a single shot at the very end of the scene and depicts a close-up of one of the small wheels found at the front of the chair, spinning noisily. A hum in the background combined with the clicking of the bearings creates a subtly threatening mechanical sound that marks the uniqueness of this gaze. This floor-level perspective appears numerous times throughout the film, particularly around or during footage of the wheelchair rugby games. Often these sequences effectively put audiences into the game; shifting the focus according to the chair's movement invites viewers to see from a player's point of view. This gaze also presents the wheelchair athletes in a superior position, so that they look down while audiences look up from the players' feet, reversing the ableist cinema's convention of directing the gaze down when viewing disabled persons.

One sequence using this gaze precedes the final game of the 2002 International Championships between the United States and Canada. Here the camera twice moves at ground level the length of the gymnasium—once toward each of the teams who sit arranged as if for a team photo. The shot uses time-elapsed techniques so that the approach is blisteringly rapid, and the soundtrack heightens the energy with music, featuring a fast-riffing electric guitar, pounding bass beat, and clashing cymbals. When the camera's eye arrives at their feet, the teams look down with stern faces and crossed arms. They are everything that is absent in the conventional ableist image of the paraplegic: they are powerful, self-controlled, superior, tough, and very impressive. Moments later another sequence using this wheel's-eye view encourages audiences to imagine what it is like to play the sport, as a shot dramatically throws viewers into the game. This shot contravenes all the traditional accoutrements of ableist cinema. Audiences look up at the players, the movement is uncontrollably fast paced—almost reckless— and the background noise of people yelling and grinding wheels is punctuated with loud crashes. Most significantly, the shot depicts an impending collision: the view swerves toward one of the chairs, which grows rapidly to fill the field of vision. An instant before the chairs hit, the audience is spared viewing the actual moment of contact, but it does hear the crash and is warned symbolically that expectations of the body disabled are about to be wrecked.

One of the longest sequences to continually use the wheel's-eye view is the scene that segues between the players' arrival in Athens and their entrance to the Olympic stadium. This extensive shot, again done with time-elapsed techniques, literally wheels viewers into the facility. It passes through gates and doorways, turns corners, goes through security checkpoints, and crosses courtyards, ultimately arriving at a large sign reading, "Athens 2004." Like the similar shots described above, viewers are put in the position of the athletes themselves, encouraging adoption of their perspective. The shot also reveals an extremely accessible facility through which the wheelchair user can move freely and rapidly. The view is empowering; viewers are "going places" and doing so very rapidly. Thus, the sequence symbolizes the rising status of the Paralympian and other disabled athletes. The ableist's eyes are opened further by the next rapid sequence of Paralympic competition. It begins with the rather familiar images of wheelchair racers and sprinters with spring-like prosthetic feet but then quickly shows activities typically absent from coverage such as quadriplegic volleyball, weight lifting, and wheelchair fencing. Combined, these images of Paralympic sport and the wheel's-eye view of the arrival create a clear subtext: looking from a different perspective promises new sights. Overall, this theme shapes the various ways that gaze is directed by the camera. Even when technical issues intervene and require a shot that looks down on the players—as happens frequently during the sequences depicting actual game play—the camera typically locates its primary target in the upper half of the screen. In these cases when the audience does "look down," its gaze elevates the athletes instead of subordinating them.

"Don't stare" is one of the social codes that traditionally governs the act of looking at a disabled person. Murphy (1990) notes the relationship of this dictum and ableist sensibilities, arguing that parents provide the foundation for fearing disability when they punish an inquisitive child for looking too openly at people with disabilities. Not only does it make disability into a "fearsome possibility," the prohibition makes the act of looking illicit and attractive (Murphy, 1990, p. 117). Just as keeping certain parts of our bodies hidden under clothing creates the erotic potential associated with seeing them revealed, restrictions on the act of gazing upon the body disabled make such looking perversely pleasurable. To avoid censure, this illicit act of looking must be done surreptitiously, hidden from public scrutiny. Successfully performing the act thus not only puts the viewer in a position of power over the viewed, it also implies a power over society at large as the unpunished transgression suggests the viewer is "above the law." These voyeuristic pleasures do not occur if the looking involved is not prohibited: taking that which is not offered is inherent in voyeuristic pleasure. Granting permission to look or inviting the gaze shifts the power from the viewer to the viewed and places the looker at the mercy of the one observed. By letting the audience peep into the lives and bedrooms of people with disabilities, *Murderball* engages the ableist voyeur.

An early example of the way the film accomplishes this is found in two brief moments in the opening sequence showing Zupan dressing, when the camera enacts explicit stares. As noted throughout the majority of these two shots, the camera does not move; it allows Zupan to direct the gaze with his own movement. For a brief moment that occurs only once in each shot, however, the camera zooms in to stare at Zupan's body. The first stare focuses on his naked legs as he puts his feet on the chair's footrests after he has removed his pants. The shot centers on the elaborate tattoo that covers his lower left leg, but it also reveals that his legs shake with slight palsy. The second stare begins at his knees and slides up his body at the exact moment he pulls on his athletic shorts. The stares are not primarily sexual, but they become intimate and voyeuristic by providing a glimpse of nude flesh and underwear. They also allow viewers to frankly examine the physical evidence of Zupan's disability and sanction—even demand—stares at the disabled body. At the same time, the stares are guided by the camera's focus on Zupan's tattoo and his ability to dress himself. The first focus suggests that Zupan's cool tattoo is more remarkable than his shaking limbs, while the second questions the association of disability and dependency. In short, these two intimate stares encourage the voyeur to look openly, but they direct that gaze so that the viewer sees disability in ways that question ableist norms. Furthermore, because the disabled body is presented willingly and without shame, the voyeur is denied the pleasure of the illicit act. This pattern appears repeatedly in the film. Throughout the documentary, the characters put themselves on display, inviting the audience to see them—and to see them from the perspective of equals. Watching *Murderball* the viewer learns that disability is not something to fear or something from which we must look away, which counters the ableist lesson taught by the prohibition on "staring."

In effect, *Murderball* presents the point of view of the disabled athlete so that the audience views from a perspective that sees the players as powerful and heroic instead of lacking ability and pitiable. Not only does this break with the conventions associated with an ableist perspective, it also encourages the audience to identify with people with disabilities. As Lacan (1977) and others have demonstrated, the way we see—i.e., our perspectives—is central to our identity and sense of self. Adopting the gaze of the film—even if only for a short while—encourages us to see differently the issues that surround disability and to question the negative images that pervade our culture. In this way the film promotes a positive image and acceptance of the claimed identity of athletes with disabilities.

❖  DISCUSSION: *MURDERBALL,*
    MASCULINITY, AND SEXUALITY

*Murderball* presents a complex portrayal of gender and disability. While ableist culture views disabled men as "less than normal" in body type, ability, and sexuality, the film presents disabled men who draw on facets of sport to "rehabilitate" their gender identity. Specifically, by engaging in an aggressive, hard-hitting sport, the athletes in *Murderball* are able to access a conventional discourse of masculinity and, in turn, sexuality. Ironically, by framing athletes' participation as close in ability and spirit to ablebodied athletes, the film reifies traditional ableist notions of masculinity and sexuality, ultimately "othering" the athletes in a manner similar to the ablebodied gaze. This "othering" points to the thorny intersections of sport, disability, and gender, and the role of each in the rehabilitation of identity.

### The Rugby Wheelchair and "Prosthetic Masculinity"

The players' "Mad Max" wheelchairs are displayed prominently in the film. The wheelchairs, heavily fortified with welded metal pieces around the front, sides, and back, serve as battering rams with which players smash into each other in attempts to block others from getting a goal and to knock the ball out of their hands. Marty Frierson, the equipment manager for Team USA, explains, "What we do is we take these wheelchairs and make them into a gladiator, a battling machine, a Mad Max wheelchair that can withstand knocking the living daylights out of each other" (Mandel, 2005). His explanation is interspersed with shots using the wheel's-eye camera work described above, which puts the audience at the vantage point of these armored vehicles.

The filmmakers' choice to splice player narratives with action scenes frames the wheelchairs as tools used to resist common stereotypes about disabled persons as weak, helpless, and asexual. For example, shots of Zupan—headphones on and shirt off—racing his chair down the street, a determined look on his goateed face, are frequently interrupted by cuts to his on-court smashes and crashes. Following this sequence, Zupan sits in a weight room with his shirt off, exposing his taut pectorals and tattooed arms, and relates his view of ableist misconceptions about disability: "I've gone up to people and started talking shit, and they'll go 'Oh, oh, oh.' And I'll say, 'What, you're not going to hit a kid in a chair? Fucking hit me, I'll hit you back'" (Mandel, 2005). Here, his chair is barely visible as it props up on display his naked athletic torso and chest. In effect, Zupan's wheelchair and by extension all the quad rugby wheelchairs function to create a sort of "prosthetic masculinity." In other words, the film discursively positions the wheelchair as part of a masculinity commonly associated with ablebodied sport—fit, strong, able, enduring bodies punishing themselves for the love and glory of "the game." The wheelchairs stand for what the ablebodied gaze too often renders absent from disabled bodies: strength, agility, endurance, and, in essence, a masculinity usually reserved for ablebodied athletes.

The armored wheelchairs also operate as prostheses when their tough construction facilitates the brutal collisions for which the sport is named. Simply put, without these chairs neither the athletes nor their wheels would survive intact many of these violent crashes. The brute force employed shapes the sport's masculine image and the athletes claim a traditionally masculine identity by engaging in the hard-hitting behavior it demands. Current sport recreation scholarship (Huang & Brittain, 2006; Hutchinson & Kleiber, 2000) notes that disabled men are able to (re)claim their masculinity through feats of strength and athletic prowess, often enacted in disability sport. In *Murderball*, the wheelchairs themselves enable such feats of athleticism and allow the players to enact a traditionally masculine identity. This process of rehabilitating a masculine identity continues in another narrative thread: sexuality. As with the wheelchair images, this portrayal both challenges the ableist gaze and reifies it, complicating the rehabilitation of identity through disabled sport.

### (Dis)Ability and Sexuality: Ironic Framing

The historical links between sport and sexuality are numerous. Sport was, and to a certain extent still is, considered the "natural" domain of men (Messner, 2002). Quad rugby in particular, in which only 6 of the 406 athletes in league play in 2006 were women, functions as a boy's club (United States Quad Rugby Association, 2006). While much scholarship has devoted itself to the marginality of homosexuality in sport (see e.g., Chapter 2, in this volume; Pronger, 1990), next to nothing covers disabled sexualities in sport. Ablebodied sport is thought to socialize young boys into men (Whitson, 1990) as they learn "normal" behavior through sport (Messner, 2002). A narrow prescription for heterosexuality is reiterated in social interactions off the field (Burstyn, 1999), and deviations are often punished by social ostracism and physical beatings (Pronger, 1990). Heterosexuality, then, is a defining feature of athletic prowess in ablebodied sport. When communication of and about sexuality among disabled persons occurs in a sport context bursting with hypermasculine signifiers and sexist readings of the body, disabled sexuality is a doubly problematic concept; not only may disabled males be "othered" by the ablebodied gaze, these individuals may be subject to the normalizing forces of sport participation that emphasize ablebodied heterosexuality (Crosset, 1990). Just as Hardin (2003) found that images of disabled athletes are more palatable to disabled and ablebodied publics if they closely conform to ablebodied notions of athleticism, images of disabled athletes' sexuality are typically normalized as well. In *Murderball*, directors Henry Alex Rubin and Dana Adam Shapiro tackle these issues with mixed results.

Several items in the opening sequence showing Zupan dress focus attention on sexual themes. The bed, displayed prominently throughout this scene immediately behind Zupan, is unmade and appears recently used. Although he is not seen in bed with anyone, the disordered sheets imply that his bed is a site of activity, encouraging viewers to question the stereotype of the emasculated disabled male. Additionally, in the lower left of the frame of the second shot appears a metal studded leather belt, later shown worn by his ablebodied girlfriend Jess, suggesting that some of the clothes lying around the room are hers and offering mute testimony to his sexually active lifestyle.

Many of the film's scenes more explicitly focus on sex, featuring players in conversations with women about whether "it works" and footage of *Sexuality Reborn*, an explicit sex education video for people with spinal cord injuries. The film's portrayal of sexuality, while frank and unflinching, unfortunately reproduces ableist and heteronormative notions of sexuality by focusing on erections and penetrations. For example, Zupan explains some misconceptions about quads and sex: "When you break your neck, these things [holding up his hands] may be impaired, but that [pointing down to his crotch] still works" (Mandel, 2005). Significantly, he delivers this explanation in yet another shot of him with his shirt off, wheelchair just out of view flanked by weight-lifting machines, so all viewers see is a physically fit, muscular, presumably virile man. Shakespeare (1999) argues that too often the measurement of male sexuality is penetration, and that even when sexuality and disability is discussed, it is often in such ableist terms. The framing of Zupan's discussion unfortunately falls into this trap. The link to athletic ability is unmistakable, from the setting of the weight room to the display of his muscles.

This ironic discursive framing of disabled sexuality is further bolstered by shots of the athletes chatting up women while at training camp, fielding their questions about sex. Hogsett even tells one unsuspecting female a story about receiving a "bed bath" from a nurse who, excited at his first erection since his accident, runs out into the hallway of the hospital to get his mother. Tableaus like this—both of Hogsett telling this story and of the scene the story creates—resist the ablebodied notion of disabled men as asexual or impotent. Unfortunately, the emphasis is on only a particular kind of sexual ability, which reifies this ableist gaze and emphasizes the very standards it exacts on other men. This ability is inextricably connected to the athletes' ability on the rugby court through the editing and camera shots, all of which embed this sex talk as part of a typical locker room conversation by showing the athletes in their uniforms or weight rooms, presumably before or after a workout.

Similarly, the players are shown reaffirming ideal body types. In a poker game in the Team USA training facility, several players sit around a table drinking, playing cards, and talking about women. The scene depicts the conventional "guy's night out." The talk eventually turns to one player, Sam, and his personal taste in body type, about which Andy Cohn teases him: "That's number two on the list of most stupid things I heard Sam say at this camp. He said he doesn't like big tits, and that he'd dump a girl with big tits" (Mandel, 2005). The scene is ironic given that none of the male players' bodies conform to what might be called the ideal body type. The film normalizes disability and sexuality, then, by framing it as "typical guy talk." Again, while this discursive framing may challenge the ableist tendency to desexualize the disabled body, it simultaneously reaffirms many of the norms associated with the ableist gaze.

In contrast to these more ribald moments, the players are sometimes shown exhibiting a great deal of vulnerability regarding sexuality. The newly injured Cavill is shown stammering out his question to a doctor as he lies in bed: "I had a girlfriend prior to injury. And as I get discharged from here and get back to my private life, will that affect . . . how will it affect . . . will I be able to be sexually active?" (Mandel, 2005). Cohn explains wistfully that the "first full-on sex after being in a wheelchair was a great moment in my life" (Mandel, 2005). Ultimately, this vulnerability is unwoven by a loose-hanging thread in this narrative tapestry: how disabled men might "play up" their disability to attract women. What attracted Jess to Zupan, she explains, was "curiosity" and "maybe also to some extent . . . the mothering instinct." Such inclinations do not escape Hogsett. He relates: "People ask me, 'What's your approach? How do you work these women?' I'm like, fuck it, the more pitiful I am, the more the women like me" (Mandel, 2005). Through feigning more disability, more helplessness, Hogsett's practice accesses stereotypical norms of sexuality and disability too often portrayed in mainstream media. It maintains that the only, or "right," kind of sexuality involves "working" women (talking them up) in order to get them into bed and validates appealing to the ableist tendency to pity people with disabilities as an appropriate way "to score." Thus, the film depicts ableist beliefs about the sexual capacity of quadriplegic persons as "misinformed" while the values upon which those beliefs are based are left intact. Indeed, the emphasis on valuing traditional sexuality is evident in the final words of Hogsett's vignette: "I'd rather be able to grab my meat than grab a toothbrush" (Mandel, 2005).

## ❖ CONCLUSION

During a sequence of shots at the Team USA training camp, Hogsett tells a story about being at a wedding and listening to his girlfriend's relative congratulate him for being in the Special Olympics:

> And all of the sudden, I went from being the man at the wedding to the fucking retard. It was the worst feeling. What they do in the Special Olympics is very honorable. It's amazing what they can do. But this is something that is totally different . . . We're not going for a hug, we're going for a fucking gold medal. (Mandel, 2005)

In other words, these athletes raise the status of disability athletics by emphasizing the athletics and distancing them from disability. Ultimately this perpetuates division within the community of people with disabilities, reinforcing the ableist practice of valuing everyone based on their distinctiveness from an ablebodied "center." Just as the most popular images of disabled athletes were those viewed as most like the traditionally idealized athlete, this strategy for improving the image of disability sport privileges ableist assumptions about body value and norms.

Put another way, the film suggests that the ableist view is wrong—not because it applies discriminatory standards with which it devalues disability, but because those standards do not apply to these particular athletes. By implication, ableist assumptions are left intact and subtly validated. It becomes easier for ableists to see wheelchair rugby as a genuine athletic competition but only because—viewed this way—it does not threaten to upset the underlying ableist premises that oppress people with disabilities. Indeed, this perspective rigorously applies such standards against those who are unable to compete, often with a hostility—*"fucking retard"*—usually associated with virulent ableism. The scenario parallels the familiar narrative of people who maintain racist ideals but accept particular individuals of color as friends because they are seen as exceptions to those "rules."

This stance undermines the film's praiseworthy moves to improve the image of disability sport and to challenge the ableist conventions of viewing the disabled body. Unquestionably, *Murderball* presents an image of disability that differs dramatically from the stereotypes that pervade traditional media. Yet while it works to display wheelchair rugby as a sport deserving acceptance within traditional masculinist and ableist value systems, it avoids challenging those systems' discriminatory power. Rehabilitating its image may enhance the appeal of disability sport and support its ability to improve the self-esteem of athletes with disabilities, but the film also suggests the difficulty of negotiating the intersection of identity, disability, ableism, and sport. In particular, the emphasis on hypermasculinity and penetration seems to reify the ableist connection of disability and emasculation, as those who "can't get it up" are not included in the film's story. The emphasis on rehabilitation also tends to validate the damaging medical perspective of disability, as it generally views disability as a problem to be solved rather than a common life condition. Huang and Brittain (2006) concluded their study of disability sport and the negotiation of identity by arguing that athletes in these activities have the opportunity to "pin their dominant identity on that of an elite disabled athlete" which provides "a possible way out of the trap of negative identification" and "a basis from which to challenge the dominant perceptions of the medical model of disability" (p. 372). Overall, our analysis of *Murderball* supports this claim, but adds a serious caveat: These gains become suspect when such identification is based on the affirmation of ableist values and elevating disabled athletes distances them from other people with disabilities.

## ❖ REFERENCES

Ashton-Shaeffer, C., Gibson, H. J., Autry, C. E., & Hanson, C. S. (2001). Meaning of sport to adults with physical disabilities: A disability sport camp experience. *Sociology of Sport Journal, 18,* 95–114.

Baker, A. (2003). *Contesting identities: Sports in American film.* Urbana: University of Illinois Press.

Brasile, F. M. (1992). Inclusion: A developmental perspective on integration. *Adapted Physical Activity Quarterly, 9,* 293–304.

Brittain, I. (2004). Perceptions of disability and their impact upon involvement in sport for people with disabilities at all levels. *Journal of Sport and Social Issues, 28,* 429–452.

Burstyn, V. (1999). *The rites of men: Manhood, politics, and the culture of sport.* Toronto: University of Toronto Press.

Crosset, T. (1990). Masculinity, sexuality, and the development of early sport. In D. F. Sabo & M. A. Messner (Eds.), *Sport, men, and the gender order: Critical feminist perspectives* (pp. 45–54). Champaign, IL: Human Kinetics Books.

DePauw, K. P. (1997). The (in)visibility of disability: Cultural contexts and "sporting bodies." *Quest, 49,* 416–430.

Eastman, S. T., & Billings, A. C. (1999). Gender party in the Olympics: Hyping women athletes, favoring men athletes. *Journal of Sport and Social Issues, 23,* 140–170.

Ebert, R. (2005, July 22). Murderball. *Chicago Sun-Times.* Retrieved September 6, 2008, from http://rogerebert.suntimes.com/apps/pbcs.dll/article?AID=/20050721/REVIEWS/50607001

Goffman, E. (1963). *Stigma: Notes on the management of spoiled identity.* New York: Simon & Schuster.

Guthrie, S. R., & Castelnuovo, S. (2001). Disability management among women with physical impairments: The contribution of physical activity. *Sociology of Sport Journal, 18,* 5–20.

Hardin, M. (2003). Marketing the acceptably athletic image: Wheelchair athletes, sport-related advertising and capitalist hegemony. *Disability Studies Quarterly, 23*(1), 108–125.

Hardin, B., & Hardin, M. (2003). Conformity and conflict: Wheelchair athletes discuss sport media. *Adapted Physical Activity Quarterly, 20,* 246–259.

Hardin, B., Hardin, M., Lynn, S., & Walsdorf, K. (2004). Missing in action? Images of disability in *Sports Illustrated for Kids. Disability Studies Quarterly, 21*(2), 21–32.

Hartlaub, P. (2005, July 22). These rugby warriors use wheels. *San Francisco Chronicle.* Retrieved September 6, 2008, from http://www.sfgate.com/cgi-bin/article.cgi?f=/c/a/2005/07/22/DDG9JDR21J1.DTL&type=movies

Hooper, E. (2005, February 9). Game on. *Ragged Edge Online.* Retrieved on September 6, 2008, from http://www.ragged-edge-mag.com/reviews/hoopermurderball.html

Huang, C. J., & Brittain, I. (2006). Negotiating identities through disability sport. *Sociology of Sport Journal, 23,* 352–375.

Hutchinson, S. L., & Kleiber, D. A. (2000). Heroic masculinity following spinal cord injury: Implications for therapeutic recreation practice and research. *Therapeutic Recreation Journal, 34,* 42–54.

Kosma, M., Cardinal, B. J., & Rintala, P. (2002). Motivating individuals with disabilities to be physically active. *Quest, 54,* 116–132.

Lacan, J. (1977). *Écrits: A selection* (A. Sheridan, Trans.). London: Tavistock Books.

Lainson, S. (1996). Sport programming on television. *Sports News You Can Use.* Retrieved June 15, 2007, from http://www.onlinesports.com/sportstrust/sports4.html

Linton, S. (1998). *Claiming disability: Knowledge and identity.* New York: New York University Press.

Longmore, P. K. (1987). Screening stereotypes: Images of disabled people in television and motion pictures. In A. Gartner & T. Joe (Eds.), *Images of the disabled, disabling images* (pp. 65–78). New York: Praeger.

Mandel, J., & Shapiro, D. A. (Producers); Rubin, H. A., & Shapiro, D. A. (Directors). (2005). *Murderball* [Motion picture]. United States: Thinkfilm, Inc.

Martin, J. J., & Smith, K. (2002). Friendship quality in youth disability sport: Perceptions of a best friend. *Adapted Physical Activity Quarterly, 19,* 472–483.

Messner, M. A. (1992). *Power at play: Sports and the problem of masculinity.* Boston: Beacon Press.

Messner, M. A. (2002). *Taking the field: Men, women and sports.* Minneapolis: University of Minnesota Press.

Mulvey, L. (1989). *Visual and other pleasures.* Bloomington: Indiana University Press.

Murphy, R. F. (1990). *The body silent.* New York: W. W. Norton.

Nelson, J. A. (Ed.). (1994). *The disabled, the media, and the information age.* Westport, CT: Greenwood Publishing.

Norden, M. F. (1994). *The cinema of isolation.* New Brunswick, NJ: Rutgers University Press.

Pronger, B. (1990). *The arena of masculinity: Sports, homosexuality, and the meaning of sex.* London: GMP Publishers.

Puig, C. (2005, July 7). "Murderball": The wheel deal. *USA Today.* Retrieved September 6, 2008, from http://www.usatoday.com

Schell, L. A., & Duncan, M. C. (1999). A content analysis of CBS's coverage of the 1996 Paralympic Games. *Adapted Physical Activity Quarterly, 16,* 27–47.

Shakespeare, T. (1999). The sexual politics of disabled masculinity. *Sexuality and Disability, 17,* 53–64.

Smit, C. R., & Enns, A. (Eds.). (2001). *Screening disability: Essays on cinema and disability.* Lanham, MD: University Press of America.

Sparkes, A. C., & Smith, B. (2002). Sport, spinal cord injury, embodied masculinities, and the dilemmas of narrative identity. *Men and Masculinities, 4,* 258–285.

Taub, D. E., Blinde, E. M., & Greer, K. R. (1999). Stigma management through participation in sport and physical activity: Experiences of male college students with physical disabilities. *Human Relations, 52,* 1469–1484.

Thompson, D. (2005, July 22). "Murderball": Rowdy, winning, and real. *The Washington Post.* Retrieved September 6, 2008, from http://www.washingtonpost.com

Travers, P. (2005, July 14). Murderball. *Rolling Stone.* Retrieved September 6, 2008, from http://www.rollingstone.com

United States Quad Rugby Association (2006, January). *2005–2006 USQRA team representatives and RAC's.* Retrieved March 10, 2006, from http://www.quadrugby.com

Whitson, D. (1990). Sport in the social construction of masculinity. In D. F. Sabo & M. A. Messner (Eds.), *Sport, men, and the gender order: Critical feminist perspectives* (pp. 19–29). Champaign, IL: Human Kinetics Books.

# 11

# The Effects of Outcome of Mediated and Live Sporting Events on Sports Fans' Self- and Social Identities

Jennings Bryant

R. Glenn Cummins

When it comes to enacting their fanship, sports fans are in a league of their own. This admittedly grandiose claim is not without merit. Although extreme cases of fanship can be found across the social world, few domains engender the widespread passion that characterizes sportsfanship. Before we review evidence to support that statement, consider this observation offered by St. John (2004) in his examination of the extreme behavior that sometimes characterizes sportsfanship. First, he pointed to the scores reported in daily papers worldwide and urged readers to ponder the untold number of fans who followed each contest. Regarding those fans, he stated:

It's possible that some of these people had the most intense emotional experience in their lives . . . If this sounds like hyperbole, think of the most emotionally intense moments in your own life—when you realized you were in love, when your child was born, or when someone you cared for accomplished something important, like graduating from college. You were profoundly happy, but you probably didn't hug the stranger sitting next to you. Most likely, you didn't "go wild." You probably didn't tear down a goalpost. (p. 11)

Even if not all fans are guilty of such extreme behavior, social scientists have demonstrated that sports fans are distinct from other types of fans (Gantz & Wenner, 1995; Gantz, Wang, Paul, & Potter, 2006). Ostensibly, sports fans are voracious consumers of actual sports competition, both live and mediated. For example, a review of sports-related content in one U.S. television market found nearly 645 hours of sports programming in just one week's time (Brown & Bryant, 2006). Moreover, technology allows sports fans to customize their media diet like never before through services like baseball's MLB.TV Premium, which allows fans to view up to six games at once on their personal computers (Strauss, 2007). Surely the modern media landscape is a sports fan's nirvana.

The appetite for sports-related fodder hardly ends there, as fans' devotion extends well past the actual game-viewing experience. Many fans follow their favorite teams around the clock, eagerly scouring television, newspapers, radio, and online portals for team-related news (Gantz, et al., 2006; Real, 2006). Indicators of sportsfanship extend beyond media consumption to other forms of consumption as well. Bryant and Raney (2000) noted that sports fans routinely adorn themselves in all manner of team gear. Moreover, fans' consumer behavior extends beyond team-affiliated gear to products merely associated with teams via named sponsorships (e.g., Kinney, 2006; Madrigal, 2000).

Such devotion begs the question, what drives such voracious consumption? Scholars have enumerated several factors that motivate sports viewing, such as aesthetic appeal, the ability to arouse, or to facilitate social bonding (e.g., Raney, 2006; Trail & James, 2001). Of particular interest to this volume is the relationship between sports consumption and fans' own sense of identity. Sports fans follow the trials and tribulations of their favorite teams because, as we will note, it directly impacts how they view themselves, for better or for worse. This chapter examines conceptualization, theory, and evidence demonstrating that the outcome of sporting events affects how sports fans view themselves. We begin with conceptual approaches to identity in psychology and sociology; turn to two social scientific theories related to self-concept, rooting, and identity; review empirical investigations that have examined the effect of game outcome on identity; and preview a long-term investigation into the effects of a favorite college football team's winning and losing on fans' self- and social identity, as well as their perceived well-being and self-confidence.

❖  THEORY AND RELATED LITERATURE:
CONCEPTUAL APPROACHES TO IDENTITY

### William James and the Empirical Self

Central to our discussion of the impact of game outcome on sports fans is the concept of identity. As we will discuss, numerous scholars have examined the construct relative to sportsfanship, although much of this research has its roots in the broader work of psychologist and philosopher William James. One of the founders of the discipline of psychology, as well as of the philosophy of pragmatism, James (1890) devoted the longest chapter of his classic work *The Principles of Psychology* to self and identity. In one of many prescient declarations, James defines the Self in a way that is particularly useful to those studying contemporary sportsfanship:

> [A] man's [sic] Self is the sum total of all he can call his, not only his body and his psychic powers, but his clothes and his house, his wife and children, his ancestors and friends, his reputation and works, his lands and horses, and yacht and bank account. All these things give him the same emotions. If they wax and prosper, he feels triumphant; if they dwindle and die away, he feels cast down—not necessarily in the same degree for each thing, but in much the same way for all. (p. 292)

Implicitly embedded in this observation about the way we feel about the fortunes and misfortunes of what is ours—or better, what is *us*, the empirical Self—is a synthesis of ABC's *Wide World of Sports'* familiar slogan "the thrill of victory and the agony of defeat" and two contemporary theories—Social Identity Theory (SIT; Tajfel & Turner, 1986) and disposition theory (e.g., Zillmann, Bryant, & Sapolsky, 1989).

### LaFave's Identification Class and Reference Groups

James' (1890) ideas on the extended self were brought into modern psychology by LaFave (1972), who utilized the construct of Identification Class to explore the psychological mechanisms underlying humor, although that construct is equally relevant to our understanding of sportsfanship. According to his superiority theory of humor, "a 'joke' may prove especially funny when the 'good guys' beat the 'bad guys'" (p. 197), in which the so-called good guys serve as a Reference Group or identification class to the receiver interpreting the joke. Thus, reference groups are an extension of one's self, allowing for the vicarious experience of superiority via that group.

Also relevant to our examination of sportsfanship and identity, LaFave (1972) proposed that individual reference groups may combine to form macro-level groups. For example, he notes that Catholics, Baptists, and Jehovah's Witnesses all combine to form the broader group known as Christians. Analogously, sports fans align with one favorite team, but they may also support broader groups. Such is the case with a college football fan who supports (a) his or her favorite team throughout the season (individual reference group) and (b) its associated conference in post-season play (macro-level reference group). These multiple permutations of reference groups allow additional opportunities for fan associations and rooting.

### Team Identification

Wann and his collaborators (for a review, see Wann 2006a, 2006b) have amassed a considerable body of research demonstrating the central role of team identification in a variety of reception processes related to sports consumption. Wann (2006a) defines team identification as "the extent to which a fan feels a psychological connection to a team and the team's performances are viewed as self-relevant" (p. 352). Subsequent research has demonstrated that identification shapes numerous cognitive, affective, and behavioral responses to sports spectatorship, including acts of aggression (Wann et al., 2005), emotional response (Wann, Royalty, & Rochelle, 2002), and evaluations of opposing fans (Wann & Grieve, 2005). More central to this discussion is research connecting team identification and self-esteem (e.g., Wann & Pierce, 2005), which suggests that stronger fan associations with teams lead to better group and individual self-esteem and social psychological health (Wann, 2006b).

## ❖ THEORETICAL APPROACHES TO SPORTSFANSHIP AND IDENTITY

### Social Identity Theory

Much research investigating the relationship between sportsfanship, identity, and team performance has been carried out under the broad paradigm of Social Identity Theory (Tajfel & Turner, 1986). According to the theory, group membership plays a key role in the development of self identity. Groups do not exist merely as means of social categorization and sense making, but they also serve a self-referential function by helping define self identity through intergroup comparisons. People are not only *different* according to their group membership, but they are also *better* or *worse* than others. This essentially combines Festinger's (1954) Social Comparison Theory with self- and social identity. These comparisons occupy much of the predictive focus of SIT, as the "mere perception of belonging to two distinct groups—that is, social categorization per se—is sufficient to trigger intergroup discrimination favoring the in-group" (p. 13), i.e., in-group bias. Although sports are not the sole focus of SIT, its relevance is obvious. In few other contexts do "pre-fabricated" in-groups and out-groups appear as readily as in organized sports, and research has demonstrated this in-group bias in sports spectatorship (Wann & Grieve, 2005).

Having stated the importance of group affiliation to self-image, Tajfel and Turner (1986) then define social identity as "those aspects of an individual's self-image that derive from the social categories to which he perceives himself as belonging" (p. 16). Thus, for fans of a particular team, being a fan is a central part of their identity (e.g., Wann, Royalty, & Roberts, 2000). These concepts lead to three theoretical propositions, all of which suggest implications for the study of sportsfanship. First, they posit that because people strive for a positive self-concept, they also strive for a positive social identity. Within sportsfanship, this suggests that fans strive to be associated with successful teams, an argument that has received empirical support (e.g., End, Dietz-Uhler, Harrick, & Jacquemotte, 2002; Wann, Tucker, & Schrader, 1996).

Second, Tajfel and Turner (1986) proposed that a positive social identity is largely based upon favorable comparisons between the in-group and a relevant out-group. The head-to-head competition provided through sports contests allows for such comparisons via the phenomenon of Basking in Reflected Glory (BIRGing; Cialdini et al., 1976). Furthermore, Tajfel and Turner argued that intergroup comparisons are dynamic and change based upon a host of criteria. They claimed that "in-groups do not compare themselves with every cognitively available out-group: the out-group must be perceived as a relevant comparison group. Similarity, proximity, and situational salience are among the variables that determine out-group comparability" (pp. 16–17). This argument is clearly played out through the ongoing nature of the athletic season, which allows for the continual addition of new out-groups and the decreased salience of past out-groups. Sports allow for frequent and multiple comparisons with numerous out-groups to maintain a positive social identity (e.g., Boen, Vanbeselaere, & Feys, 2002; End, 2001). Moreover, research has demonstrated that sports fans often have multiple favorite teams, as well as multiple indices of success (End et al., 2002), allowing fans to maintain positive social identities by shifting focus to a winning team when another loses or by manipulating the criteria for evaluation (e.g., a winning record, post-season play, off-the-field recruiting).

Finally, Tajfel and Turner (1986) posited that when social identity is unsatisfactory, an individual will either leave the group and join another or make their group more positively distinct. Such behavior is exhibited by "fair-weather" fans who shed team allegiances in the face of loss, seen empirically through the phenomenon of Cutting Off Reflected Failure (CORFing; Snyder, Lassegard, & Ford, 1986).

The relevance of SIT to sportsfanship is most useful when reviewing Tajfel and Turner's (1986) propositions regarding how individuals react to threats to their social identity. They termed the first response Individual Mobility, in which "individuals may try to leave, or disassociate themselves from, their erstwhile group" (p. 19). This has been demonstrated through numerous empirical studies via CORFing (Snyder et al., 1986). However, because team affiliations are central to some fans' self and social identities, this option is not available to "die hard" team supporters (Wann & Branscombe, 1990).

The second response is called Social Creativity in which "group members may seek positive distinctiveness for the in-group by redefining or altering the elements of the comparative situation" (pp. 19–20). For example, the authors posited that group members may make comparisons between groups along some new dimension to achieve a more positive evaluation. In addition, group members can alter the out-group with which they are being compared to achieve a more positive evaluation. Examples from the world of college athletics help illustrate this practice. For example, fans of a school who lose to a key rival in one sport could potentially point to successes in another sport to help restore a positive social identity.

Tajfel and Turner (1986) also argued that under this tactic, fans of a subordinate in-group may seek a new out-group to allow for a more favorable comparison. Again, the world of college athletics can come to our aid. Arguably, one example is the common practice of scheduling weak out-of-conference opponents within college sports (e.g., Thamel, 2006). By doing this, in-groups are all but guaranteed the opportunity to make positive comparisons with the out-group and maintain a healthy group identity. However, Tajfel and Turner's warning of creating a "spurious rivalry" (p. 21) with inferior opponents rings particularly true. After all, landslide victories against weak opponents may bolster in-group fans' social identities, but it does little to raise a team's stock with those beyond the in-group.

Wann (2006a, 2006b) enumerated a host of additional coping mechanisms in accordance with SIT by which highly identified sportsfans learn to deal with threats to their identity. These include biased recollections of team performance (e.g., remembering past victories); externalizing team failures (e.g., blaming officials); derogating fans of the opposing team so as to alter the dimension of comparison; retroactive pessimism (reporting after team losses that the fan secretly had doubts concerning the team's chance of success); and proactive pessimism (increased pessimism as a contest draws nearer).

### Disposition Theory of Sportsfanship

Additional insight regarding the importance of fans' affiliations with teams is provided by the Disposition Theory of Sportsfanship (Raney, 2006; Zillmann, Bryant, & Sapolsky, 1989). Although the theory does not employ the term identification, associations between fans and teams in the form of dispositions are at the heart of the theory. Dispositional affiliations are formed with teams and/or players based on many factors, such as geographical proximity (e.g., the "home-team"; Owens & Bryant, 1998) or storylines created by sports commentary (e.g., Bryant, Brown, Comisky, & Zillmann, 1982). Although these dispositions may vary in intensity, for many fans the associations are central to their identity. As Bryant and Raney (2000) indicated:

> Today's ardent sportsfan adds team and player jerseys, team hats of all shapes and colors, face and body paint, and weird but clearly identifiable costumes or apparel (e.g., cheeseheads, elephant trunks). These symbols clearly mark one not only as a fan, but as a die-hard, true-blue, unadulterated, as-I-live-and-breathe, in-your-face fan. (p. 162)

The theoretical propositions of the disposition theory of sportsfanship reflect the intellectual influence of LaFave's (1972) aforementioned superiority theory of humor and identification class. Analogous to that theory, Zillmann et al. (1989) suggested the following:

1. Enjoyment derived from witnessing the success and victory of a competing party increases with positive sentiments and decreases with negative sentiments toward that party.

2. Enjoyment derived from witnessing the failure and defeat of a competing party increases with negative sentiments and decreases with positive sentiments toward that party. (p. 257)

Zillmann et al. (1989) further added: "The optimal condition for enjoyment is the contest in which an intensely liked player or team defeats an intensely disliked player" (p. 257). Thus, dispositional affiliations with teams and/or players are at the heart of enjoyment. Absent those affiliations, spectators either do not experience enjoyment or find alternate reasons for their appreciation of a contest (e.g., quality of play: Zillmann et al., 1989; roughness of play: Bryant, Comisky, & Zillmann, 1981; and suspense: Bryant, Rockwell, & Owens, 1994).

The authors (Zillmann et al., 1989) summarized a body of evidence to support these theoretical propositions. They first conducted an experiment utilizing participants' preexisting dispositions toward two NFL teams, the Minnesota Vikings and St. Louis Cardinals.[1] The naturally occurring variation in participants' feelings allowed for a factorial design with varying levels of disposition: positive, neutral, and negative. In a head-to-head contest between those teams, the authors observed the effects of students' dispositions toward those teams in successful offensive plays such that "a positive disposition toward a team tended to enhance the appreciation of offensive plays successfully executed by that team" (p. 258). These findings were likewise echoed by participants' sentiments toward the final outcome of the game.

Next, the disposition theory of sportsfanship was supported outside the research laboratory through a common form of fan behavior, cheering. Zillmann et al. (1989) cited data from a field study of fan responses during actual game play where the results again were in line with the predictions of disposition theory. They found that "failing plays of the visiting team were nearly as much applauded as successful plays of the home team" (p. 260).

Additional evidence demonstrates how dispositional affiliations with athletes and teams are formed along a number of criteria. For example, Sapolsky (1980) provided evidence that viewers formed dispositions toward sports teams along ethnic lines. In addition, Zillmann et al. (1989) cited data from an investigation involving the 1976 U.S. men's Olympic basketball game where participants reported greater enjoyment seeing the U.S. team score when compared with the opposing team. Moreover, the greatest enjoyment was reported when baskets were scored by team members who also played at Indiana University, where the study participants attended school. Thus, spectator enjoyment varied as a function of their dispositions toward both the team and individual players.

The disposition theory of sportsfanship has also been manifested in the commentary of sports broadcasters. For example, Owens and Bryant (1998) examined the effects of home team or "homer" announcers on viewers' enjoyment of televised sports. They argued that home team announcers present an obvious bias by focusing commentary largely on one team. Their findings demonstrated spectators' preference for this practice, as "'homer' commentary resulted in greater levels of excitement during the contest and greater overall enjoyment for the home team fans as compared to the excitement and enjoyment level of the visiting fans" (Owens & Bryant, 1998, p. 2). In sum, this body of evidence demonstrates the robustness of the disposition theory of sportsfanship and the importance of dispositions toward teams and players in fans' enjoyment of sports spectatorship.

### Effects of Game Outcome on Identity

*BIRGing, Blasting, CORFing, and COFFing*: The various predictions of SIT have found considerable empirical support in the form of numerous image-maintenance and image-enhancement techniques. Sports fans are adept at employing a variety of tactics to maintain a positive social identity, either by strengthening ties to successful groups, severing or reducing ties to unsuccessful groups, or derogating rival groups. All of this is done in the hopes of improving observers' evaluations of valued group memberships.

One of the first of such image maintenance techniques to be examined is Basking in Reflected Glory (*BIRGing*). Cialdini et al. (1976) coined the phrase in their examination of people's tendency to "share in the glory of a successful other with whom they are in some way associated" (p. 366). They presented BIRGing as an image-maintenance technique in line with the principles of Heider's (1958) balance formulation and Festiner's (1957) Cognitive Dissonance Theory. In short, people wish to be positively associated with things that are evaluated positively because "observers to these connections tend to evaluate connected objects similarly" (Cialdini et al., 1976, p. 374). Failure to evaluate connected objects similarly produces the unpleasant psychological state known as dissonance. In the context of sportsfanship, they predicted that people would choose to be publicly associated with a winning team in order to share in its positive evaluation.

The authors detailed a series of studies that demonstrated empirical support for BIRGing. In one study, Cialdini et al. (1976) found that students were significantly more likely to wear clothing associated with their school on the Monday after a winning football game when compared to when the team lost. Moreover, data collection occurred across seven university campuses, demonstrating the robustness of the phenomenon. A second study examined the use of the pronouns "we" versus "they" in descriptions of games won and lost. They found that the personal pronoun "we" was used significantly more often when participants were prompted to recall victories versus defeats (e.g., "we won," versus "they lost").

Cialdini and Richardson (1980) later introduced the concept of *Blasting* as an additional image-maintenance technique. Just as BIRGing serves to increase positive associations with positively evaluated objects, Blasting serves to decrease evaluations with negatively associated objects. In the context of sportsfanship, such behavior manifests itself as derogating or "blasting" a disliked opponent or rival so as to cast it in a negative light. Not only did Cialdini and Richardson find support for Blasting, but their data also suggested that participants are particularly likely to engage in such behavior after suffering a threat to their self-esteem in the eyes of an observer.

Snyder and his collaborators (1986) advanced this line of research by demonstrating yet another image-maintenance technique, Cutting Off Reflected Failure (*CORFing*). With this technique, individuals seek to sever ties with negatively evaluated groups to avoid damaging associations with the group. To test this phenomenon, they had participants take part in a group task, after which the experimenter gave either positive evaluations, negative evaluations, or no evaluations. They found that participants in the negative feedback condition reported more anxiety, depression, and hostility than participants given positive feedback. Moreover, participants in the negative feedback condition were less likely to wear team badges and reported less desire to take part in a group presentation of their team's work.

An additional image-maintenance technique, Cutting Off Future Failure (*COFFing*) was introduced by Wann, Hamlet, Wilson, and Hodgest (1995) as a means of explaining why some individuals refrain from BIRGing after group success. They defined the phenomenon as a

distancing tactic in which individuals decline the opportunity to bask in the glow of victory of a successful group and consequently enhance their ego. Rather, these persons decide not to publicly announce their membership in an attempt to protect their ego from future damage. (pp. 382–383)

Wann et al. (1995) demonstrated support for COFFing by having research participants engage in a creativity task in the guise of a competition with senior art majors. Participants who were told that they had outperformed the art students were less likely to want to meet their competition if they believed that they still faced a second round of competition relative to those who believed the competition was over. Thus, if individuals fear the possibility of future failure, they may refrain from basking in the glow of victory.

Scholars have since conducted numerous studies demonstrating the robustness of these phenomena in both interpersonal and mediated settings. For example, evidence suggests that BIRGing extends to online behavior via fan visits to team Web sites (Boen et al., 2002) and posts to a team's online message board following wins versus losses (End, 2001). In addition, Wann and Branscombe (1990) demonstrated that fans' strength of affiliation with a team is a key mediating variable in these image-maintenance techniques. Their data revealed that CORFing is not an option for highly identified fans, as that fanship represents a crucial component of their self-image.

### Effects on Optimism, Pessimism, and Self-Esteem

The research presented thus far regarding the impact of team affiliation has involved public displays of behavior, occupying the realm of interpersonal processes. As such, one question not addressed is the extent to which team affiliations influence intrapersonal processes such as mood, optimism, and self-esteem evaluations. For example, Cialdini and Richardson (1980) proposed that just as BIRGing and Blasting serve to influence social identity, they may have similar influence on one's self identity. However, their data did not explicitly test this suggestion. Similarly, Boen et al.'s (2002) study of fan traffic to team Web sites posited such media use as a private form of BIRGing that allows fans to "ruminate and relive the strong positive emotions attached to the victory" (p. 778). Thus, it merely suggests intrapersonal effects of game outcome.

Evidence does support the argument that game outcome affects fans' mood states. For example, Wann, Dolan, McGeorge, and Allison (1994) examined the impact of team identification and game outcome on changes in spectators' mood states. Their results showed the largest increase in fans' positive affect after a difficult win and the largest decrease in affect after a difficult loss. In addition, because highly identified fans are unable to distance themselves from the team after a loss (i.e., CORF), "these fans experience unfavorable emotions such as sadness, anger, and discouragement" (p. 359). In addition, Snyder et al. (1986) reported significant differences in participants' experience of negative affect (i.e., anxiety, depression) after group failure relative to group success. In addition to changes in affect, sports may also elicit a sense of optimism regarding one's favorite team. Research has documented a so-called "allegiance bias" (Markman & Hirt, 2002), whereby fans who strongly identify with a team report biased recollections of past victories and are likewise overly optimistic of their team's potential for future success (Wann & Dolan, 1994).

More interesting, however, is evidence that demonstrates effects beyond the immediate domain of sports. For example, Schwarz, Strack, Kommer, and Wagner (1987) found that sports spectators reported being more satisfied with their lives in general, with their work and income, and even with national issues after viewing their national team win a soccer game, compared to responses prior to the game. The opposite was true after witnessing a tie, with reported satisfaction decreasing in that situation.

Based on that research, Schweitzer, Zillmann, Weaver, and Luttrell (1992) examined the extent to which game outcome affected other areas of fans' psyche. They hypothesized that game outcome would affect participants' evaluations of the likelihood of a feared event such that fans of a losing team would report increased estimates of such an event, whereas fans of a winning team would report decreased estimates of a feared event. In their study, students at two rival universities viewed a head-to-head competition between the schools. After the game, participants completed measures of mood as well as estimates of the chances that Iraq would enter into armed conflict with the United States. Participants were also asked to report estimated casualties in the conflict. Results showed that fans of the losing team thought the conflict was significantly more likely than fans of the winning team. In addition, fans of the losing team predicted greater loss of life relative to fans of the winning team. Thus, viewing a favorite team suffer defeat induces a general state of gloom that influences sports' fans outlook on the world.

Similar effects have been documented when examining the financial sector. Edmans, García, and Norli (2006) present a wealth of data showing that "losses in soccer matches have an economically and statistically significant negative effect on the losing country's stock market" (p. 1). Moreover, they demonstrate the same effect with international cricket, rugby, ice hockey, and basketball games. Most impressive is the robustness of their data set. After combining data regarding all the above sports across a cross-sectional sample of 39 countries, the authors based their conclusions on 2,600 independent observations. Again, the impact of game outcome goes far beyond simple changes in affect.

What these studies do not address is the extent to which group successes and failure are internalized as personal successes and failures as suggested by SIT. Hirt, Zillmann, Erickson, and Kennedy (1992) provided empirical support for this hypothesis in a series of studies. They began by conceptualizing the self "as a set of internalized roles or identities" (p. 725). As such, any threat to one's identity is treated as a threat to the self. In the case of sports spectatorship, when a winning team suffers defeat, the fan feels as though he or she has personally suffered defeat. The implications for success and defeat should thus include changes in fans' predictions of future success and failure. Likewise, implications for the fan include changes in affect as well as changes in predictions of one's own future success and failure. To test these predictions, student participants were recruited to view a broadcast of a men's basketball game at their home university. After viewing either a team victory or defeat, participants were asked to report estimates of future team success as well as their own mood state. Participants were later asked to predict their own performance on a series of tasks under the guise of a second, independent study.

Results suggested "the outcome of the game strongly affected subjects' estimates of their team's future performance" (Hirt et al., 1992, p. 728). More importantly, there was also some evidence that the success was internalized, as participants in the win condition reported higher estimates of their own abilities on subsequent mental and motor skills tasks. After viewing a team victory, participants reported stronger confidence in their own abilities relative to those who viewed a team loss. Moreover, subsequent path analysis suggested that although team performance affected participants' moods, changes in mood did not mediate the observed effects. Thus, although team losses resulted in negative affect, mood per se was not to blame for the decreased estimates of team or personal success.

In addition, analogous to Wann and Branscombe's (1990) findings, Hirt et al. (1992) found that the strength of affiliation with the team also played a significant role in shaping fans' post-game responses. They added, "The fact that the effects were observed only for those subjects who reported high levels of fanship suggest that an identity must be of sufficient importance and prominence for these effects to occur" (p. 736).

## ❖   METHODOLOGICAL APPROACH

### Avid Fans, Extreme Identity: Alabama-Auburn Football

To systematically examine how winning and losing affects avid sports fans' self- and social identities, Bryant and his associates (Bryant et al., 2007) examined diverse effects of the outcome of Alabama-Auburn football games over a 20-year period.[2] Often referred to as *A War in Dixie* (Maisel & Whiteside, 2001), the annual football game between The University of Alabama Crimson Tide  and the Auburn University Tigers, known as the Iron Bowl, is one of the greatest rivalries in sports. *Sports Illustrated* ranked the rivalry as the second greatest in all of sports and the greatest in college football, and the cable sports network ESPN ranked it as college football's number one rivalry ("Some Crimson Tide," 2007). Not only does the outcome of the game determine who will have so-called "braggin' rights" in the state of Alabama for the next year, the rivalry regularly has implications for who will play in the SEC (Southeastern Conference) championship game. As St. John (2004) noted in his look inside one season of Alabama football, "If you were a scientist hoping to isolate the fan gene, Alabama would make the perfect laboratory" (p. 1). As such, it represents the ideal opportunity for a longitudinal, real-world examination of the impact of game outcome on fans' self- and social identities.

During the 20-year span of this investigation, Auburn won 12 of the games (60%), and Alabama won 8 (40%). Alabama won the SEC title three times (1989[3], 1992, 1999) and the national championship once (1992); and Auburn won the SEC title three times (1988[4], 1989, 2004) and was undefeated one year (2004). On the negative side of the equation, both teams were also on NCAA probation once during this period.

### Survey Procedure

During the week following each Iron Bowl game played between 1987 and 2006, Bryant et al. (2007) conducted research on Alabama and Auburn sportsfans' self- and social identities via a variety of procedures, including the collection of archival data (e.g., sales of team paraphernalia, food and beverage sales), personal interviews, focus groups, and telephone surveys.[5] In this report, findings are limited to a small number of questions from the 20 telephone surveys only. Each of the 1987–2006 telephone surveys featured 300 completed interviews (overall N = 6,000) with a probability sample of State of Alabama residents who self-identified as either an Alabama fan or an Auburn fan and who indicated that they had watched most, if not all, of the preceding Iron Bowl game, either in the stadium or on television.[6]

Among the 60 questions asked each Alabama and Auburn football fan interviewed during this 20 years of telephone surveys were four that were concerned primarily with self- and social identity and sportsfanship. These featured items are:

(1) "How avid an Alabama/Auburn (the team identified depended on responses to prior questions) fan do you consider yourself to be?" Response options ranged from 0 (not avid at all) to 10 (as avid as anyone possibly can be).

(2) "How important is your being an Alabama/Auburn fan to your overall self-concept?" Responses to this social identity item could range from 0 (not important at all) to 10 (extremely important).

(3) "How good have you felt about yourself so far this week?" Responses to this self-esteem question ranged from 0 (extremely lousy) to 10 (fantastic).

(4) "How much self-confidence have you had overall about the personal, professional, and business decisions you have made so far this week?" Responses could range from 0 (not confident at all) to 10 (as confident as anyone can possibly be).

All data were analyzed by game, by coaching era (e.g., Pat Dye, Terry Bowden, and Tommy Tuberville for Auburn; Bill Curry, Gene Stallings, Mike Dubose, Dennis Franchione, and Mike Shula for Alabama), by team preference, by outcome, and a number of other ways. However, for this report we have collapsed all data to the extent possible and report the findings only by team preference (Alabama, Auburn) and game outcome (Alabama wins/Auburn loses, Auburn wins/Alabama loses).

❖  RESULTS

As can be seen from examining the data for the first item ("How avid a fan") presented in Table 11.1, which reveals the mean scores for the items related to game outcome and team fanship, Alabama and Auburn fans are loyal, even diehard, fans independent of Iron Bowl outcome. Although mean fanship scores for both groups of fans were

**Table 11.1**    Mean Scores of Items Related to Identity of Alabama and Auburn Fans as Affected by the Outcome of the Iron Bowl Games

| Item | Alabama fan/Alabama wins | Alabama fan/Alabama loses | Auburn fan/Auburn wins | Auburn fan/Auburn loses |
|---|---|---|---|---|
| 1. How avid fan | 8.73 | 8.44 | 8.52 | 8.27 |
| 2. Importance of fanship to self-concept | 8.03[c] | 6.51[a] | 7.69[b] | 6.55[a] |
| 3. Felt about self | 8.57[b] | 5.43[a] | 8.46[b] | 5.51[a] |
| 4. Self-confidence | 9.03[b] | 7.19[a] | 8.96[b] | 7.29[a] |

**Note:** Comparisons are horizontal only (i.e., within item). Means having different superscripts differ significantly at $p < .05$ by Newman-Keuls' test following an overall statistically significant $F$-ratio from an analysis of variance.

slightly lower when their team lost, this decrease did not reach statistical significance. Thus, degree of fanship was not affected for either Alabama or Auburn fans by whether their team won or lost the previous Saturday.

In contrast, the importance of their fanship (i.e., identity with their team) to their overall self-concept was markedly affected by game outcome. For fans of both teams, when their team won, their identity as an Alabama/Auburn fan was deemed more important than when their team lost. Apparently some "distancing" process takes place within self-identity when a favorite team loses, undoubtedly for the purpose of psychological self-preservation. The effects on this item were more pronounced for Alabama fans than for Auburn fans, which were derived from a more extreme integration of their team identity into their self-concept when Alabama won. This may well be symptomatic of how desperate Alabama fans have been for a win of late (Auburn has won the last six Iron Bowl games), which undoubtedly was a factor in the widespread fan support for offering a record-breaking salary to new head Alabama football coach Nick Saban in 2007 (Maske, 2007).

In terms of the effects of winning and losing on how fans felt about themselves, clearly winning and losing made a major difference for both Alabama and Auburn fans. Fans of both teams reported feeling significantly better about themselves when their team won than when they lost.

Finally, the findings for the effects of a beloved team winning or losing on self-confidence in personal, professional, and business decisions made in the recent past were pronounced for fans of both teams. Whenever their team won, fans apparently felt more confident about all sorts of personal and professional decision-making than they did when their team lost. Winning and losing obviously matter psychologically, not just when we do it personally, but also when our teams win or lose. Our self-identity, or at least certain aspects of such, is apparently directly linked to our social identity as a fan.

❖  DISCUSSION

Taken altogether, this vast body of research demonstrates that for sports fans, both being a fan and being viewed as a fan are critical components of a person's identity. This association with a team is one that fans readily and creatively boast about in victory through a variety of external markers, including clothes, team regalia, interpersonal behavior, and much more. However, in defeat, this association is one that is not easily shed, and fans must suffer along with their team. As a result, research has also shown us that fans are just as creative at coping with a team defeat. They can look forward to next season, look backwards at a past victory, or focus on a different team entirely to restore their positive self and social identity. What drives this fervent behavior? Research demonstrates that rooting for a favorite team is a crucial component of why we watch sports in the first place. It brings us together and allows us to experience euphoric highs. Our yearning to see our team win forces us to suffer great anxiety during a game and experience equally great jubilation in victory. Finally, we know that for sports fans, a team loss is taken as a personal defeat, and a team win is taken as a personal victory. The joy of victory can enhance one's self-esteem, and the agony of defeat can inflict just as strong a blow to one's self-image.

The original research reported here illustrates the concepts described in the literature review by demonstrating the extremes of sportsfanship endemic to Alabama and Auburn football as well as the significant impact of game outcome on fan identity. Clearly, our research participants view themselves as die-hard team supporters, and being a fan was central to their self-identity. Nonetheless, these fans did exhibit signs of distancing behavior after a team loss by reporting that being a fan was less central to their own self-concept. This response is distinct from CORFing (Snyder et al., 1986) or other responses originally suggested by SIT (Tajfel & Turner, 1986). These results suggest that Alabama and Auburn fans seek to renegotiate their identities to make team fanship less central to their self-concept. Nonetheless, as Wann and Branscombe (1990) noted, highly identified fans are unable to simply shed team allegiances due to wavering team performance. For our participants, team associations are deeply engrained, and as a result, fans must suffer along with their team.

The negative impact of these associations is evident in how Alabama and Auburn fans felt about themselves and their personal abilities following team wins and losses. For ardent fans, team losses are internalized as personal defeats (Hirt et al., 1992), and the impact of team performance has been demonstrated on a global scale (Edmans et al., 2006). Such was the case in our investigation, as fans of both Alabama and Auburn felt significantly worse about themselves following a team loss when compared with a victory. This blow to our participants' self-esteem also manifested itself in judgments about their abilities in personal and business decisions, which saw significant decreases following team losses when compared with victories. Given this response, it is of little surprise that the ebb and flow of team wins and losses is reflected not only in how we view ourselves, but also in our day-to-day lives.

## ❖ REFERENCES

Boen, F., Vanbeselaere, N., & Feys, J. (2002). Behavioral consequences of fluctuating group success: An Internet study of soccer-team fans. *Journal of Social Psychology, 142,* 769–781.

Brown, D., & Bryant, J. (2006). Sports content on U.S. television. In A. A. Raney & J. Bryant (Eds.), *Handbook of sports and media* (pp. 77–104). Mahwah, NJ: Lawrence Erlbaum.

Bryant, J., Brown, D., Comisky, P. W., & Zillmann, D. (1982). Sports and spectators: Commentary and appreciation. *Journal of Communication, 32*(1), 109–119.

Bryant, J., Comisky, P. W., & Zillmann, D. (1981). The appeal of rough-and-tumble play in televised professional football. *Communication Quarterly, 29,* 256–262.

Bryant, J., Gibson, R., Owens, J., Davenport, S., Rockwell, S. R., Love, C., Raney, A. A., Cummins, R. G., & Fondren, W. (2007). *The effects of Alabama and Auburn football on the social, psychological, and economic well-being of Alabama's citizens.* Tuscaloosa, AL: Institute for Communication & Information Research.

Bryant, J., & Raney, A. A. (2000). Sports on the screen. In D. Zillmann & P. Vorderer (Eds.), *Media entertainment: The psychology of its appeal* (pp. 153–174). Mahwah, NJ: Lawrence Erlbaum.

Bryant, J., Rockwell, S. C., & Owens, J. W. (1994). "Buzzer beaters" and "barn burners": The effects on enjoyment of watching the game go "down to the wire." *Journal of Sport & Social Issues, 18*, 326–339.

Cialdini, R. B., Borden, R. J., Thorne, A., Walker, M. R., Freeman, S., & Sloan, L. R. (1976). Basking in reflected glory: Three (football) field studies. *Journal of Personality and Social Psychology, 34*, 366–375.

Cialdini, R. B., & Richardson, K. D. (1980). Two indirect tactics of image management: Basking and blasting. *Journal of Personality and Social Psychology, 39*, 406–415.

Edmans, A., García, D., & Norli, Ø. (2006, May). *Sports sentiment and stock returns.* Paper presented at the 16th annual Utah Winter Finance Conference, Salt Lake City, UT.

End, C. M. (2001). An examination of NFL fans' computer mediated BIRGing. *Journal of Sport Behavior, 24*, 162–181.

End, C. M., Dietz-Uhler, B., Harrick, E. A., & Jacquemotte, L. (2002). Identifying with winners: A reexamination of sport fans' tendency to BIRG. *Journal of Applied Social Psychology, 32*, 1017–1030.

Festinger, L. (1954). A theory of social comparison processes. *Human Relations, 7*, 117–140.

Festinger, L. (1957). *A theory of cognitive dissonance.* Evanston, IL: Row & Peterson.

Gantz, W., Wang, Z., Paul, B., & Potter, R. F. (2006). Sports versus all comers: Comparing TV sports fans with fans of other genres. *Journal of Broadcasting & Electronic Media, 50*, 95–118.

Gantz, W., & Wenner, L. A. (1995). Fanship and the television sports viewing experience. *Sociology of Sport Journal, 12*, 56–74.

Heider, F. (1958). *The psychology of interpersonal relations.* New York: Wiley.

Hirt, E. R., Zillmann, D., Erickson, G. A., & Kennedy, C. (1992). Costs and benefits of allegiance: Changes in fans' self-ascribed competencies after team victory versus defeat. *Journal of Personality and Social Psychology, 63*, 724–738.

James, W. (1890). *The principles of psychology* (Vol. 2). New York: Henry Holt.

Kinney, L. (2006). Sports sponsorship. In A. A. Raney & J. Bryant (Eds.), *Handbook of sports and media* (pp. 295–310). Mahwah, NJ: Lawrence Erlbaum.

LaFave, L. (1972). Humor judgments as a function of reference groups and identification classes. In J. H. Goldstein & P. E. McGhee (Eds.), *The psychology of humor: Theoretical perspectives and empirical issues* (pp. 195–210). New York: Academic Press.

Madrigal, R. (2000). The influence of social alliances with sports teams on intentions to purchase corporate sponsors' products. *Journal of Advertising, 19*(4), 13–24.

Maisel, I., & Whiteside, K. (2001). *A war in Dixie.* New York: HarperCollins.

Markman, K. D., & Hirt, E. R. (2002). Social prediction and the "allegiance bias." *Social Cognition, 20*, 58–86.

Maske, M. (2007, January 4). Saban leaves Dolphins to coach Alabama. *The Washington Post*, p. E5. Retrieved September 8, 2008, from LexisNexis Academic database.

Owens, J. W., & Bryant, J. (1998, July). *The effects of a hometeam ("homer")
announcer and color commentary on audience perceptions and enjoyment of
a sports contest.* Paper presented at the meeting of the International
Communication Association, Jerusalem, Israel.

Raney, A. A. (2006). Why we watch and enjoy mediated sports. In A. A. Raney
& J. Bryant (Eds.), *Handbook of sports and media* (pp. 313–329). Mahwah,
NJ: Lawrence Erlbaum.

Real, M. (2006). Sports online: The newest player in mediasport. In A. A. Raney
& J. Bryant (Eds.), *Handbook of sports and media* (pp. 171–184). Mahwah, NJ:
Lawrence Erlbaum.

Sapolsky, B. S. (1980). The effect of spectator disposition and suspense on the enjoyment of sports contests. *International Journal of Sports Psychology, 11,* 1–10.

Schwarz, N., Strack, F., Kommer, D., & Wagner, D. (1987). Soccer, rooms,
and the quality of your life: Mood effects on judgments of satisfaction with
life in general and with specific domains. *European Journal of Psychology,
17,* 69–79.

Schweiter, K., Zillmann, D., Weaver, J. B., & Luttrell, E. S. (1992). Perception
of threatening events in the emotional aftermath of a televised college
football game. *Journal of Broadcasting & Electronic Media, 36,* 75–82.

Snyder, C. R., Lassegard, M. A., & Ford, C. E. (1986). Distancing after group
success and failure: Basking in reflected glory and cutting off reflected
failure. *Journal of Personality and Social Psychology, 51,* 382–388.

Some Crimson Tide/Auburn Tigers Trivia. (2007, November 23). *The Tuscaloosa
News,* p. D15.

St. John, W. (2004). *Rammer jammer yellow hammer: A journey into the heart of fan
mania.* New York: Crown.

Strauss, R. (2007, July 17). Tech me out to the ballgame. *PC Magazine, 26,* 17.

Tajfel, H., & Turner, J. C. (1986). The social identity theory of intergroup behavior. In S. Worchel & W. G. Austin (Eds.), *Psychology of intergroup relations*
(2nd ed., pp. 7–24). Chicago: Nelson-Hall Publishers.

Thamel, P. (2006, August 23). In college football, big paydays for humiliation.
*The New York Times,* p. A1.

Trail, G. T., & James, J. D. (2001). The motivation scale for sport consumption:
Assessment of the scale's psychometric properties. *Journal of Sport Behavior,
24,* 108–127.

Wann, D. L. (2006a). The causes and consequences of sport team identification.
In A. A. Raney & J. Bryant (Eds.), *Handbook of sports and media* (pp. 331–352).
Mahwah, NJ: Lawrence Erlbaum.

Wann, D. L. (2006b). Understanding the positive social psychological benefits
of sport team identification: The team identification-social psychological
health model. *Group Dynamics: Theory, Research, and Practice, 4,* 272–296.

Wann, D. L., & Branscombe, N. R. (1990). Die-hard and fair-weather fans:
Effects of identification on BIRGing and CORFing tendencies. *Journal of
Sport and Social Issues, 14*(2), 103–117.

Wann, D. L., Culver, Z., Akanda, R., Daglar, M., DeDivitiis, C., & Smith, A.
(2005). The effects of team identification and game outcome on willingness

to consider anonymous acts of hostile aggression. *Journal of Sport Behavior,*
*28,* 282–294.

Wann, D. L., & Dolan, T. J. (1994). Influence of spectators' identification on
evaluation of the past, present, and future performance of a sports team.
*Perceptual and Motor Skills, 78,* 547–552.

Wann, D. L., Dolan, T. J., McGeorge, K. K., & Allison, J. A. (1994). Relationships
between spectator identification and spectators' perceptions of influence,
spectators' emotions, and competition outcome. *Journal of Sport & Exercise*
*Psychology, 16,* 347–364.

Wann, D. L., & Grieve, F. G. (2005). Biased evaluations of in-group and
out-group spectator behavior at sporting events: The importance of team
identification and threats to social identity. *Journal of Social Psychology, 145,*
531–545.

Wann, D. L., Hamlet, M. A., Wilson, T. M., & Hodges, J. A. (1995). Basking in
reflected glory, cutting off reflected failure, and cutting off future failure:
The importance of group identification. *Social Behavior and Personality,*
*23,* 377–388.

Wann, D. L., & Pierce, S. (2005). The relationship between sport team identification and social well-being: Additional evidence supporting the team
identification-social psychological health model. *North American Journal of*
*Psychology, 7,* 117–124.

Wann, D. L., Royalty, J., & Roberts, A. (2000). The self-presentation of sport
fans: Investigating the importance of team identification and self-esteem.
*Journal of Sport Behavior, 23,* 198–206.

Wann, D. L., Royalty, J. L., & Rochelle, A. R. (2002). Using motivation and team
identification to predict sports fans' emotional responses to team performance. *Journal of Sport Behavior, 25,* 207–216.

Wann, D. L., Tucker, K. B., & Schrader, M. P. (1996). An exploratory examination of the factors influencing the origination, continuation, and cessation
of identification with sports teams. *Perceptual and Motor Skills, 82,*
995–1001.

Zillmann, D., Bryant, J., & Sapolsky, B. S. (1989). Enjoyment from sports spectatorship. In J. Goldstein (Ed.), *Sports, games, and play: Social and psycholog-*
*ical viewpoints* (2nd ed., pp. 241–278). Hillsdale, NJ: Lawrence Erlbaum.

### ❖ NOTES

1. Now the Arizona Cardinals.

2. The study of the psychological impact of these rivalry football games is
a relatively small part of our comprehensive study of the social, psychological,
and economic impact of Alabama and Auburn football, 1987–2006. We are
deeply grateful for the support of the Research Funds of the Ronald Reagan
Chair of Broadcasting, which provided the bulk of the support for this longitudinal investigation.

3. Alabama, Auburn, and Tennessee tied (6–1-0) in 1989, prior to the intro-duction of the SEC championship game.

4. Auburn and LSU tied (6–1-0) in 1988.

5. Professional interviewers of the Institute for Communication Research of the University of Alabama conducted the first five telephone surveys on which the present report is based. The remaining 15 surveys were conducted by one of three different professional research firms under contract with the first author.

6. Our research determined that fans who go to the trouble and expense of attending an Iron Bowl game "live," at the Stadium (either Birmingham's Legion Field, Auburn's Jordan-Hare Stadium, or Alabama's Bryant-Denny Stadium) typically are, in the parlance of the day, "Super Fans" or " uber fans." For example, our research revealed that each fan spent an average of $246 per person on their Iron Bowl game day experience between 1995 and 2005.

# 12

# The Institutional(ized) Nature of Identity in and Around Sport(s)

### Kelby K. Halone

To consider the role of identity in the domain of sport is no small undertaking. If entertained authentically (Clair, 1999), such a query initially begs for the consideration of an array of questions: What is the relationship between identity and sport? How do communication dynamics contribute to issues of identity in sport? Where might one confidently locate identity in sport? How do the media contribute to our understanding of identity in sport? How does identity become enacted around sport? When does identity become "organized" in the domain of sport? How might one know they are examining identity in sport when they claim to do so? Where (and how often) does identity become (re)produced in sport? What role do human-mediated interactions play in our understanding of identity in sport? How do issues of identity become consumed in sport? How do communication and sport scholars contribute to (and/or detract from) our understanding of identity in and around sport? How does one confidently know whether (or if) one has a clear understanding of the relationships that exist among dynamics of communication, identity, and sport? While these questions are clearly suggestive versus exhaustive in scope, one may begin to see how attempting to articulate a comprehensive answer for each question is far from a commonplace intellectual undertaking.

The goal of this chapter is to facilitate (rather than legislate) a discussion on the potential relationships that exist among communication, identity, and sport.[1] In order to accomplish this goal, I am recommending that (a) scholars must first identify the institutional character of sport, and, in order to sufficiently do so, (b) scholars must outline those communication processes that literally give rise to such institutional forms. While scholars have begun to consider the communicative nature of institutional processes (Heritage, 2005; Lammers & Barbour, 2006), media (Bernstein & Blain, 2003; Morris, 2006), sport (Halone, 2008; Kassing, et al., 2004), and identity (Eisenberg, 2006; Hall, 1996) as distinct concepts, this chapter examines how these concepts are potentially interconnected by illustrating how issues of identity in sports media are *inherently* communicative phenomena that give rise to the institutional nature of sport. Engaging in this objective should provide newfound clarity for understanding the institutional(ized) nature of identity in and around the domain of sport(s).[2]

## ❖ (RE)CONNECTING THE SCHOLARSHIP ON IDENTITY IN AND AROUND SPORT(S): STRIVING FOR "ACCURACY" (VERSUS BEING "RIGHT")

In the previous chapters, each scholar embraced certain intellectual assumptions (whether cognizant or not) about the (a) nature of identity, communication, and sport; (b) relationships that potentially exist among identity, communication, and sport; and (c) consequential role of identity, communication, and sport. It is the nature of these assumptions that has enabled the authors to entertain certain claims, develop particular arguments, and advance various conclusions throughout their work. While each chapter has provided newfound insight for its readers, such work must also be productively situated among each other if it is to collectively advance theory and research on this emerging and important issue. What I offer in this chapter are some preliminary considerations at a global level that might enable future opportunities for comparative discussions between (and across) each chapter at a local level.

This objective will be accomplished five-fold. First, the macro-micro nature of communication, identity, and sport is outlined. Second, potential relationships that exist among communication, identity, and sport are considered. Then, various options from which to examine the nature of identity are offered. Next, a theoretical conceptualization of identity in and around sport from the standpoint of sport communication is articulated. Finally, a communication theory of the institutional(ized) nature of identity in and around sport is advanced. Engaging in these respective steps should enable newfound opportunities to clarify the role of identity in the domain of mediated sport.

To that end, the forthcoming information offered is being advanced in the spirit of ultimately striving for intellectual "accuracy" versus being academically "right." Allow me to provide some subtle yet significant distinctions between these two standpoints. Scholars who are trying to be "right" will rarely admit that they are ever "wrong." In order to obtain the goal of intellectual "accuracy," one must ultimately operate from a standpoint of "incorrectness" in order to (eventually; hopefully) obtain it. Scholars who want to be "right" (un)intentionally do so with self*ish* gratifications in mind. Scholars who strive for "accuracy" (un)intentionally do so with self*less* gratifications in mind. Scholars who are seeking "accuracy" will fully realize that they may be incorrect. Scholars who are trying to be "right" will rarely desire (or stand) to be corrected. Scholars who are trying to be "right" will endeavor to "legislate" *their* perspective. Scholars who are seeking "accuracy" will want to "facilitate" *a* perspective. Those who are seeking "accuracy" will rarely admit they are ever "right." Those who are trying to be "right" will rarely understand their need for more "accuracy."

One has nothing to lose when attempting to strive for "accuracy." One has ultimately lost everything when one is attempting to be "right." What I offer in this chapter is an opportunity to facilitate collective clarity on an important issue rather than facilitate personal charity through this writing. Therefore, to begin—in the hopes of *accurately* facilitating a discussion on issues of identity in mediated sport—I am recommending that scholars must first entertain the macro-micro nature of communication, identity, and sport.

## ❖ THE MACRO-MICRO NATURE OF COMMUNICATION, IDENTITY, AND SPORT

If scholars want to understand how issues of identity surface throughout the domain of mediated sport, they must first consider the potential intersections that exist among dynamics of communication, identity, and sport. In order to accomplish this task, one must consider the degree to which these dynamics are potentially similar in scope and status. Scholars have recognized that social knowledge will not adequately progress until it is understood in micro-level (local) and macro-level (global) terms (Baxter & Montgomery, 1996; Ellis, 1999; Halone, 2006; Lannamann, 1991; Leeds-Hurwitz, 1995; Taylor, 1993). Therefore, one must (a) first consider whether dynamics of communication, identity, and sport are concepts that may be characterized in micro-macro terms, and (b) then determine whether these concepts may be fashioned in similar terms. Figure 12.1 offers an opportunity to consider the potential relationships that exist among dynamics of communication, identity, and sport.

As the figure denotes, dynamics of communication, sport, and identity all meet those necessary conditions for being classified in micro-macro terms. Dynamics of sport may be understood with respect to a specific *domain* of reference (e.g., NCAA athletics) as well as a specific *locale* for analysis (e.g., NCAA track and field). Dynamics of communication may also be understood with respect to *law*-like patterns (e.g., NCAA *regulations*) as well as its *rule*-like patterns (e.g., NCAA sport-specific *guidelines*). Dynamics of identity may likewise be understood with respect to a *generalized* orientation (e.g., identity of NCAA student athletes), or a *specified* orientation (e.g., identity of NCAA track

**Figure 12.1**    The Macro-Micro Nature of Communication, Identity, and Sport

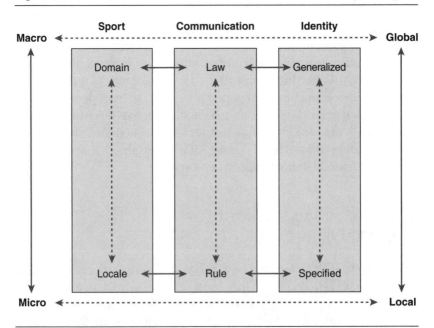

and field athletes). Worthy of note is that the frames (Goffman, 1974) that constitute these macro-micro concepts may be characterized on a continuum; they are fluid rather than fixed in scope. For example, in light of the aforementioned examples, one could have easily made the *domain* of sport "NCAA track and field" and the *locale* for analysis "Big XII track and field." The *law*-like patterns could have been "Big XII track and field regulations," while the *rule*-like patterns could have been "University of Oklahoma track and field guidelines." The dynamics of identity could have been *generalized* among "Big XII track and field athletes" and *specified* among "University of Oklahoma track and field athletes." The macro-micro nature of these examples may be teased out even further (e.g., Conference versus University specific sport [sport]; Coach-regulated guidelines versus team-constituted rules [communication]; indoor/outdoor track and field student athletes versus cross-country student athletes [identity]). Understanding the manner and degree to which a scholar employs macro-micro theorizing in their work—and is (in)consistent in their understanding of such distinctions—will ultimately affect what one can claim to know about dynamics of communication, identity, and sport.

### Theorizing the (Un)Intended Consequences of Potentially Similar Concepts

It appears that macro-micro dynamics of communication, identity, and sport *may* be understood in similar terms. If this might be the case, then one must question what (un)intended outcomes (Giddens, 1984) consequentially arise (Sigman, 1995) when viewing these dynamics in a similar light. I argue that two consequences potentially arise: "additive" (regulation-based) consequences, and "formative" (constitution-based) consequences.

#### "Additive" Consequences: The Regulation of Potentially Similar Concepts

One consequence is "additive" in nature. Such thinking fosters a "regulative" approach to examining how dynamics of communication, identity, and sport relate to one another. This may lead one to assume that any two of the three dynamics may literally *regulate* (i.e., thereby "equaling") the presence of the other. The following examples illustrate such thinking:

$$\text{Sport} + \text{Communication} = \text{Identity}$$

$$\text{Communication} + \text{Identity} = \text{Sport}$$

$$\text{Identity} + \text{Sport} = \text{Communication}$$

These combinations are plausible if one takes an "additive" approach to theorizing dynamics of communication, identity, and sport.

### "Formative" Consequences: The Constitution of Potentially Similar Concepts

Another consequence is "formative" in nature. Such thinking fosters a "constitutive" approach to examining how dynamics of communication, identity, and sport relate to one another. This may lead one to assume that any two of the three dynamics may literally *constitute* (i.e., thereby "giving rise to") the presence of the other. The following examples illustrate such thinking:

Sport + Communication → Identity

Communication + Identity → Sport

Identity + Sport → Communication

These combinations are plausible if one takes a "formative" approach to theorizing dynamics of communication, identity, and sport.

Given these two options, one might ask if either is more "accurate" than the other, and, if so, what would be the criteria for *ultimately* determining such a decision. Such a determination can be accurately made when one further (dis)entangles the specific relationships that potentially exist among dynamics of communication, identity, and sport.

## (Dis)Entangling the Potential Relationships Among Communication, Identity, and Sport

In order to confidently determine whether the "additive" or "formative" consequences to understanding dynamics among communication, identity, and sport are both legitimate options from which to function, one must further clarify those operational assumptions that potentially exist when positioning dynamics of communication, identity, and sport with one another (Cooren & Taylor, 1997; Putnam, Phillips, & Chapman, 1997). I offer three potential options from which to clarify such assumptions.

### A "Containment" Perspective on Communication, Identity, and Sport

A *containment* perspective exists when the existence of one concept *results from* the existence of another concept. People refer to one concept as it originates from within (or out of) another (e.g., "communication 'in' sport"). The necessary conditions for this relationship are more rigid in nature (i.e., in order for "communication" to occur, "sport" must exist). Here, one concept is viewed as existing within a relatively unquestioned structure (e.g., "identity 'in' sport"). The following examples illustrate such thinking:

> Identity "in" Sport
>
> Communication "in" Sport
>
> Communication "in" Identity

The consequence of such thinking results in privileging one concept (i.e., sport as primary) over the other (i.e., communication as secondary), thus fostering a "dependent" relationship.

### A "Production" Perspective on Communication, Identity, and Sport

A *production* perspective exists when the existence of one concept *prompts* the existence of another concept. People refer to one concept as giving rise to another, yet the latter concept is not entirely dependent upon the former (i.e., "communication 'around' sport"). In this view, "identities" produce "sport," and "sport" produces "identities." The necessary conditions characterizing the relationship are hinged upon one another but are conditions that are not absolute (e.g., "identities" may arise from the domain of "sport," but "sport" is only one domain from which "identities" may ultimately arise). The following examples illustrate such thinking:

| *Identity and Sport* | *Sport and Communication* | *Communication and Identity* |
|---|---|---|
| Identity → Sport | Sport → Communication | Identity → Communication |
| Sport → Identity | Communication → Sport | Communication → Identity |

The consequence of such thinking results in understanding one concept (i.e., sport) in its relative position with another (i.e., communication), thus fostering an "interdependent" relationship.

### An "Equivalence" Perspective on Communication, Identity, and Sport

An *equivalence* perspective exists when the existence of one concept is understood as being similar with another concept. People refer to one concept as if they were referring to another (e.g., "communication 'and' sport" or "communication 'is' sport"). Here, the two terms may be viewed synonymously, whereby each may be viewed similarly yet are accounted for in different ways. No necessary conditions are typically outlined that prompt the presence of the other. (i.e., as "communication" and "sport" are viewed as potentially similar phenomena). The following examples illustrate such thinking:

| Identity and Sport | Sport and Communication | Communication and Identity |
|---|---|---|
| Sport = Identity | Sport = Communication | Identity = Communication |
| Identity = Sport | Communication = Sport | Communication = Identity |

The consequence of such thinking results in understanding one concept (i.e., sport) as relative(ly equal) to another (i.e., communication), thus fostering an "interchangeable" relationship.

### Reconsidering the (Dis)Entangled Relationships among Communication, Identity, and Sport

If the previous distinctions have begun to facilitate a heightened sense of uncertainty (or angst) regarding how scholars might begin to appropriately consider dynamics of communication, identity, and sport, then one might kindly contend that facilitators of this discussion have been *accurately* enacting their respective roles. Determining whether one is conceptualizing dynamics of communication, identity, and sport in "regulative," "constitutive," or "equivalent" terms will ultimately determine whether one is producing knowledge with goals related to "effect" (i.e., regulation), "outcome" (i.e., constitution), or "understanding" (i.e., equivalence). An inability to clarify these respective concepts at a theoretical level will ultimately lead to unclear analyses and findings in any research endeavor (Berger, 1994).

What the previous perspectives (and consequences) begin to offer the reader is an opportunity to clearly understand what constitutes the "figure" (i.e., what is privileged; focused on) and the "ground" (i.e., what is denied; given up) in any scholarly undertaking. Thus, the question remains: How might one begin to understand the potential relationships that exist among communication, identity, and sport so that one is *accurately* developing newfound knowledge on/about/around it? From what has been offered thus far, it appears that one could "logically" place each respective concept in relative position with one another without violating any canons of formal logic. If dynamics of communication, identity, and sport have the potential to be similar in their scope (at one end), and hold the promise of being conceptually equivalent in their observable status (at the other), how might one confidently determine how to (re)position these dynamics so as to be theoretically clear in any form of systematic inquiry?

### Working Toward a Clarified Understanding of Communication, Identity, and Sport

These earlier observations might lead one to conclude that, while the "logical" consequences that surround such actions are not entirely incorrect, such actions—if striving for *accuracy*—become ultimately incomplete. One candidate option for consideration may be to theoretically assess these dynamics in a *pragmatic* fashion. When one pragmatically looks at these dynamics in relative position to each another, one must begin to consider each concept in both their "abstract" and their "literal" terms. The following analytical exercise serves to clarify this option.

A common intellectual practice that I have developed, in my attempt to compare abstract theoretical concepts, stems from taking various abstract (theoretical) concepts and seeing if (or how) they may be examined in literal (observable) terms. Given that this section of the chapter seeks to clarify the potential relationships that exist among dynamics of communication, identity, and sport, it would be in scholars' best interest to assess the degree to which such dynamics can be understood in *literal* terms. An exchange drawing upon the following format provides an example of how to pragmatically compare abstract concepts in literal terms:

**Question:** Can one have instances of "communication" outside of instances of "sport"?

**Answer:** Certainly. Instances of "communication" (e.g., in relationships; in organizations) make themselves available outside of the domain of sport.

**Question:** Can one have instances of "sport" outside of instances of "communication"?

**Answer:** One might be hard-pressed to see how instances of sport could *literally* manifest themselves without some instance of "communication" (i.e., those [non]verbal messages that constitute and regulate the domain of sport).

The same pragmatic comparison could be made about the potential interplay that exists between dynamics of "communication" and "identity."[3] A pragmatic analysis of these concepts clarifies the centrality of one concept (i.e., communication) to another (i.e., sport). The profound irony surrounding this exercise is that the credibility of the communication discipline continues to remain in collective question (Deetz & Putnam, 2001). Why would one question the credibility of a discipline whose primary phenomenon of disciplinary interest (i.e., the message) *literally* gives life to abstract (theoretical) concepts?

It would not seem illogical to conclude that—while concepts of communication, identity, and sport may all be viewed as abstract theoretical phenomena—the concept of "communication" is the *only* one of the three that has a *direct* observable equivalent (i.e., one can *literally* point to "messages" in order to verify its existence). One *cannot* directly point to concepts of "identity" and "sport" without some reliance upon "communication" to do so. While one can have instances of "communication" without instances of "identity," or instances of "communication" without instances of "sport," one cannot have instances of "identity" or instances of "sport" without instances of "communication."[4] Thus, one could pragmatically conclude that more scholarly attention should be given to the role of "communication" and how this concept *literally* gives rise to the institutional(ized) nature of identity in and around sport. However, prior to providing this attention that the concept of communication may *accurately* deserve, one must first consider how dynamics of "identity" might be understood in light of these newfound (i.e., communication-based) observations.

## ❖ (DIS)PLACING DYNAMICS OF IDENTITY IN AND AROUND SPORT

If previously drawn observations appear to be valid, one might then begin to consider how dynamics of identity might be (or have been) previously examined in the absence of possessing a clearly communication-based understanding of it. What follows are six ways that dynamics of identity may be (or have been) previously examined in and around the domain of sport. These include how dynamics of identity have been: (a) formed, (b) ascribed, (c) presented, (d) prioritized, (e) located, and (f) focused upon.

## Forms of Identity in and Around Sport

The *form* in which an "identity" (in)directly surfaces in and around sport may be viewed on a continuum representing two standpoints: sports identities ←→ athletic identities. A *sport identity* is a standpoint that is *inclusive* in nature; it becomes developed through processes of *identification with* sport. This identity is typically embodied though the *observation of sport* and becomes collectively manifest through *fans* of sport. An *athletic identity* is a standpoint that is more *exclusive* in nature; it becomes developed through processes of *identification through* sport. This identity is typically embodied vis-à-vis *participation in sport* and becomes individually or collectively manifest through *athletes* of sport. These standpoints may be developed in either a segmented (distinct) or an integrated (combined) fashion (Ashforth, 2001).

## Ascribing Identity in and Around Sport

The manner in which identity is *ascribed* in and around sport may be viewed on a continuum representing two distinct standpoints: internal identity ←→ external identity. An *internally ascribed* identity is *authentic* in its orientation. It is something that occurs *naturally* and is *experienced* directly. It is an identity that is *self-acknowledged*, which enables an individual to be a *subject* of their choosing. An *externally ascribed* identity is typically *imposed* on others by others. It is something that transpires *artificially*, thereby becoming an *observed* identity by others. It is an identity that is ultimately *other-acknowledged*, which causes an individual to be an *object* of others' observations and (re)actions.

## Presenting Identity in and Around Sport

The manner in which identity is *presented* in and around sport may be viewed on a continuum representing two standpoints: private identity ←→ public identity. A *private identity* is one that is *genuine* in its orientation. It is one that may be *covered* periodically with a goal of personal *protection* in mind. It is an identity that represents an individual's *back stage* (Goffman, 1959). A *public identity* is one that may be *fabricated* in its orientation. It may be one that is typically *exposed*, which makes it available for *projection* on a public scale. It is an identity that represents an individual's *front stage* (Goffman, 1959).

### Prioritizing Identity in and Around Sport

The manner in which identity is *prioritized* in and around sport may be viewed on a continuum representing two standpoints: primary identity ←→ secondary identity. A *primary* identity is one that is *central* in its orientation. Given its centrality, it is one that is deemed *important*, thus giving rise to *consequential* implications and outcomes. A *secondary* identity is one that is *peripheral* in its orientation. Given its peripheral status, it is one that may facilitate a sense of *indifference*, potentially giving rise to *inconsequential* implications and outcomes.

### Locating Identity in and Around Sport

The manner in which identities may be *located* in and around sport may be viewed as a public-private phenomenon that may be understood in micro-macro terms. Figure 12.2 provides a visual illustration of how dynamics of identity may vary in terms of its scope and status.

Identities may surface and develop locally while remaining private at the individual level (i.e., personally), and they may reside between two individuals (i.e., relationally). These identities can exist among multiple individuals (i.e., among a group or a team) or become available throughout larger collectives of people (i.e., in various organizational venues). These identities may be distributed en masse (i.e., in mediated form) and may be systematically revealed at a public level (i.e., culturally). Such identities may also become manifest in a cross-cultural fashion (i.e., internationally). The manner and degree to which an identity becomes privately or publicly negotiated is contingent upon its network structure (Stohl, 1996) and those respective channels that a given network operates (Rogers, 2004).

### The Foci of Identity in and Around Sport

The *focus* of an identity in and around sport may be viewed in terms of how much analysis/scrutiny it receives. The foci of identity may emphasize topics or issues such as sex differences (i.e., male/female), gender differences (i.e., masculinity/femininity), sexuality (i.e., gay/lesbian/hetero-normative [pre]dispositions), race (i.e., genetic [pre]dispositions), ethnicity (i.e., co-cultural [pre]dispositions), nationality (i.e., [inter]cultural [pre]dispositions), socioeconomics (i.e., financial privilege/despair), disability (i.e., the [un]able-bodied), age (i.e., [inter]generational dynamics/lifespan), organizations (i.e., decision-making), and international affairs (e.g., cross-cultural differences).

**Figure 12.2**   Locating Identity in and Around Sport

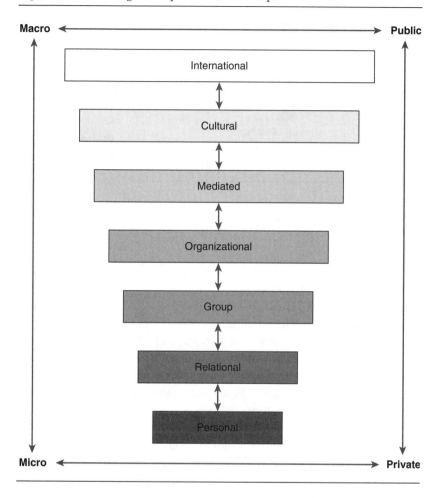

### The Negotiated Nature of Identity in and Around Sport

While each dynamic of identity provides a distinct lens from which to understand how identity becomes manifest in and around sport, each ultimately operates in some combination with one another. Figure 12.3 provides a suggestive illustration of how these dynamics are negotiated in and around sport(s).

The visual provides a three-dimensional space that conceptually illustrates the manner and degree to which dynamics of identity work in synergistic combination with one another. Each dynamic respectively contributes to defining one facet of the overall identity dynamic, which provides a global understanding of how identities in and around sport

**Figure 12.3**   The Negotiated Nature of Identity in and Around Sport

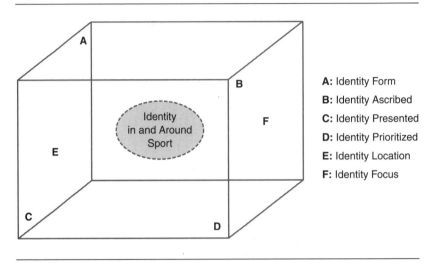

differentially surface. The visual also provides a $2 \times 2 \times 2 \times 2 \times 6 \times 11$ factorial design from which to operationally develop a host of propositions that may lead to future research on issues of identity in and around sport. This translates into over 1,000 different identity orientations that remain open for future consideration and scholarly exploration.

While this proposed model may seem plausible in its introduction, one should logically inquire about (a) whether the model clearly accounts for the role of "communication," and, if so, (b) "where" might one direct one's attention to examining "communication" in the model. While one could propose that the lines holding the box together represent those interactions that allow each identity dynamic to "come into conversation" with each other, one can begin to see what (un)intentional consequences surface when attempting to theoretically link abstract concepts with each other. What remains unanswered is how dynamics of identity in and around sport become *communicatively* manifest.

❖ (RE)CONCEPTUALIZING IDENTITY IN AND
   AROUND SPORT: PERSPECTIVE FROM THE
   STANDPOINT OF SPORT COMMUNICATION

The previous section sought to consider how dynamics of identity may be conceptually understood in and around sport and how abstract theoretical concepts may mask those processes that give rise to their *literal* existence. This section seeks to examine how dynamics of identity become *communicatively* manifest in and around the domain of sport.

### Toward a Communicative Paradigm of Identity in and Around Sport

As Kassing et al. (2004) noted, "Although the actual performance of sport is a physical activity, communication in, around, and about sport influences both the physical performance of athletes and the social construction of the sporting experience" (p. 374). The nature of these communication processes "take[s] place within a context or discourse that articulates a powerful set of values and beliefs about how people do sport and who can do sport" (Kassing et al., 2004, p. 377). Such sport communication processes ultimately give rise to dynamics of identity in and around sport, revealing which identities become acknowledged or denied, and how certain identities become privileged or ignored.

Failing to acknowledge the inherently communicative nature of sport prevents scholars from acknowledging those messages that literally give rise to the constitution and regulation of sport (Halone, 2008; Halone & Billings, in press). Kassing et al. (2004) proposed that scholars begin to examine the phenomenon of sport communicatively in all of its variants: enacting sport, organizing sport, (re)producing sport, and consuming sport. Figure 12.4 provides a newfound conceptualization of how identity in and around sport may be understood in communicative terms.

The model proposes that the nature of identity in and around sport may be observed through processes of enacting, organizing, (re)producing, and consuming messages. Identity first comes into fruition through *discursive enactment.*[5] Once the identity at hand is enacted, it becomes *interactively organized.* The manner in which the identity becomes organized will influence its degree of *communicative (re)production.* The degree to which a given identity becomes (re)produced will affect how it becomes *symbolically consumed.* The component parts of the model suggestively serve to illustrate the fluid, dynamic, and interdependent nature of identity in and around sport.

While this model has been initially portrayed in a "sequential" fashion, it is important to note that not all identities in and around sport may follow such a "linear" path. Where a respective identity in and around sport resides (i.e., at the point of enactment; organization; (re)production; consumption) will determine its relative scope and perceived status in the domain of sport. For example, dynamics of race (Denham, Billings, & Halone, 2002; Jarvie, 2000; also see Chapter 8 and Chapter 9 in this volume) and gender (Billings, Halone, & Denham, 2002; Theberge, 2000;

**Figure 12.4**   A Communicative Conceptualization of Identity in and Around
Sport

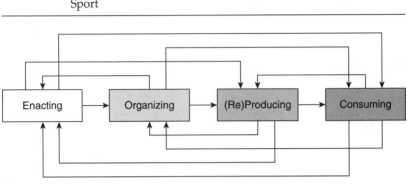

also see Chapter 2, Chapter 3, Chapter 4, Chapter 5, and Chapter 6 in
this volume) have been historically prominent issues that have both
characterized and defined the domain of sport. One might contend that
the communicative presence, degree, force, and strength to which each
of those respective "identities" have become communicatively "nor-
mal(ized)" throughout sport is hinged upon the degree to which those
identities have become symbolically perpetuated (in its enactment; its
organization; its (re)production; its consumption) throughout the institution of sport. The same, perhaps, could not be said about identity
issues of age or (dis)ability (see Chapter 10, in this volume); they have
yet to reach a certain level of "interactive recognition" or "communicative distinction" throughout the institution of sport.

Thus, dynamics of identity in and around sport should not be considered isolated events that have little consequence to the domain of
sport; its presence *literally* constitutes and regulates the institution of
sport. Recognizing the inherently communicative nature of identity—in
all of its variants—enables one to see how all issues of sport are truly
"identify-able." The "identify-able" nature of various topics and issues that
become communicatively perpetuated throughout sport (un)intentionally
facilitate the symbolic infrastructure that enables or constrains its institutional status. What follows is a framework of how the communicative
nature of identity gives rise to the institutional(ized) nature of sport(s).

❖  (RE)CONSIDERING THE INSTITUTIONAL(IZED)
    NATURE OF IDENTITY IN AND AROUND SPORT(S)

The previous section explained how identity dynamics in and around sport
become discursively enacted, interactively organized, communicatively

**Figure 12.5**    The Institutional(ized) Nature of Identity in and Around Sport

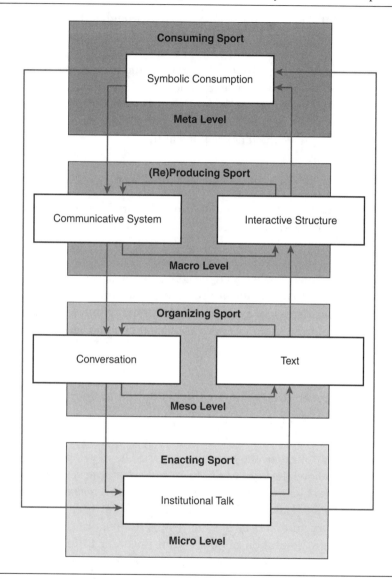

(re)produced, and symbolically consumed. While this model is helpful in understanding the level and degree to which identity dynamics *theoretically* contribute to the institutional(ized) nature of sport(s), one must also consider how these dynamics *empirically* give rise to the institutional(ized) nature of sport(s). Figure 12.5 provides a visual illustration of how these theoretical dynamics become empirically manifest—in micro, meso, macro, and meta terms—throughout the domain of sport.

### The Micro Level: Enacting the Institution of Sport

The institution of sport becomes enacted through its *institutional talk* (Heritage, 2005). Such micro-level talk on/about/around sport(s)—contrary to popular contemporary belief—is not "cheap" nor is it merely about "nothing." It *literally* serves as the basis from which one understands sport as one currently knows it. Thus, in order to understand how a certain identity issue has become institutional(ized) throughout sport, one must first focus upon the nature of its talk and how that talk frames the identity issue at hand.

### The Meso Level: Organizing the Institution of Sport

The institutional talk on/about/around sport does not remain idle. Given its topical and symbolic status, it becomes open to processes of *organizing* (Taylor, 1999) at a meso level. Institutional talk literally surfaces in *conversation;* such conversations serve as a *text* for future interaction(s). The interplay between the conversation and its text (and vice versa) gives rise to the *organized* nature of the institution of sport. Thus, in order to clearly assess a certain identity issue within the institution of sport, one must examine those conversations and texts that have organized that given issue at hand.

### The Macro Level: (Re)Producing the Institution of Sport

The manner and degree to which any identity issue becomes organized determines the manner and degree to which an issue becomes *(re)produced* throughout the domain of sport. The development of certain conversations/texts gives rise to an *interactive structure.* The nature of these interactive structures, in turn, gives rise to a *communicative system* of meaning (Halone, 2008). The interplay that becomes fostered between a structure and its system fosters its *(re)productive* potential throughout the institution of sport. Thus, in order to further understand a certain identity issue within the institution of sport, one must take into account those interactive structures and communicative systems that have become perpetuated at a macro level.

### The Meta Level: Consuming the Institution of Sport

The manner and degree to which an identity issue becomes enacted, organized, and (re)produced determines the manner and degree to which that respective issue becomes *consumed* throughout the domain of sport (Shrum, 2002). The consumption of sport may be understood as a meta-level process; the degree to which an identity issue becomes consumed at its level of enactment, organization, and/or (re)production determines the degree to which an identity issue remains "identify-able" as such throughout the institution of sport. Thus, in order to readily understand a certain identity issue within the institution of sport, one must understand the degree to which that issue has become symbolically consumed at a meta level.

## ❖ REFLECTING UPON THE DISCUSSION ON, ABOUT, AND AROUND COMMUNICATION, IDENTITY, AND SPORT: LET THE CONVERSATION CONTINUE . . .

The goal of this chapter was to facilitate (rather than legislate) a discussion on the potential relationships that exist among dynamics of communication, identity, and sport. In order to capitalize upon this goal, I offered that scholars must first identify the institutional character of sport, and, in order to sufficiently accomplish this, scholars must outline those communication processes that literally give rise to such institutional forms. This was accomplished five-fold.

First, the macro-micro nature of communication, identity, and sport was outlined. Readers were provided an opportunity to understand how dynamics of communication, identity, and sport could be viewed in micro-macro terms and to recognize what the (un)intended consequences might be if/when theorizing dynamics of communication, identity, and sport in similar terms. Second, potential relationships that existed among dynamics of communication, identity, and sport were considered. Readers were provided an opportunity to consider the myriad ways in which dynamics of communication, identity, and sport may be (inter)related in abstract terms and to understand what consequences potentially surface when one does not theorize about such abstract dynamics in a pragmatic light.

Next, the ways in which the phenomenon of identity in and around sport may be examined were offered. Readers were provided an opportunity to consider the various ways in which one can theoretically consider dynamics of identity in and around sport and to entertain what consequences potentially surface as a result of not making a direct theoretical link between issues of identity in and around sport and the phenomenon of communication. Then, a sport communication conceptualization of identity in and around sport was articulated. Readers were provided an opportunity to consider what the phenomenon of identity might look like communicatively and how a communication-based conceptualization of identity in and around sport enables an opportunity to examine the institutional underpinnings of sport. Finally, a communication theory of the institutional(ized) nature of identity in and around sport was advanced. Readers were invited to consider how communication-based phenomena *literally* drive the institutional(ized) nature of sport(s) and how issues of identity in and around sport potentially become the catalyst for enacting, organizing, (re)producing, and consuming the institutional(ized) nature of sport.

I also provided readers with an opportunity to (re)consider whether they approach intellectual endeavors with a symbolic posture of seeking intellectual "accuracy" or being academically "right." At this juncture of the chapter, the facilitator of this discussion has begun to question whether (or if) the goals communicated at the outset of the chapter have *accurately* come into fruition. The "result" of this query is ultimately contingent upon how (or if) the messages outlined in this chapter ever become enacted, organized, (re)produced, and consumed in forthcoming interactions. At this juncture of intellectual inquiry, one may confidently claim that we have symbolically arrived at the communicative end of a new interactive beginning.

To that end, I leave the readers with a two-fold "conclusion" for the prospect of future deliberations. First, Figure 12.6 provides a synergistic framework from which to examine how proposed dynamics of identity in and around sport become differentially manifest at an empirical (i.e., observable) level. Attempting to use this framework as you reflect upon the previous chapters will provide an opportunity to assess, verify, and/or modify several of the claims that I have collectively offered for scholarly inspection.

Finally, I ask the readers to revisit several of those questions that I initially advanced at the outset of this chapter, as they reflect upon the collective work in this book. Examine if, whether, or how each respective scholar provided an (in)direct answer to the following: What is the relationship between identity and sport? How do communication dynamics contribute to issues of identity in sport? Where might one confidently locate identity in sport? How do the media contribute to our understanding of identity in sport? How does identity become enacted around sport? When does identity become "organized" in the domain of sport? How might one know they are examining identity in sport when they claim to do so? Where (and how often) does identity become

**Figure 12.6**    A Dynamic Framework for Future Research on Identity in and Around Sport(s):

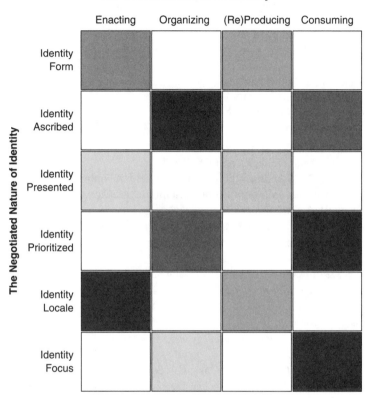

(re)produced in sport? What role do human-mediated interactions play in our understanding of identity in sport? How do issues of identity become consumed in sport? How do communication and sport scholars contribute to (and/or detract from) our understanding of identity in and around sport? How does one confidently know whether (or if) one has a clear understanding of the relationships that exist among dynamics of communication, identity, and sport? If I have upheld my facilitative role sufficiently well, the readers of this book will realize that striving to understand the role of identity in the domain of mediated sport is no small intellectual undertaking. The contributing authors, and the analyses offered herein, have provided ample evidence to accurately verify this claim.

## ❖ REFERENCES

Ashforth, B. E. (2001). *Role transitions in organizational life: An identity-based perspective*. Mahwah, NJ: Lawrence Erlbaum.

Baxter, L. A., & Montgomery, B. M. (1996). *Relating: Dialogues and dialectics*. New York: Guilford Press.

Berger, C. R. (1994). Evidence? For what? *Western Journal of Communication, 58*, 11–19.

Bernstein, A., & Blain, N. (Eds.). (2003). *Sport, media, culture: Global and local dimensions*. Portland, OR: Frank Cass.

Billings, A. C., Halone, K. K., & Denham, B. E. (2002). "Man, that was a pretty shot": An analysis of gendered broadcast commentary surrounding the 2000 men's and women's NCAA Final Four basketball championships. *Mass Communication & Society, 5*, 295–315.

Clair, R. P. (1999). Standing still in an ancient field: A contemporary look at the organizational communication discipline. *Management Communication Quarterly, 13*, 283–293.

Cooren, F., & Taylor, J. R. (1997). Organization as an effect of mediation: Redefining the link between organization and communication. *Communication Theory, 7*, 219–259.

Deetz, S., & Putnam, L. L. (2001). Thinking about the future of communication studies. *Communication Yearbook, 24*, 1–14.

Denham, B. E., Billings, A. C., & Halone, K. K. (2002). Differential accounts of race in broadcast commentary of the 2000 men's and women's final four basketball tournaments. *Sociology of Sport Journal, 19*, 315–332.

Eisenberg, E. M. (2006). *Strategic ambiguities: Essays on communication, organization, and identity*. Thousand Oaks, CA: Sage.

Ellis, D. G. (1999). Research on social interaction and the micro-macro issue. *Research on Language and Social Interaction, 32*, 31–40.

Giddens, A. (1984). *The constitution of society: Outline of a theory of structuration*. Berkeley: University of California Press.

Goffman, E. (1959). *The presentation of self in everyday life*. New York: Doubleday-Anchor Books.

Goffman, E. (1974). *Frame analysis: An essay on the organization of experience*. Boston: Northeastern University Press.

Hall, S. (1996). Introduction: Who needs "identity"? In S. Hall & P. du Gay (Eds.), *Questions of cultural identity* (pp. 1–17). London: Sage.

Halone, K. K. (2006). Organizing (un)healthy dialectics of work-life balance: An organizational communication response to The *Opt-Out Revolution*. *Electronic Journal of Communication, 16*(3/4). Retrieved from www.cios.org

Halone, K. K. (2008). The structuration of racialized sport organizing. *Journal of Communication Inquiry, 32*, 22–42.

Halone, K. K., & Billings, A. C. (in press). The temporal nature of racialized sport consumption. *American Behavioral Scientist*.

Heritage, J. (2005). Conversation analysis and institutional talk. In K. L. Fitch & R. E. Sanders (Eds.), *Handbook of language and social interaction* (pp. 103–147). Mahwah, NJ: Lawrence Erlbaum.

Jarvie, G. (2000). Sport, racism, and ethnicity. In J. Coakley & E. Dunning (Eds.), *Handbook of sports studies* (pp. 334–343). Thousand Oaks, CA: Sage.

Kassing, J. W., Billings, A. C., Brown, R. S., Halone, K. K., Harrison, K., Krizek, B., Meân, L. J., & Turman, P. D. (2004). Communication and the community of sport: The process of enacting, (re)producing, consuming, and organizing sport. *Communication Yearbook, 28,* 373–408.

Lammers, J. C., & Barbour, J. B. (2006). An institutional theory of organizational communication. *Communication Theory, 16,* 356–377.

Lannamann, J. W. (1991). Interpersonal communication research as ideological practice. *Communication Theory, 1,* 179–203.

Leeds-Hurwitz, W. (1995). Introducing social approaches. In W. Leeds-Hurwitz (Ed.), *Social approaches to communication* (pp. 3–20). New York: Guilford Press.

Morris, M. (2006). *Identity anecdotes: Translation and media culture.* London: Sage.

Putnam, L. L., Phillips, N., & Chapman, P. (1997). Metaphors of communication and organization. In S. R. Clegg, C. Hardy, & W. R. Nord (Eds.), *Handbook of organizational studies* (pp. 375–408). London: Sage.

Rogers, E. M. (2004). A prospective and retrospective look at the diffusion model. *Journal of Health Communication, 9,* 13–19.

Shrum, L. J. (2002). Media consumption and perceptions of social reality: Effects and underlying processes. In J. Bryant & D. Zillman (Eds.), *Media effects: Advances in theory and research* (2nd ed., pp. 69–96). Mahwah, NJ: Lawrence Erlbaum.

Sigman, S. J. (1995). Introduction: Toward study of the consequentiality (not consequences) of communication. In S. J. Sigman (Ed.), *The consequentiality of communication* (pp. 1–14). Hillsdale, NJ: Lawrence Erlbaum.

Stohl, C. (1996). *Organizational communication: Connectedness in action.* Thousand Oaks, CA: Sage.

Taylor, J. R. (1993). *Rethinking the theory of organizational communication: How to read an organization.* Norwood, NJ: Ablex Publishing.

Taylor, J. R. (1999). What is "organizational communication"? Communication as a dialogic of text and conversation. *Communication Review, 3,* 21–63.

Theberge, N. (2000). Gender and sport. In J. Coakley & E. Dunning (Eds.), *Handbook of sports studies* (pp. 322–322). Thousand Oaks, CA: Sage.

## ❖ NOTES

1. In order to productively engage in a theoretical discussion about these dynamic phenomena, it is necessary to frame the discussion with concepts that are potentially parallel in scope. While one could possibly employ "media" in

place of "communication," one would ultimately be committing—at this respective juncture—an error of theoretical abstraction. Media is an empirical phenomenon that is a sub-set of all communication phenomena (i.e., we ultimately understand "media" as such because of our ability to communicate about it [not the reverse]). Therefore, in order to productively understand how the media contributes to issues of identity in sport, one must generally consider the phenomenon of communication first as it (may) pertain(s) to issues of identity and sport.

2. The parentheses are being employed with a three-fold purpose: (a) as a means to remain consistent with the philosophical undercurrent that gives rise to this work (i.e., that processes are concurrently productive and reproductive [hence a (re)productive understanding]; that such processes have both intentional and unintentional consequences [hence its (un)intentional consequences]); (b) to remain consistent with how scholars of sport communication have conceived of these respective dynamics (Kassing et al., 2004); and (c) to achieve clarity with brevity in word count.

3. While, admittedly, one could argue that all messages are inherently identifiable, thereby making "identity" a closer empirical companion to "communication," one would still have to logically conclude that one remains unable to make something identifiable unless there is some symbolic (i.e., "communicative") undercurrent to ultimately render it as such.

4. This claim is being offered for scholarly consideration as a statement of fact. I remain dialogically patient as I await a substantive rebuttal to this claim.

5. The terms "discursive," "interactive," "communicative," and "symbolic" are being used to illustrate the various ways in which empirical phenomena are inherently linked to properties of "communication" in general; they may be—at this juncture of theoretical exploration—used in an interchangeable fashion. The discipline of communication has yet to progress to a stage where these concepts have become empirically distinguishable from one another.

# Index

# About the Editors

**Andrew C. Billings** (PhD, Indiana University, 1999) studies sports communication and mass media, particularly focusing on the negotiation of identity within televised sport. He holds a degree in Communication & Culture from Indiana University and has received several teaching awards for his work in the classroom. His scholarship has been published in areas as diverse as *Journal of Communication, Journal of Broadcasting & Electronic Media, Journal of Sport & Social Issues, Communication Yearbook,* and *Mass Communication and Society,* and he has won top paper awards from conferences for the National Communication Association, Broadcast Education Association, and Southern States Communication Association. In all, he has published over 40 refereed journal articles and book chapters and delivered over 60 research presentations in national and international forums. His first book, *Olympic Media: Inside the Biggest Show on Television,* was published by Routledge in 2008.

**Heather L. Hundley** (PhD, University of Utah, 1999) is a Professor at California State University, San Bernardino. She teaches graduate and undergraduate courses in mass media including media history, media and culture, media law, interpretative approaches, seminar in mass media, and digital culture. Her research interests include gender, feminism, sport, pop culture, law, and health related issues such as portrayals of alcohol consumption, cancer, and sexual promiscuity. Hundley has published in scholarly journals such as *Visual Communication Quarterly, Communication Reports, Journal of Broadcasting & Electronic Media, Journal of Men's Studies, The Journal of Intergroup Relations, Journal of Popular Film and Television* and *American Behavioral Scientist.* She has book chapters in *Critical Approaches to Television, Transmitting the Past: Historical and Cultural Perspectives on Broadcasting,* and *Critical Thinking about Sex, Love, and Romance in the Mass Media: Media Literacy Applications.*

# About the Contributors

**Kim L. Bissell** (PhD, Syracuse University, 1999) is an Associate Professor in the Department of Journalism at the University of Alabama and is the Southern Progress Corporation Endowed Professor in Journalism. She teaches undergraduate courses in photojournalism and magazine editing and design and teaches graduate courses in the social effects of mass media and research methods. Her research interests are in health and visual communication, with a concentration on body image distortion in adolescent girls and women and the role of sport in the development of body image. Her other research examines anti-fat bias in adolescents and health communication messages in children's television programming. Her recent research has been published in the *Journal of Communication, Journalism & Mass Communication Quarterly, Journal of Broadcasting and Electronic Media, Journal of Sports Media, Atlantic Journal of Communication,* and the *Journal of Promotion Management.* Prior to her graduate work, she worked as a sports photographer for the University of Florida's information publication services and worked as a news photographer covering collegiate and professional sports for *The Observer-Reporter* in Washington, Pennsylvania.

**Michael L. Butterworth** (PhD, Indiana University, 2006) is an Assistant Professor in the School of Communication Studies at Bowling Green State University where he teaches courses in rhetorical criticism, democratic theory, and cultural studies. His research focuses on sport and political culture, with a particular interest in how history, democratic politics, and sport share an emphasis on contestation (agonism). He is committed to politically engaged scholarship that both contests sport's democratic failures and envisions democratic possibilities found in and through sport. His work has appeared in *Critical Studies in Media Communication, Communication and Critical/Cultural Studies, Western Journal of Communication,* and the *Journal of Sport and Social Issues.*

**Jennings Bryant** (PhD, Indiana University, 1974) is CIS Distinguished Research Professor, holder of the Reagan Endowed Chair of Broadcasting, and Associate Dean for Graduate Studies and Research at the University of Alabama. He received the university's Blackmon-Moody Outstanding Professor Award for 2000 and was President of the International Communication Association in 2002–2003. In 2006, he received a Distinguished Scholar Award from the Broadcast Education Association and was elected a Fellow of the International Communication Association. He is Advisory Editor of the 11-volume *International Encyclopedia of Communication.* Author or editor of 28 scholarly books or textbooks, Bryant has published more than 120 articles in peer-reviewed journals, has written more than 180 chapters published in edited scholarly books, and has delivered more than 200 papers at conventions of national and international professional associations. His primary research interests are in entertainment theory, mass communication theory, media effects, and media and children.

**James L. Cherney** (PhD, Indiana University, 2003) is an Assistant Professor in the Department of Communication at Miami University in Oxford, Ohio, where he teaches graduate and undergraduate courses in rhetorical criticism, critical theory, public address, and disability rhetoric. He and several colleagues at the university recently succeeded in establishing a minor program in disability studies that incorporates courses across several disciplines. He has published essays and reviews engaging disability issues in such journals as *Argumentation and Advocacy,* the *Quarterly Journal of Speech,* and *Disability Studies Quarterly.* His previous work on disability and sport includes an analysis of the Supreme Court case *Casey Martin v. PGA, Inc.* that appeared in *Case Studies in Sport Communication* (Praeger, 2003).

**R. Glenn Cummins** (PhD, University of Alabama, 2005) is an Assistant Professor in the Department of Electronic Media and Communications in the College of Mass Communications at Texas Tech University. His research interests include entertainment theory and media effects, and he has examined numerous areas of media content including sports media, music videos, reality television, and horror films.

**Bryan E. Denham** (PhD, University of Tennessee, 1996) is Charles Campbell Professor of Sports Communication in the Department of Communication Studies at Clemson University. He studies political and sports communication, media effects, and quantitative research methods. He has published articles addressing the impact of newspaper and magazine journalism on the formation of public and organizational policy, issue framing, attribution of news sources and story definition, and gender and ethnicity issues in mass communication and public opinion. His articles have appeared in publications such as the *Journal of Communication*, *Communication Theory*, the *Journal of Applied Communication Research*, *Journalism & Mass Communication Quarterly*, the *International Journal of Sport Communication* and the *Journal of Sports Media*.

**Andrea Duke** (PhD, University of Alabama, 2008) is an Assistant Professor at Trinity University in San Antonio, Texas. Her research interests focus on sports media, with an emphasis on gender, cultural stereotypes, body image issues, masculinity/femininity, and entertainment. She has been published in the *Journal of Promotional Management*, and has co-authored book chapters in the *Handbook of Sports and Media* and *Investigating the Use of Sex in Media Promotion and Advertising*. She is also the founder of Athletica Consulting Company, whose clients include San Antonio Sports Foundation, GoGirlGo! San Antonio, and the Women's Sports Foundation.

**Benjamin D. Goss** (Ed.D., The University of Southern Mississippi, 1999) serves as an Assistant Professor in the entertainment management program within the Department of Management and College of Business Administration at Missouri State University in Springfield, Missouri. Goss has twice taught in Missouri State's joint business degree program with Liaoning Normal University in Dalian, China. He is a cofounder and the editor-in-chief of the forthcoming *Journal of Sport Administration & Supervision* and has authored or co-authored several peer-reviewed refereed journal articles, one book chapter, and numerous trade journal articles. His research agenda centers largely on organizational behavior in sport and sport marketing. Goss's vita includes 56 professional conference presentations, including 29 at the international and national levels. He serves on the review boards of the *Journal of Business Cases & Applications* and the *International Journal of Business Disciplines*, and he served for three years on the *Sport Marketing Quarterly* review board.

**Kelby K. Halone** (PhD, University of Oklahoma, 1998) is in the Department of Communication Studies at West Virginia University. His research agenda theoretically and empirically examines the pragmatic intersection of relational processes and processes of organizing, how institutional processes become communicatively manifest at micro and macro levels, and how face-to-face and mediated processes interactively contribute to cultural dynamics underlying (inter)group, relational, and organizational health. He has published in outlets such as *Communication*

*Yearbook, Journal of Communication Inquiry, American Behavioral Scientist, Mass Communication & Society, Electronic Journal of Communication, International Journal of Listening, Communication Quarterly, Communication Reports,* and *Sociology of Sport Journal.* In addition to his academic endeavors, he has professional experience working in, and consulting for, corporate business, state government, athletic administration, and health organizations.

**Marie Hardin** (PhD, University of Georgia, 1998) has been an Associate Professor of journalism at Penn State University since 2003, is director of the university's Center for Editing Excellence, and is associate director of its Center for Sports Journalism. She teaches classes in reporting, editing, and sports media. Her research concentrates on diversity, ethics, and professional practices in sports media; her work has been published in *Journalism & Mass Communication Quarterly, Women in Sport and Physical Activity Journal, Sex Roles, Newspaper Research Journal, Mass Communication & Society, Journal of Sports Management* and *The Howard Journal of Communications,* among others. She received the Deans' Award for Integrated Scholarship in 2005. Before completing her PhD, she worked as a newspaper reporter and editor; she has also worked as a freelance magazine writer.

**Kurt Lindemann** (PhD, Arizona State University, 2006) is an Assistant Professor in the School of Communication at San Diego State University, where he teaches graduate and undergraduate classes in ethnography, performance studies, and organizational communication. His interest in disability and sport stems from growing up with a father who was a wheelchair marathon road racer and participating with him in long-distance races. His research focuses primarily on the ways gender and identity are performed in organized and mediated contexts, and has garnered numerous top paper awards from national and regional communication associations. He is currently finishing up a four-year ethnographic study of wheelchair rugby players. His work has been published in *Text and Performance Quarterly, Journal of Communication, Western Journal of Communication,* and *Disability Studies Quarterly.*

**Mary G. McDonald** (PhD, University of Iowa, 1995) is an Associate Professor in the Department of Kinesiology and Health, and an affiliate with the Women's Studies program at Miami University in Oxford, Ohio. Her scholarship focuses on feminist and cultural studies of sport, the media, and popular culture and explores power relations as constituted along the axes of race, class, gender, and sexuality. She is coeditor with Susan Birrell of *Reading Sport: Critical Essays on Power and Representation* (Northeastern University Press, 2000), an anthology that explores the representational politics of sport celebrities and controversial incidents in sport. McDonald is guest editor of a special issue of the *Sociology of Sport Journal*, "Whiteness and Sport," published in 2005. She is also a former president of the North American Society for the Sociology of Sport.

**Lindsey J. Meân** (PhD, University of Sheffield, 1995) is an Assistant Professor in the Department of Communication Studies at Arizona State University. Primarily taking a social constructionist perspective, her research interests are identities, discourses, language, and culture with a particular interest in sport, gender, race, diversity, and organizations. Her work has been published in journals such as *Discourse and Society*, *Communication Yearbook*, and *Sex Roles*, and she is the coauthor, with Angela Goddard, of the textbook *Language and Gender* (2000; 2nd ed., 2007).

**Andrew L. Tyler** is a recent graduate from the DeVos Sport Business Management program at the University of Central Florida (UCF), earning masters degrees in both Sports Business Management and Business Administration in 2006. While at UCF, Drew served as a graduate assistant for Dr. Richard Lapchick. Alongside Lapchick, Drew helped to prepare the 2004 Racial and Gender Report Card, served as student editor for *New Game Plans for College Sport*, and coauthored *100 Heroes*. A Clemson University undergraduate, Drew also amassed a great deal of experience in professional athletics working for the Orlando Magic, Memphis Redbirds, and Charlotte Knights. Drew currently serves as Director of Operations for the Missouri Valley Conference in St. Louis, Missouri.

**Lawrence A. Wenner** (PhD, University of Iowa, 1977) is the Von der Ahe Professor of Communication and Ethics in the College of Communication & Fine Arts and the School of Film & Television at Loyola Marymount University in Los Angeles. He is former editor of the *Journal of Sport and Social Issues* and his books on sport and communication include *MediaSport* and *Media, Sports, and Society*. His new book (with Steven Jackson), *Sport, Beer, and Gender in Promotional Culture*, will be published by Peter Lang in 2008.

**Erin Whiteside** is a PhD, student at Penn State University, studies in the college of communication's Center for Sports Journalism, and assists in research areas that include gender and diversity issues in sport and sports media. Her work has been published in *Newspaper Research Journal*, *Mass Communication & Society* and *Visual Communication Quarterly*. Before beginning her PhD, studies, she worked in the sports industry for Major League Baseball as a publications editor and for Penn State athletics as a public relations manager.

# Supporting researchers for more than 40 years

**Research methods have always been at the core of SAGE's publishing program.** Founder Sara Miller McCune published SAGE's first methods book, *Public Policy Evaluation*, in 1970. Soon after, she launched the *Quantitative Applications in the Social Sciences* series—affectionately known as the "little green books."

Always at the forefront of developing and supporting new approaches in methods, SAGE published early groundbreaking texts and journals in the fields of qualitative methods and evaluation.

Today, more than 40 years and two million little green books later, SAGE continues to push the boundaries with a growing list of more than 1,200 research methods books, journals, and reference works across the social, behavioral, and health sciences. Its imprints—Pine Forge Press, home of innovative textbooks in sociology, and Corwin, publisher of PreK–12 resources for teachers and administrators—broaden SAGE's range of offerings in methods. SAGE further extended its impact in 2008 when it acquired CQ Press and its best-selling and highly respected political science research methods list.

From qualitative, quantitative, and mixed methods to evaluation, SAGE is the essential resource for academics and practitioners looking for the latest methods by leading scholars.

For more information, visit **www.sagepub.com**.